Greenhill Books

Beachhead Assault

David Lee

Beachhead Assault

The Story of
the Royal Naval Commandos
in World War II

Foreword by Tony Parsons

Preface by Ken Oakley

Greenhill Books, London
Stackpole Books, Pennsylvania

Greenhill Books

Beachhead Assault
The Story of the Royal Naval Commandos in World War II

First published 2004 by Greenhill Books/Lionel Leventhal Limited
Park House, 1 Russell Gardens, London NW11 9NN, England
and
Stackpole Books, 5067 Ritter Road, Mechanicsburg, PA 17055, USA

British Library Cataloguing-in Publication Data

Beachhead assault : the story of the Royal Naval Commandos in World War II
1. Great Britain. Royal Naval Commandos – History
2. World War, 1939–1945 – Commando operations – Great Britain
3. World War, 1939–1945 – Amphibious operations
I. Title
940.5'45941

ISBN 1-85367-619-5

Library of Congress Cataloging-in Publication Data available

Maps, Appendix 1 and text figure drawn by Phil Andrews

Printed and bound in Great Britain by
Creative Print and Design (Wales), Ebbw Vale

For the Commandos

Contents

Illustrations

Maps

Foreword

by Tony Parsons

They are leaving us now, these old heroes, the men who so proudly wore the uniform and carried the Fairbairn Sykes knife of the Royal Naval Commandos. Even the youngest among them, the roaring teenage boys who saw action at Dieppe and Sicily and Normandy and Elba and Salerno, are in the twilight of their lives.

But what true heroes they were, and their exploits, recalled now in peacetime by those of us who remain, their children and grandchildren, seem more extraordinary as time goes by. Every page of this book is covered with tales of an almost suicidal courage, and the human cost of the freedom we enjoy today is there in every line.

This is a good time to recall the history and deeds of the Royal Naval Commandos. For too long their incredible story has been neglected.

The Royal Naval Commando Association itself disbanded in the spring of 2003. Former RN Commandos will of course meet and gather as long as two of them are left alive to draw breath. But nothing marked the relentless passage of time like the dissolution of the Royal Naval Commando Association.

The boys became men, and the men have now passed into history. The book you are holding is that history made flesh and blood and bone.

The thing that I have been proudest of in my entire life is the fact that my father was a Royal Naval Commando. My father said very little about his wartime experiences, and what he revealed was invariably self-deprecating and dismissive. But there was a Distinguished Service Medal at the back of a drawer and a huge starburst of scar tissue down one side of his torso. In all the ways that matter, that said it all.

Perhaps other former Commandos spoke to their families about what they had seen and done, but I suspect not. Where would they begin? How could we possibly understand? And these men, who fit any definition of the word hero that you care to name, were not the kind to boast.

I met other Royal Naval Commandos over the years, and I know that my father loved them like brothers. It was only after my dad's death, as I sifted through the photographs of a lifetime, that I got some sense of the vast number of Commandos who gave their lives on those murderous foreign beaches.

Here was the great divide. The ones that came home, and the ones, and there were so many of them, who did not.

We have lost so many of the Royal Naval Commandos in recent years; to cancer, to old age, to time. But there was a generation of friends who never made it off the beaches of World War II, and this book reminds us, and we need constant reminding, of their sacrifice.

Many of the Commandos who never came home died in combat before their adult lives had really begun. This book honours them, as well as the men who came home to start the families that we grew up in.

If you were the son of a Royal Naval Commando, then you were always aware of this family of ghosts who could never be left behind and never forgotten.

All the fallen brothers.

First in, last out. Fighting for their lives on the beaches of Nazi-occupied Europe at the age when the contemporary British teenager is doing his A levels and dreaming about a gap year. A Beach Party meant something quite different in 1942.

David Lee has written a wise, thoughtful history of the Royal Naval Commandos that is both illuminating and incredibly moving. This is military history that reminds us that every Commando was somebody's son, somebody's loved one.

This is what I understood about my father's years as a Royal Naval Commando. They were fighting for something, but it wasn't an abstract concept like country or freedom. The men of the Royal Naval Commando fought for each other.

First in, last out. They shared experiences that are quite literally beyond our imagination. But this book attempts to record those experiences, and tries to understand. It also records the voices of the remaining Royal Naval Commandos, those who survived, and who live today, and collects their memories and allows them to speak for themselves, before their voices are gone for ever.

For those of us who were their children, it seems inconceivable that one day soon the last of them will be gone. But what will remain for ever are their deeds, the memory of their brotherhood, and the enormous debt we owe them.

Preface

by Ken Oakley

On behalf of my Royal Naval Commando Association friends, I welcome this book about us and our work on the beaches during the many landings of World War II.

We received many awards for our work but all were hidden under the designation 'Royal Navy' because of the Wartime Secrets Act; it was never 'Royal Naval Beach Commandos' or 'Royal Naval Commandos'. My own unit, Fox Commando, was awarded five Distinguished Service Medals, two Mentioned in Dispatches, two Croix de Geurre, three Distinguished Service Crosses and one Bar to the DSC for D-Day. My own Mentioned in Dispatches was for Sicily.

I served two years at sea (1940–2) on the cruiser HMS *Neptune* and the battleship HMS *Queen Elizabeth* before being drafted into Combined Operations. After Lord Louis Mountbatten took command of Combined Operations an order was sent out for Royal Naval men to be trained to Commando standard for the beach landings. This training was carried out at HMS *Armadillo*, Ardentinny, and at Achnacarry and Inverary, as well as at many other places in Scotland.

My unit took part in the landings in North Africa, Sicily and Normandy. In 1945 I was promoted to Leading Seaman, and in the same year I was married and the best man was Sidney Compston DSM whom I helped to rescue on D-Day. In 1947 I finished my seven years' service in the Royal Navy.

In 1983 I joined the Royal Naval Commando Association and was pleased to meet and 'swing the lamp' again. I was invited to join the Committee and accepted the position of Chairman, in which capacity I was invited to the VE Day Reception and Dinner at the Guildhall. It was a wonderful occasion which I will never forget.

Now that the Association has disbanded I am very pleased the Commandos will continue to have a voice in this book. Thank you.

Author's Preface

World War II saw a new type of elite soldier. The Commandos. But the Commandos never belonged to just one branch of the Armed Forces during World War II.

The Army, Royal Marines, Royal Air Force and Royal Navy all had their own Commandos although of these only the Marine Commandos remain today. They were brought together under Combined Operations Command, which organised training, raids into enemy territory and amphibious landings.

The Royal Naval Commandos were sailors who became elite soldiers. Unlike all the other Commandos which were known by numbers, these units were denoted by letter from A Commando to W Commando.

After the war they were disbanded and generally ignored by history, which instead concentrated on the Army and Marine Commandos. The Royal Naval Commando Association itself disbanded in early 2003 after some twenty years of bringing together the former Commandos.

For the amphibious landings on the coasts of mainland Europe, Africa and the Far East, the Royal Navy determined it would not only transport the Army but also deliver it to a beach under Royal Navy control. If a retreat were ordered the Navy would also see the Army safely back off the beach.

The film *Saving Private Ryan* opens with the landings on the Normandy beaches and gives a good idea of what the Royal Naval Commandos experienced on the beaches where they fought.

To the Royal Naval Commandos went the honour of being first in and last out, and this is their story.

Acknowledgements

My grateful thanks go to all those members of the Royal Naval Commando Association and others who provided their recollections for this book and without whom it could not have been written.

The book started back in January 2003 when I wrote to all the members of the Royal Naval Commando Association as well as to others who served with them but who did not belong to the Association.

I asked them for their accounts of their careers with the Commandos and many responded with detailed recollections, diaries and notes written at the time. Others invited me to visit them, and I have spent many happy hours in different parts of the country listening to the Commandos talking about the war and their part in it.

Rather than list them individually here, their names are recorded along with their stories in the chapters of this book. I am very grateful to them all and I have used their material with their permission. Official reports where quoted are all from the Public Record Office.

Sadly not all the Commandos whose accounts appear in this book are still alive. In those cases I am grateful to the families I could trace for allowing me to use the accounts they wrote before they died. As I finished writing the book I received word that John Savory had died. His gentle humour and ready willingness to answer my many questions were a great help along the way. His account is in the book.

Of course World War II brought together many people in the Armed Forces who joined up merely for the duration. The Royal Naval Commandos were no exception and many disrupted peacetime careers to join the Navy thinking they would go to sea as sailors, little imagining that they would end up as elite soldiers. Witness the large number of accounts in this book from Royal Naval Volunteer Reserve (RNVR) officers and the smaller number of general service Royal Naval (RN) officers.

After the war many returned to civilian life. But it was not until 1981 that the Royal Naval Commando Association was formed. It ran until 2003 when it was disbanded. The Association did not restrict its membership to Royal Naval Commandos but also welcomed members of the Royal Naval Beach Signals, who went through the Commando training and who served with the Commandos on the beaches, the Landing Craft Obstacle Clearance Units (LCOCU), the Combined Operations Bombardment Units and the Levant Schooner Flotilla. Their accounts are also included in this book.

Special thanks go to Ken Oakley, the Chairman of the Association, for his inspiration in getting me started and for his very considerable help, and also to George Fagence who started the Association and whose help was similarly invaluable.

Special thanks too go to Tony Parsons for taking time out of a very busy schedule to write the Foreword to the book.

I am hugely grateful to Ken Barry, whose knowledge of the history of the Royal Naval Commandos is unrivalled, for checking the manuscript through for factual errors, for suggesting some additions to the text, and for answering a continual stream of questions along the way.

I also owe grateful thanks to Leonard Lloyd who helped me considerably with technical queries as well as finding fellow Telegraphists from the Bombardment Units for particular operations.

I am likewise very grateful to Bill McGrann and Ron Hicks who gave me valuable help with the Elba chapter. Bill's brother George McGrann was killed with A Commando, and Ron Hicks's cousin Alan Davis was killed with O Commando, both at Elba.

Finally my thanks go to James Dunning for permission to quote from his book about Achnacarry, *It Had to Be Tough*, to Adrian Webb at the UK Hydrographic Office for D-Day tidal information, and to Dr Simon Robbins at the Imperial War Museum for dealing patiently with my many requests for information.

'The war will be won or lost on the beaches'
Field Marshal Erwin Rommel

CHAPTER 1

Beginnings

August 1942 was hot and dry. The sunshine was especially welcome because the early part of the summer had been awful. For the men of the Royal Naval Beach Parties, later to become the Royal Naval Commandos, the warm weather meant a pleasant few weeks billeted in the Marine Hotel, Cowes, on the Isle of Wight. They had been there since their planned operation had been cancelled due to bad weather in late June. Every day they made their way to the beach where they exercised with the Army, practising landings. What made this spell at Cowes even more agreeable was the unusual self-victualling arrangements of these particular Royal Naval Beach Parties; a group of Wrens looked after all their culinary needs.

The 18th August dawned fine and clear. For the Beach Parties a routine trip to Portsmouth later in the day to pick up a landing craft was planned. The first sign that this was going to be a different kind of day came when the men were issued with next-of-kin cards and ammunition for their guns. Their landing craft was loaded up with Churchill tanks, and instead of returning to Cowes that afternoon it headed out into the English Channel to rendezvous with the rest of the Assault Force. They sailed through the night to their destination. It was 19th August 1942 and they were going to Dieppe.

Royal Naval Beach Signal Party No. 3 had also been enjoying the fine weather. The sunshine and warmth had meant a pleasant few weeks at the village of Crondall, near Farnham in Surrey. Instead of exercising in the rain as they had been doing at Inverary in the west of Scotland, in the countryside around Crondall they basked in the sunshine or sweated on their cross country runs.

On 18th August at 9 a.m. the signallers paraded in the morning sunshine. But this parade was different. Instead of going out into the countryside on exercise the signallers were ordered to board a couple of coaches which had arrived earlier that morning. Ominously, the windows were blacked out. By midday the coaches were in Portsmouth. The signallers were ordered straight from the coaches into landing craft. No. 3 Section boarded LCT 127, together with Canadian tanks and engineers.

Alongside other craft in the flotilla they made their way out to a point between Portsmouth and the Nab Tower lighthouse in the Solent, where they dropped anchor for the night. At 2 a.m. the next morning they too set sail for Dieppe.

Sunrise on 19th August was at 05.50 and heralded another fine day. But for the Naval Beach Parties the sunshine and chalk cliffs which run along the coastline around Dieppe were already obscured by the smokescreen laid down by the Navy and the RAF. Operation Jubilee to seize Dieppe was underway. But the element of surprise, which had been a critical factor in the success of the raid, had been lost. En route to Berneval, a village east of Dieppe, No. 3 Army Commando ran into a German convoy. That was the moment that things started to go wrong.

1097069 AC2 Royal Air Force W/Operator Kenneth Prestidge, attached Royal Naval Beach Signals

All went well until the early hours of 19th August. Numerous star shells filled the air and all hell was let loose; a savage battle took place with many casualties. We had run into a small coastal convoy and were attacked time and time again, sustaining more casualties. Personnel on the craft were killed and wounded and everyone helped each other as much as possible. My wireless set No. 18 was blown to pieces, and so along with others I looked after those in need of help.

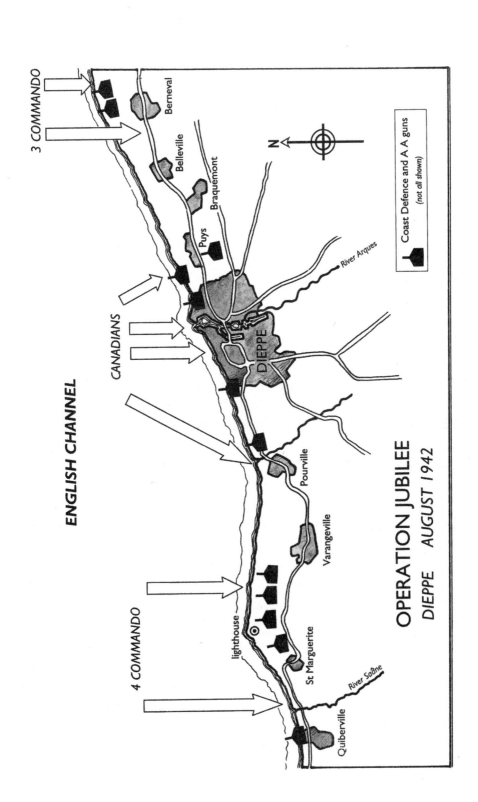

ENGLISH CHANNEL

3 COMMANDO

4 COMMANDO

CANADIANS

Berneval
Belleville
Braquemont
Puys
River Arques

DIEPPE

Pourville

Varangeville

lighthouse

St Marguerite

River Saône

Quiberville

N

OPERATION JUBILEE
DIEPPE   AUGUST 1942

Coast Defence and A A guns
(not all shown)

Dawn came and we were assisted by other landing craft. Several pilots who had been shot down were picked up and taken aboard. One pilot took over a gunner's job, and rescues from the sea were numerous. I saw more acts of bravery in eight or nine hours than most people see in a lifetime.

Come lunchtime we had orders to return to the UK, which we did with great sadness, shattered beyond belief and dog tired.

The men of the Royal Naval Beach Parties were under orders to control the landings on each of the beaches as well as to cover any withdrawal. Most did not return. Their officers were appointed Beachmasters, and in overall charge of the Beach Parties was Commander Lambert RN, designated the Principal Beachmaster. As was normal practice, the beaches had been given the names of colours. From the west they were: Orange Beach One (the village of Varengeville); Orange Beach Two (just East of the River Saane); Green Beach (the village of Pourville); White Beach (Dieppe); Red Beach (Dieppe); Blue Beach (the village of Puys); Yellow Beach One (the village of Berneval); and Yellow Beach Two (the village of Belleville).

But the encounter with No. 3 Army Commando had forewarned the Germans and they were waiting. Not only that, but the raid's planners had not known that the Germans had turned Dieppe into a fortress with large numbers of gun positions overlooking the beach, either in plain view or camouflaged.

Because of that early encounter with the German convoy, only eighteen Commandos from No. 3 Army Commando, including the second in command, Major Peter Young, made it onto the beaches at Berneval, with some fifty Commandos managing to land at the nearby beach at Belleville. The larger group fought their way through the defences on the beach, but when the defenders from the battery counter-attacked the Commandos were all captured or killed. However, they had succeeded in diverting attention from the smaller group of Commandos who had climbed a steep gully on the cliff face and who only came under fire as they moved through the village of Berneval itself.

From Berneval the Commandos could fire at the battery, which they annoyed enough for one of the guns to traverse round to try and shell them instead of the ships out at sea. With ammunition running out the Commandos shot up an observation post before retreating to their landing craft for the journey back. On the other side of Dieppe, No. 4 Army Commando successfully landed and knocked out the German battery at Varengeville in a textbook operation before retreating back to the beach and the boats.

On Green Beach at Pourville, the Canadian South Saskatchewan Regiment landed successfully, although not without mishap. On the way in some men had been injured in their landing craft before they even reached the beaches.

Dawson Biggs, Coxain Naval Party 1745, assault landing craft, Green Beach

We ran into a bit of trouble before we even got there. There was a violent explosion in the large compartment that had been allocated to the Saskatchewan Regiment. During the arming of the hand grenades one accidentally went off in a full box, which injured about twenty men.

I went to investigate and opened the big sliding door, when I saw a scene of blood and smoke. I closed the door and reported to the bridge as we had orders not to involve ourselves with the Canadians.

After this mishap we finally arrived at Pourville. We landed safely on Green Beach. We expected a sandy beach, which would have been ideal for landing craft, but it was full of polished pebbles where we landed, and as we jumped out we got soaking wet.

Dawn was just breaking and it was a fine summer's day. Not a shot was fired and I went with some of the Canadians I had got friendly with nearly as far as the wall. I returned as the tide was coming in. It was easy to return to the landing craft.

However, from then on things started to go wrong for the Canadians. After overcoming some initial resistance and moving into the village of Pourville, they were unable to overrun the western flank of Dieppe. Added to this, their supporting troops from the Canadian Cameron Highlanders arrived late, some having been to the wrong beach. They retreated the way they had come, finally arriving back at the beach where they fought off the Germans with the help of the Naval Beach Parties.

Dawson Biggs, Coxwain Naval Party 1745, assault landing craft, Green Beach

When the order came to evacuate we made six hellish trips with each landing craft. We used to call the airforce men 'Brylcreem boys', but not any more. We would not have made it but for the fact that they laid down brown smoke to cover the retreat as we were dragging Canadians and No. 4 Commandos through the water.

The wounded were taken to a large tank landing craft with a thick rope ladder slung over the side and were dragged up by fair means or foul. Those that could make it went up the Jacob's ladder of any vessel available. The Germans pounded them from the cliff top with the ferocity of hell.

Back on Green Beach the Beachmaster, Lieutenant Commander Redvers Prior DSO DSC RN, and his Assistant Beachmaster, Lieutenant Millar RNVR, were both wounded. Lieutenant Commander Prior had tried to arrange for a naval bombardment but had failed because of the absence of a Naval Beach Signal Section. Both ended up being captured, although Redvers Prior managed to escape and make his way through Europe to safety.

At Blue Beach things had been even worse. The landing craft had come under fire from one hundred yards out, and this was so intense that the Beachmaster's own landing craft could not make it onto the beach. The Commanding Officer of the Royal Regiment of Canada made it to the top of the cliff with a small party of men but there they were cut off and forced to surrender. The losses on this beach were heavy, with twenty-four out of thirty-seven officers, and 459 out of 516 other ranks posted, killed, wounded or missing. Some landing craft did make it with a few survivors, but Blue Beach suffered the worst casualties of the day.

At Dieppe (Red Beach and White Beach) itself, the Canadian Essex Scottish and the Royal Hamilton Light Infantry were the attacking force, with the Fusiliers de Mont Royal in reserve. They were supported by the 14th Canadian Army Tank Battalion. They landed at 05.23. The success of the attack depended on the landing forces immediately getting into Dieppe to take control. But from the outset things started to go wrong. Ahead of the attacking force, the Royal Naval Beach Parties landed on the beach at Dieppe where the sea wall extends out to cover the mouth of the River Arques.

Able Seaman Michael McFadden, Royal Naval Beach Party, later L Commando

We were under orders not to show ourselves in our khaki uniforms. The only piece of kit we had that showed us as Royal Navy were our sailor's hats. If we thought we could be seen we had to put on blue overalls.

On board our landing craft were three Churchill tanks, an armoured car, and a long tube full of TNT. We were to sail in alongside a sea wall and put the tanks ashore on a shale beach, bear off, sail up this river and help with the TNT pipe to try and block the river. At the end of the sea wall we were told was just a factory. But it was like a fort, guns firing from the windows. The three tanks got onto the beach and faced heavy fire. They got stuck on the beach.

The naval ratings manning the machine guns forward and aft on our landing craft were cut to pieces.

When we moved off the beach the chains holding the bow door were smashed, leaving the door just hanging into the water. The TNT plan was out. So we sailed up and down picking people out of the water. They discovered a shell embedded in the ammo store – luckily for us it never went off.

Some signals personnel did make it onto the beach at Dieppe. Although organised separately they were effectively the Royal Naval Beach Party signallers and were a crucial part of the operation. Their absence had already been felt on Green Beach, but things were no better for them.

Signalman Ron Wallbank, Royal Naval Beach Signals Section No. 3

Together with some of my shipmates I was embarked on LCT 127 (Lieutenant Commander MacPherson RNR commanding) together with Canadian tanks and their engineers. We were allocated to Red Beach (Eastern Sector) and reached the beach with the first waves. The tanks got off the beach but only one managed to get over the wall, the others being blown out of action. Our LCT was badly damaged – first the ramp mechanism was smashed, so that the ramp itself just dropped and hung underwater as soon as the craft went astern.

Secondly, as the LCT turned to face seaward, a shell hit the aft side of the bridge superstructure, killing and wounding some of the permanent crew. The explosion tipped open the door of the Bofors guns' ammunition locker, which was thankfully dowsed by the bursting water tank above, otherwise I would probably not be writing this.

Sub Lieutenant Ray Evans DSC RNVR, Royal Naval Beach Signals, later Commanding Officer Royal Naval Beach Signals Section No. B5

As the LCT approached, orders had been given, correctly, to open the doors and lower the ramp prior to beaching. As the craft stopped, the tank crews thought they had arrived, went out into deep water, and were drowned.

Due to the depth of the water, radio equipment could not be landed and the main force was shrouded in smoke and out of V/S range. A number of tanks had landed from other craft but appeared to have been knocked out by anti-tank fire or had lost their tracks on the stony beach. No movement appeared to be taking place. There was a lot of noise from various small and heavy guns and a factory on the front was burning.

The main problem appeared to be from unrevealed machine-gun emplacements in the west cliff and from artillery pieces located at the base of the fort. No Beach Parties seemed to be operating. The main action appeared to be in the vicinity of the Casino. The radio would not work within the confines of the LCT.

A number of swimmers from sunken craft had now reached the LCT, and they were in great danger from enemy fire coming at the craft. Also on board was a large batch of Bangalore torpedoes and demolition charges, intended to demolish the beach obstacles. The order to withdraw was eventually given and it was in the ensuing struggle to get to a craft, under heavy fire, that a large number of casualties occurred.

647456 LAC Royal Air Force W/Operator Jack Payton, attached Royal Naval Beach Signals

I was on an ML [motor launch] escorting R-boats which were due to land at Dieppe. Just before we came into Dieppe we heard the BBC announcing the invasion of Dieppe – this was before we had even landed! The R-boats went into the shore where the Canadians landed, while the ML stayed out at sea patrolling the waters and laying the occasional smokescreen, a couple of hundred yards or so from the beach at Dieppe itself. We were knocked about a bit and there were quite a few casualties from shells hitting the boats. I had a grandstand view from the upper deck, from where I could see the German soldiers firing at us from the houses on the front.

The situation was confused and the Military Force Commander, not knowing the true state of affairs on the beach, decided to send in the reserve as well as the Royal Marine Commandos, whose cutting-out mission on the harbour had been abandoned. They too came under heavy fire as they went in and Lieutenant Colonel J. Phillips in command of the Marines sacrificed his own life by donning a pair of white gloves and signalling to his force behind him to retire behind the smoke screen. In doing so he saved many from certain death. By late morning the troops were coming back off the beach and causing problems for the landing craft. But there were just too many men and disaster loomed.

Lieutenant P. Ross RNVR, Beachmaster White Beach

With the help of the Beach Party these [troops] were quickly loaded and had just shoved off when there was a rush of military personnel towards the departing craft. In order to stop this I plunged into the sea and made for the nearest craft. I reached it and gave orders to go full speed astern to get clear, but the few extra men who had managed to scramble aboard, together with timely enemy fire, upset the trim of the craft and she sank. Another of the remaining craft received a direct hit and also sank.

With the situation fast becoming impossible, a final attempt was made to pick up troops from the beaches.

Commander G. Lambert RN, Principal Beachmaster

I observed about eight LCA making for White Beach and was proceeding along the beach to meet them when they were heavily attacked by bombs from German aircraft while still some way off. Meanwhile about half a dozen other LCA were seen heading for Red Beach. These duly made the land through heavy fire and deployed perfectly just below the strong point. Lieutenant Bibby took charge of the loading, but all except one were struck by mortars or shells as they were backing away and the troops had to be brought on shore again through heavy fire. The only surviving officer of the boats which had been sunk was Lieutenant H. R. Hobday RNVR of HMS *Princess Beatrix*. It was subsequently reported to me that it was this officer who led these boats in and it was hard luck that his boat should have been hit on its way off after a fine attempt to rescue troops in almost hopeless circumstances.

After this incident, which left us busy for some time, it was noticed that the horizon was clear of shipping and the Brigadier (W. W. Southam) was informed that it was unlikely that any more would be sent. He was rallying his men to further efforts but they were too exhausted for much exertion. Casualties were getting heavy, and although we kept up small-arms fire as individuals, we could not reduce the increasing fire directed at us from the cliff tops. I then set out to return to Beach HQ about a furlong to the eastward to talk things over with the PMLO [Principal Military Landing Officer], but a heavy barrage was put down and it was necessary to lie very flat until it ceased. When it suddenly stopped, Germans could be seen approaching the promenade, and our troops had begun to surrender. I returned to the strong point, being met by Lieutenant Bibby who told me that the soldiers had had enough and had run out of ammunition.

We decided to try to escape by swimming out to a sunken LCT with its bows afloat and lie up in it until dark. The Germans had no compunction about firing at us all the way out, but we got on board. However, the rising tides engulfed the bows and as we were too exhausted to swim, the current took us close in to the breakwater where we were picked up by the enemy.

Back on the beach Lieutenant Ross and his Beach Party joined the remaining Canadian troops in fighting the Germans. But with ammunition running low they bowed to the inevitable and surrendered. Some of the assault landing parties had not been able to make it onto the beaches at Dieppe as intended and were forced instead to remain on their original ships out at sea. But this was not necessarily a safe option during the assault on Dieppe.

Signalman Norman Weston, Royal Naval Beach Signals

I as a Visual Signalman, a Radio Operator and one more rating, a Coder, boarded HMS *Fernie* and set sail, from which during the night we were to be transferred to an assault landing craft, from which we were to go ashore and carry out the job we had to do, namely to keep communications open. However, during the night the craft was sunk, apparently by a German E-boat, so we were left to do what might be appropriate.

We took up a position just away from the activity and the wireless operator set up his radio and we were helping to write messages for passing onto the bridge. It was a very hectic sort of a day, no let up ashore, but we didn't realise that conditions were as bad as they were for the people that were having to land there.

I can't say I felt very happy with the situation, but we were kept very busy, putting down a huge smoke screen along the edge of the shore, firing a salvo of shells, before going back a little way out to sea, then repeating the operation. The sky was pretty full with aircraft throughout the day, both German and our own, and consequently we were engaged quite a lot in recovering pilots who had ditched their planes after being shot down.

Sometime later in the day, when it seemed like this was as bad as it was going to get, there was a big bang! I blacked out for a while and came to below decks where a medical officer was working on me to dislodge shrapnel from various parts of my body, including a piece in my head which had pierced my steel helmet and was embedded there.

There was another piece in my chest and lots of smaller pieces in my arms. The piece in my head was removed, but the piece lodged in my chest had to stay there in spite of the Medical Officer probing for it without anaesthetic! He did tell me it had only entered the muscle part of my chest and that it would eventually work its own way out. Sure enough many years later it did work its way near the surface – about the size of a small fingernail.

The shell which had hit HMS *Fernie* had exploded just after 12.30. Shortly after this the decision was taken to abandon the whole operation. With the loss of HMS *Berkeley*, the flotilla made its way back to Newhaven, a journey punctuated by German air attacks which were fought off by the RAF.

For the Royal Naval Beach Parties the journey home was a sombre affair. They were told their losses at Dieppe were eleven officers out of thirteen, and fifty men out of sixty-seven. They arrived in Newhaven at teatime and, after sleeping overnight in Newhaven station, returned to Scotland.

Royal Naval Beach Signal Party No. 3 arrived back in Newhaven at 8 p.m. The next morning they returned to Crondall for another week. The Beach Signal Parties had lost one-third of the 120 who had started out that morning.

Norman Weston was admitted first to the Royal Haslar Hospital at Portsmouth and then to Stoke Mandeville Hospital, where he made a full recovery. It had been a day none of the survivors would ever forget. When the flotilla returned home it had left behind two thousand men as prisoners and nearly one thousand dead. Many lives had been lost but lessons had been learned.

Most importantly for the Royal Naval Beach Parties, the Dieppe raid had reinforced the need for a properly trained and run Beach organisation. Given the importance of their work in securing and controlling the beaches, their role would be enhanced and their numbers increased. They would be trained to Commando standard and become Royal Naval Beach Commandos and later just Royal Naval Commandos.

After Dieppe, the Royal Naval Beach Signal Parties were reformed and more units were created with the numbers B1 to 18. Although they remained separate units, to all intents and purposes they were the Royal Naval Commando Signals Sections.

These were timely moves because the Royal Navy needed both the Commandos and the Signallers for the subsequent invasions in North Africa, Europe and the Far East. And to form the new Commandos the Navy looked to its own officers and ratings, some of whom would only see service in the Commando khaki.

Immediately after Dunkirk in 1940 Captain Gerald Garnons-Williams DSO DSC RN had formed a small group of Naval officers and ratings to man an assorted collection of vessels for the initial raids across the Channel. In 1941 the first sailors for the new Royal Naval Beach Parties arrived in Scotland.

Petty Officer Gordon Holwill, A Commando

I was waiting to be sent to my next ship when four of us, Beacham, Rimmer, Murphy and myself, found ourselves on a train travelling north to a large house at Cove on the eastern shore of Loch Long.

We arrived at Cove on 2nd November 1941 and found that we were the first members of what was then to be called a Beach Party. The idea was that a Naval force was to be formed to be first on a beach during an invasion of enemy territory. We being the first became A Beach Party.

With an eye to the future course of the war, Winston Churchill ordered the creation of Combined Operations under Admiral Roger Keyes. Combined Operations would bring together the Army, Royal Navy and Royal Air Force for the purpose of raiding enemy territory and eventually getting the Allies back into Europe.

To facilitate this, Combined Operations would have its own organisation and its own training centres. In 1941 Admiral Keyes was replaced by Commodore Lord Louis Mountbatten whose first raids at Vaasgo, Bruneval and St Nazaire had been successes. These and other smaller raids had an important effect on morale both at home and in occupied Europe, especially as the press hyped them up. In early June 1942 No. 6 Army Commando was sent across the English Channel to the village of Hardelot near Boulogne. The purpose of the raid was to attack a radar station and secure some advanced-ground radar equipment. In the event the Commandos were called back to the boats before this could be achieved, with some not even making it onto the beach at all.

Telegraphist Malcolm Robinson, Royal Naval Beach Signals Section No. B5

When we hit the beach, for what would have been a dry landing, it quickly became apparent that we had picked a wrong spot because as the ramp was lowered machine-gun fire erupted from both sides and tracers could be seen crossing just in front of our bows.

At the same time I had the impression a couple of the leading Commandos, who were braced for a quick take-off, might have made the beach, but with hindsight I think I was probably mistaken. At any rate the German fire was very accurate across out bows and to step out into that would probably have been suicidal. Consequently the ramp was hastily raised, and the boat officer, a Sub Lieutenant, decided to pull off, presumably with a view to trying to re-beach at a less unfriendly spot.

However, attempts to kedge off proved ineffective and we appeared to be well and truly stuck. Situated starboard side, midships, I was keeping my head well down, the more so as my aerial seemed to be attracting attention from the German gunners. The Subby instructed me to radio that we were stuck, which I did only to receive the terse response, 'Pipe down!'

By this time the machine-gun fire had been joined by mortar shells which started to land uncomfortably close, and it may have been this that prompted our kedge winch into effective action because, at last, with the help of engines astern, we managed to ease off the beach. By then it seemed that everyone else was withdrawing so we also headed out seawards.

When they finally reached home they found reporters and photographers waiting to turn the raid into headlines for public consumption; 'Commandos Are Home', proclaimed the London *Evening Standard*.

Having taken part in these early raids after 1940, the first operation mounted by properly constituted Naval Beach Parties was in May 1942 against the island of Madagascar, codenamed Operation Ironclad. Madagascar was occupied by the pro-German Vichy French authorities, and the worry for the Allies was that the Japanese might wish to use it as a Naval base from which to attack Allied shipping in the Indian Ocean.

The key port on the island was at Diégo Suarez on the east side, which was accessible through a narrow entrance from the sea. The plan was for the Navy to land No. 5 Amy Commando on beaches some ten miles away and they would cross a peninsula and take the port. The Principal Beachmaster for Operation Ironclad was Edward Gueritz, a Lieutenant RN who had been one of the early Beach Party officers under Lieutenant P. U. Bayly RN at Largs in Scotland. As Principal Beachmaster, Gueritz had to put up a list of the officers he wanted to take with him.

Rear Admiral Edward Gueritz CB OBE DSC

I had to choose the officers for the Beach Party. I was warned that the Admiral was likely to take the opposite view to mine – sure enough he said, 'Thought so – you're taking the best – I'll give you the others except one chap.' Of course, I had picked the ones I did not want and ended up getting only one chap I did not want.

The landings themselves were not opposed although resistance was encountered further inland. A skilful piece of navigation brought the force into Courier Bay after the minesweepers had first swept the channel.

Rear Admiral Edward Gueritz CB OBE DSC

We went in at night – we later found from French orders that they believed it impossible to approach by night. The Commandos landed from the *Winchester Castle* and took a battery while the crew was asleep. It was a hot night, still and bright. The Navigator wanted to fix the moon and the landmarks as the problem was finding the right beach. I was the Principal Beachmaster and went in after the Assistant Beachmaster and Beachmaster in that order. There was practically no resistance at that stage. The casualties were due to the defences further inland which were well manned by Senegalese Colonial troops. I was there for four days in all.

Petty Officer Gordon Holwill, A Commando

The crew of the LCA landed us in the wrong place and we found trees growing in the water between us and the beach. As we were struggling over the roots of these trees someone shouted that a snake had touched his leg – the ensuing haste to reach dry land must have frightened any snakes for miles around!

After three days the French surrendered the port after a detachment of Royal Marines attacked from the opposite side to No. 5 Army Commando, who encountered fierce resistance in the west. Subsequent resistance in other parts of the island meant the Beach Parties had to participate in further landings in the south, leading to the eventual surrender of all Vichy forces on the island. However, this was not before the Beach Parties had struggled with the inexperience of the 22nd East African Brigade, who lacked any amphibious training, and it was the men of the Beach Parties who had to drive the vehicles off the landing craft to ensure they all got ashore safely.

After the Madagascar landings the shape and role of the newly created Royal Naval Beach Commandos gradually emerged from discussions within Combined Operations. For each landing a Principal Beachmaster would be appointed with the rank of Lieutenant Commander. Below him there would be a Beachmaster with the rank of Lieutenant and below him there would be Assistant Beachmasters with the rank of Sub Lieutenant. The Beachmaster would be in charge on the beach and would outrank all Army officers.

By the end of 1942 an official definition of a Beach Commando had emerged. To avoid confusion with the Army, letters would be used to denote each Commando. The first to be formed were C, D, E, F and G Commandos, or Charlie, Dog, Easy, Fox and George in the phonetic alphabet of the time. The Madagascar Beach Parties became A and B Commandos, or Able and Baker. The original Beach Parties at Dieppe had operated as C, D or H Parties, and they became C, D and H Commandos.

Definition of a Beach Commando, Combined Operations HQ 18.12.42

(a) *The Unit.* An RN Beach Commando consists of sufficient officers and men to handle the craft required to land a brigade, their attached troops, vehicles and stores. It consists of 10 officers and 66 ratings, composed of 1 Principal Beach Master, 3 Beach Masters, 6 Assistant Beach Masters, 3 Petty Officers, 6 Leading Seamen, 18 Able Seamen and 39 Ordinary Seamen.

(b) *The Sub-Unit.* Each Commando is divided into three parties. Each party contains sufficient officers and men to handle the craft required to land a battalion. It consists of 1 BM, 2 ABMs, 1 PO, 6 ABs, 13 Ordinary Seamen. The three parties are in the charge of the PBM.

(c) Commandos are distinguished by alphabetical letters and the parties by numbers, e.g. Beach Commando E consists of Beach parties E1, E2, E3 in charge of PBM (E).

These new Commandos would need new officers and ratings. First they would need to be recruited. Then they would have to be trained.

CHAPTER 2

Training

Every sailor in the Royal Navy dreams of commanding his own ship. For many officers the glamour of commanding a destroyer was a strong attraction but World War II also gave Naval ratings the chance of independent command. In early 1943 a group of Naval ratings were each given the chance to command one of His Majesty's assault landing craft at Dartmouth. The illusion of high Naval command was reinforced by the ratings' accommodation in the Officers' Naval Training School, an experience only spoilt by the fact that the officers' single beds had been removed, so the ratings slept on the floor. As things turned out, it was fortunate that the Royal Naval Commandos were able to offer one rating a convenient way out of his difficulties.

Able Seaman George Fagence, H Commando

We were in line ahead in Dartmouth harbour when a Messerschmitt 190 came down the harbour spewing bullets everywhere. They used to come in via Brixham harbour, round the back of Dartmouth, down the harbour and out to sea.

I was skipper of an LCA assault craft, the steering was a metal pillbox. Up front the bullets knocking out chunks of wood and the roar of engines as the plane went overhead were my first awareness. I immediately ducked my head inside – a mistake – as going flat out I ran smack bang into the side of a small drifter. Crash! Crash! Sharp look up, the front door was hanging off. Full astern, so there we were going full backwards with my head down in the pillbox. The strafing had stopped, but another ominous sound could be heard – rending, screeching, tearing.

I took a quick look aft. The foreshore was a sheet of concrete and I was sitting there high and dry about ten feet up on the foreshore, as dead as a dodo, realising me Lawds at the Admiralty would have my guts for garters.

I went up in front of the officer and received wrath of the gods and ambled off down the corridor. Now here was a lucky thing. The notice board was in the corridor and I took a quick butcher's – it said, 'Volunteers Wanted for Special and Hazardous Service'.

A way out. I took off for the Drafting Office, saw the Chief, God bless his cotton socks, and the very next day I packed my kit and was off to Scotland, which is how I came into the hands of Rommel of the North and how me sinking one of their Lordships' landing craft died a silent death. So I lost my first command.

'Rommel of the North' was Lieutenant Colonel Charles Vaughan, who was in charge of the Combined Operations Commando training base at Achnacarry. This base was the main Army Commando training centre but was also used to train Royal Naval Commandos.

At least George Fagence was able to volunteer. Another group of sailors were in Portsmouth after the Dieppe raid in 1942 when they found themselves 'volunteering' for the Commandos in a more traditional services manner.

Able Seaman Lofty Lucas, G Commando

We were stood on the square with all our kit and the Chief Petty Officer came up and put his arm down the middle of us. 'All those to the left, get into the lorries!' And that was our initiation into the Commandos.

Even officers could find themselves in the Commandos by default rather than by design.

Lieutenant Commander Jack D'Arcy RNVR, Principal Beachmaster R Commando

In my interview with the Captain of the Staff College I had expressed a preference for Coastal Forces but unfortunately I had omitted to mention whose coast. Whereas MTBs (motor torpedo boats) and MLs (motor launches) were largely concerned with defending Britain's coastline, Combined Ops would be far more interested in attacking the enemy's coastline.

Other recruits happened to be in the right place at the right time when they answered the call for volunteers. Ray Bromley had served on the Tribal-class destroyer HMS *Mohawk* from the time she was built to her last action when she was sunk off Tunisia in 1941. Instead of being posted to another ship he volunteered for special duties. Likewise Maurice Pascall, who joined the Royal Naval Commandos after escaping from Singapore, a journey which had taken him through the jungles of the Far East to Java with the Japanese snapping at his heels, and onto Australia.

Many of the recruits did not go to sea after basic training – they went straight to the Commandos. But for all those who volunteered or were simply sent to be Commandos, their destination for their training was the west of Scotland. Here there are mountains, moors, lochs and beaches – the perfect place to train the Royal Naval Commandos.

The nature of the training was the subject of some head scratching by the Admiralty. Here, after all, was a new Naval organisation, which was breaking new ground in its training and operational deployment. In 1943 the Admiralty finally pronounced on the subject.

Admiralty Docket No. 10647/43

The RNBC (Royal Naval Beach Commando) is a buffer between the Naval and Military aspects and consequently their training must have a 'two-service' bias; it cannot be based entirely on 'Looking only towards the sea' or 'only towards the land', but it must be something between the two.

One of the early Commandos to undergo this naval and military training was G Commando. Having filled its ranks from the parade ground at Portsmouth in 1942, it carried out much of its training at Inverary.

Able Seaman Albert Cattell, G Commando

We practised landings on the lochs with proper gunfire with the Army. The RAF had a couple of Mustangs and they used to dive bomb the beach, simulating real battles.

Inverary was just a village, but down the Loch (Fyne) they built a big naval station. It is a deep water loch where they can get big transports up, destroyers and everything. We were there for ages. We were up in the mountains always on exercises, courses, route marches, working with the Army. From there we went all round Scotland – Largs, Irvine, Troon, the Isle of Arran. We found shallow beaches on the Dumfries Coast, reminiscent of foreign beaches. We were practising landings all the time. The Beach Party went in first. You carried signs with you. The Beachmaster, who was usually the senior officer, stopped in the middle of the beach, you fanned out, you checked the beach for mines and any obstructions in the water.

If there was enemy fire we were taught, down door and away you go to secure the perimeter of the beach first against the enemy – that way you've got a chance. Then you come back and put these road signs up to guide the craft in. Then you would return until the craft came in and the invasion started. You returned to your infantry position on the perimeter. You were being a soldier then.

I was a bodyguard to an officer, Lieutenant McLennan, for the simple reason that I could use a six-gun service revolver. Once you secured the beach and pushed the enemy back a bit and it was clear of obstructions you signalled the landing craft to come in and the actual invasion started and the troops went through you and inland. We did deep-water reconnaissance depending on the coxwain. We had maps which showed if it was a shelving beach or deep water – they dropped us in deep water many a time.

A deep-water reconnaissance involved the Commandos linking hands and forming a line at right angles to the sea. The tallest would be on the seaward side and the shortest would be on the beach side. The line would then wade through the sea marking any obstructions for landing craft and organising their disposal by blowing them up. At least that was the theory. The problem for the Navy was that having the tallest man in the Commando in the deepest part of the water deprived an officer of the chance to show some leadership.

Sub Lieutenant Joe Bramble RNVR, Assistant Beachmaster M Commando

Without doubt this was one of the most unpopular tasks, especially in the cold waters of a Scottish Loch in mid-winter. Worse, we were informed that the Assistant Beachmaster was to be at the end of the line. A dozen of us held hands at arm's length and walked through the water with the unfortunate Assistant Beachmaster as Tail End Charlie in the deepest water. With water touching my chin there was no escaping the freezing water and my lack of height was a distinct disadvantage. The obvious answer was to promote a tall Seaman to the tail end job. Alas, this was strictly *verboten*. It was the Assistant Beachmaster's job and we were told it was a matter of pride that the officer had the dirty end of the stick.

Because of the planned expansion of the Royal Naval Commandos throughout 1942, the Royal Navy decided that it needed a proper Naval establishment in which to train them. Lieutenant P. U. Bayly RN, who was Principal Beachmaster at the time, and Lieutenant Roger Wake RN found the perfect place at the small village of Ardentinny on the edge of Loch Long which flows into the Firth of Clyde.

However, there was the practical problem of how to acquire the place for the Royal Navy. When Bayly asked his superior officer, Mountbatten himself, the reply came back, 'Why not write a cheque?' Soon, the forestry camp and Glenfinart House at Ardentinny became the new home of the Royal Naval Commandos, and Nissen huts appeared for the first intake. Apart from being the principal training establishment for the Commandos, Ardentinny was also their main base, and it was to here that they returned after each operation.

First, in accordance with Naval law, the place had to have a proper ship's name. Lieutenant Roger Wake had a stuffed armadillo at home which he promised to donate to the new establishment, which, as a result, was officially called HMS *Armadillo*. In fact the stuffed armadillo never arrived, but the name stayed. Although this was the place where sailors became Commandos, the Navy ensured that they remained Royal Navy through and through. Royal Naval officers in Combined Operations Headquarters were already known for going up the gangway to their cabins rather than up the stairs to their rooms. At HMS *Armadillo* the parade ground was also the quarterdeck and Glenfinart House housed the wardroom rather than the mess.

However, one cherished Naval tradition which had to be abandoned was the wearing of Naval uniform, or blues. As soldiers on the beaches the Commandos would obviously have to wear khaki, and this was another reason why they were definitely not the Navy's favourite fighting force.

Sub Lieutenant Derek Dowsett RNVR, Assistant Beachmaster, R Commando

I learned very early that we were like red rag to a bull to some RN officers, who saw us as a poorly disciplined rabble of a private army.

Rabble or not, the newly khaki-clad Commandos needed training for the beaches, and for most new arrivals at Ardentinny the training had a fixed pattern.

Able Seaman Fred Simpson, T Commando

Each day at 7 a.m. the men were collected on the parade ground at the flag. Then breakfast, then sent on an assault course up the river. We ran up the path, the whistle blew twice. We had to jump in the river fully clothed. Then over the assault course, including scaling walls, through broken tyres. There was one large rope between two large trees. Each man had a toggle rope (a six-foot length of rope with a toggle at one end and an eye at the other) which was used to slide down between the two trees. After that we ran through the camp to the jetty, dived in and swam back to the beach.

At midnight there were speed marches: march a mile and run a mile. After about seven miles we returned to camp for cups of cocoa. That was a typical day's training.

Officers were expected to do exactly the same training as the ratings, and few were given the reception given to the officers of W Commando in December 1943. W Commando was all Canadian, and their officers were greeted by the Commanding Officer of the base, Commander E. Davis RN, and a Marine band playing 'O Canada'.

The Canadians soon gained a reputation for pranks. Apart from trying to find a suitable mate for the Commander's spaniel, one of their number also let off a thunderflash in the wardroom fireplace. Unfortunately for the Canadians, the chimney flue in the wardroom was shared by the Commander up the stairs, and his cabin was soon enveloped in a cloud of greasy smoke. Because U and V Commando officers were also in the wardroom at the time, punishment could not be confined to the Canadians. Bar privileges for all officers were removed for forty-eight hours.

Apart from fitness, all the Commandos had to be trained in the finer arts of warfare. The Commandos were taught skills such as how to drop off a lorry travelling at 30 mph, or do a parachute roll and end up in a fighting position. They were expected to become proficient in the use of rifle, revolver, tommy gun and anti-tank gun, as well as explosives for clearing obstructions on the beaches. The assault course was a daily treat for the trainees, and the instructors would liven things up by throwing thunderflashes as close to the crawling Commandos as they dared.

One essential skill was the art of tackling barbed wire, which the Commandos practised together as a group. Although it sounds dangerous, in fact the technique for cutting and crossing barbed wire was surprisingly safe.

Sub Lieutenant Jack Gaster RNVR, Assistant Beachmaster J Commando

It was easier for one member to throw himself bodily onto the roll with his arms protecting his face and for the other members of the group to run over his back. It sounded like suicide, but in fact rarely did 'the bridge' get hurt as the wire gave under him like a spring, and by the time it was his turn to cross the wire was invariably flat. I know, because I always seemed to get the job, maybe it was because I was a little heavier than the others, or maybe I had the thickest skin.

The training sessions were punctuated by exercises with the Army. There was constant practising of landings, by day and night. If, during one of these exercises, the officer in charge decided that a landing craft had been hit, the Commandos had the unenviable job of wading out into the freezing waters of the loch to take it out of the exercise by pushing it into deep water. Although the exercises were designed to be as realistic as possible, sometimes there were advantages to letting the Army get the better of the Commandos.

Able Seaman Fred Simpson, T Commando

Lots of training involved skirmishes against the Army in the woods. We surrendered to them one morning because they had porridge for breakfast.

The Beach Signals units were also required to train to Commando standard so that they could accompany the Commandos onto the beaches, although because of the nature of their duties on the beach their base was another Royal Navy shore base or 'stone frigate', HMS *Dundonald* at Troon.

Signalman Bernard Stone, Royal Naval Beach Signals Section No. B5

Training started right away. Rising at six, going out onto Troon golf course, just wearing a pair of shorts to do physical training, including tossing a telegraph pole up into the air and catching it to come down onto alternate shoulders. We boarded a very old tramp steamer, HMS *Keren*, and sailed round the various Scottish lochs doing assault landings on beaches in freezing waters.

What the inhabitants of some of these remote villages must have thought! They would go peacefully to bed and wake up to find a fully manned naval wireless station sitting on their doorsteps, and in some cases set up in one of their storage sheds. We went on schemes in civilian dress, with no money or papers, and with the Police and the Army trying to find us. Teaching us to operate in enemy territory. Unarmed combat, weapon training and landings with live ammunition being used all became part of the day's work until, without realising it, I suppose we had become a tightly knit fighting unit.

Some also went to another Combined Operations training centre, Dorlin House, which was further up the west coast. Here they benefited from survival training from one of the country's leading experts, who was keen to teach survival without any modern help.

Petty Officer Telegraphist John Savory, Royal Naval Beach Signals Section No. B7

Surgeon Commander Murray Levick lectured on diet and smokeless fire – we later found that petrol in the sand gave better results.

Levick had been the surgeon on Captain Scott's ill-fated 1910–13 Antarctic expedition. He had stayed behind on the run to the Pole itself, but had gone to look for Scott and his companions when they did not return. He wore shorts in Scotland in both the summer and winter months.

At the end of their training, supplies permitting, the Commandos were issued with their Commando knives and green berets. Some Commandos went onto finish their training at the Army Commando Training Centre at Achnacarry, but for those whose training was exclusively at Ardentinny this was the moment when they passed out as fully qualified Commandos.

G Commando were also honoured with a visit from the Commanding Officer at Achnacarry, Lieutenant Colonel Charles Vaughan, to present their berets and knives at the passing-out parade.

Able Seaman Andrew Henderson, G Commando

At the end of our time at Ardentinny there was a passing-out parade when we received our green beret and Commando knife from Colonel Vaughan. We had the option of marching down the pier in full marching order with all our pouches, jumping in the loch and swimming the hundred yards back. At one point I though I was going to drown as everything filled up with water, but there were lots of others there to help.

If anything came to symbolise the Commandos in World War II it was the Commando knife, designed by William Fairbairn and Eric Sykes. Fairbairn and Sykes had first met as members of the Shanghai Municipal Police Force, which maintained law and order in the International Settlement on the Shanghai waterfront. Fairbairn was Assistant Commissioner of Police and head of the Riot Squad. Sykes was a reserve Police officer in charge of the Sniper Unit. In the years up to 1940 Shanghai was probably the most violent city the world has ever seen. The Shanghai Municipal Police Force seized more illegal drugs each year than all the American Police forces combined.

Murder, kidnapping, corruption and drugs were all commonplace, and the Police routinely had to arrest criminals armed with guns and knives, and who possessed an expert knowledge of Chinese and Japanese martial arts.

After an encounter with a gang of criminals in 1908, when Fairbairn was beaten up and left for dead, he enrolled at a ju-jitsu school and became the first foreigner outside Japan to gain the black belt. He then took on the training of all Police recruits and used his experience in dealing with the thugs of the Shanghai waterfront to teach the rookie Policemen unarmed tactics.

In 1931 Fairbairn established the Shanghai Police Armoury, and it was here that the Fairbairn Sykes Commando knife was first conceived and made. The starting point was a hunting knife and a couple of bayonets. The key difference between this knife and daggers of old was that the Fairbairn Sykes knife was designed not only to thrust but to cut and slash as well. Its flexibility gave it a decisive edge over the bayonet.

In 1940, at the suggestion of the Chief Inspector of Small Arms, Fairbairn and Sykes visited Wilkinson Sword in London. Although at this stage there were no firm orders for their Commando knife, Fairbairn and Sykes managed to persuade John Wilkinson-Latham to manufacture a quantity of the knives for sale. To demonstrate the correct use of the knife, Fairbairn astonished Wilkinson-Latham by suddenly grabbing a ruler and engaging Sykes in a mock knife fight. The knife would be made. There were many variations on the original design, some of which featured knuckle-dusters around the hilt. Whichever way you looked at it, the Commando knife was a lethal weapon.

Able Seaman George Fagence, H Commando

This weapon was carried as a last resort. I do know it lived up to its reputation, as during practice I accidentally stuck it into Florrie Ford's back and he went down like a sack of chaff. It's OK – he lived.

Both the knife and armed and unarmed combat were to become synonymous with the Commandos. The training made them dangerous fighters and could be very realistic. In 1942 Fairbairn, by then a Major, took a class at Inverary for G Commando.

Able Seaman Albert Cattell, G Commando

We did unarmed combat with a Marine Major in a school. He was about forty- or fifty-odd then, but he threw us about like rag dolls. He got a loaded gun, a Webley .45, and said to stick it in his back. 'Now when I move, you pull the trigger.' Sodding mad he is, I thought. 'That's an order. As soon as you see me move you pull the trigger.'

I said, 'I'll blow your spine apart.'

He said, 'You'll be too late.' I thought, he'll never get out of this. 'What I'm trying to demonstrate is you never push a gun into the enemy's back, you never get that close.' As soon as he moved I pulled the trigger. My arm was over there, bang! We couldn't fathom out how he did it; but he did it with all of us. The trick was, before your brain could get to your trigger finger, the signal, he'd turn round. If you were right-handed he'd turn to the left, so as he came round his left arm knocked that away, his right hand at your throat or your eyes. If the bloke with the gun is left-handed you do it opposite – you don't knock the gun across his body, that would kill him because it would take a second or so and the trigger finger would work. So you knock it away from the body. We fancied ourselves, in our twenties, fit as fiddles, hard as nails, and this chap was grey haired, close cropped. With stubble. He chucked us about. He was old enough to be our father but he was fit.

Although unarmed combat was designed for use on the enemy, there were occasions when it could come in useful against unruly elements on the British side. In 1944 most of the Levant Schooner Flotilla was celebrating Christmas in a hotel bar on the Greek Island of Khios. This was an undercover force which used motorised Greek coastal trading vessels called caiques and MTBs to carry out reconnaissance work and to land SAS and SBS parties to reconnoitre and raid the German-held islands in the area.

Wireless Telegraphist Leonard Robinson DSM, Levant Schooner Flotilla

One drunken SAS soldier who was constantly making trouble had pulled out his revolver and was threatening the orchestra that if they did not play 'The Dirty Dockyard Ditty' he would shoot them. Naturally the audience took it as a joke, but the hotel manager called out the Naval patrol. A jeep with the Naval Duty Officer and patrolmen pulled up alongside our MTB and the officer called me over. I knew him well from months before. He said to me, 'There is a madman with a gun threatening the orchestra if they don't play his tune in the hotel. If I go in and confront him and if he should strike me there will be a court martial but if you go in and disarm him he will just get Jankers.'

So I walked into the bar. The drunk was standing on a table stripping off his clothes to the music and he was down to his underpants. I simply walked over to him and ordered him to pack it in. He brought the revolver down to point it at my head. I grabbed his wrist and continued his downward thrust, past my head with my left hand. I next put my right arm between his legs and heaved him across my shoulders in a fireman's lift. Then I gripped his right forearm with my right hand and released my left hand on his right wrist to put the revolver's safety catch to the 'on' position. Now I was in a position to remove the weapon from his grasp without it being fired.

After training at HMS *Armadillo* many Commandos went to Achnacarry to finish off their Commando training. Achnacarry was the principal Army Commando training centre. The Commanding Officer, Lieutenant Charles Vaughan, stamped his personality on the whole place. Vaughan had been a private soldier in World War I, rising to Regimental Sergeant Major with the Coldstream Guards. In World War II he was summoned to create a Commando training regime second to none. Vaughan, the 'Rommel of the North', was exactly the right man for the job. He created a demanding regime, which was as strong on realism as it was on training.

The first sight which greeted new arrivals at Achnacarry was a series of graves with headstones engraved with inscriptions such as, 'This man failed to keep his rifle clean,' or, 'This man stood on the skyline.' It had a salutary effect. So did the live firing exercises.

Able Seaman George Fagence, H Commando

Lofty was to the right, alongside me, in one of these assimilated exercises where live ammo is used. (Vaughan had twin Vickers machine guns and sprayed the ground haphazardly all around you.) Lofty, prone on the ground, did a horizontal airlift, fell over backwards and passed out. I did a quick check; he had blood pouring from his right bum cheek.

Before the exercises started the Royal Naval Commandos were addressed by Vaughan, who welcomed them to Achnacarry with a speech which seemed designed to stiffen them up.

Lieutenant Commander Maurice Vernon Redshaw, Beachmaster N Commando, later Principal Beachmaster Q Commando and K Commando

We marched straight onto the parade ground as on the previous course, 42 Royal Marine Commando marched off. We were addressed by the Commandant, Lieutenant Colonel Vaughan of the Buffs. He more or less informed us we had come there to learn how to die like soldiers. We were all issued with denims and rifles and from then onwards followed the most strenuous time I shall ever know. The weather was very cold and the hills were full of snow. Immediately after breakfast each morning we fell in, wearing denims and battle order, officers and ratings in the same file, for inspection. Denims had to be free of mud, webbing blancoed, brasses polished, and rifles immaculate, after inspection, which was rigid. We proceeded over the assault course, through mud and water and snow and how cold was that water coming down from the mountains. Our lives were made up of inspections, assault courses, speed marches, cliff climbing, and a thousand ways of endeavouring to demoralise raw soldiers. Only one of the ratings couldn't make the grade and he was returned to *Armadillo*. It seemed to rain all the time, and I'm sure we all hated Achnacarry at first, then, gradually without our being aware, it seemed to change. We learned to laugh at hardship. Actually the only thing that had changed was ourselves. They taught us that we were on the winning side of the war.

Although the training was hard, the instructors were always remembered as being out of the ordinary. They never bullied; they wanted their students to pass, and they were prepared to go that extra mile to help them achieve that.

Able Seaman Michael McFadden, L Commando

One of our chaps couldn't make it on the toggle slide. Later that evening the instructor came round to find him and coached him personally to do it.

The assault course at Achnacarry had to be undertaken every day. N Commando had taken very seriously the part of the introductory speech about the Naval Commandos not letting the side down. To the puzzlement of another one of the Royal Marine Commandos undergoing training at the same time, N Commando promptly broke the assault-course record.

Leading Seaman Ray Bromley, N Commando

We were sent off in ten batches at ten-minute intervals. The batches were called A, B, C, D, E, F etc. and we decided to pull a fast one on the Marines. One of our Petty Officers spoke to C batch and said, 'When you get back you become A,' and so we broke the record! When we were leaving Achnacarry, one of the Royal Marine Sergeants said, 'By the way, how did you break the record?' To which we replied, 'Tell you what – we'll buy you a drink after the war and tell you then!'

Most of the instructors were battle-hardened veterans. One who was not but who nevertheless left a lasting impression on many Commandos was Stanley or Sonny Bissell, an Olympic wrestler and black-belt martial artist. He was one of the Metropolitan Police intake into the Commandos, and when he passed through Achnacarry he was persuaded by Colonel Vaughan to stay on as an instructor.

Able Seaman George Fagence, H Commando

The six and a half foot instructor, a black Dan, two and a half feet across the shoulders, made it all look so easy as he threw us through the air, his legs were like telegraph poles. Luckily, he was only on half-power and my arm placed to block his shin miraculously never broke. But I still cry when I think about it! This individual was also our knife-fighting instructor.

Although unarmed combat was all part of the Achnacarry experience, the camp itself was not the first place where the students were introduced to the Achnacarry way of Commando training. Instead, it all started at Spean Bridge railway station where the lorries were waiting for them.

Sub Lieutenant Clifford Claughton, Assistant Beachmaster H Commando

Our party was met at the station by an Army sergeant complete with lorry and driver. Didn't seem big enough to take our seventy-plus bodies. Not intended to. Kit loaded aboard, the seven-mile journey to Achnacarry was on foot. The sergeant was about six feet tall with legs up to his armpits. He didn't waste any time in getting us all fell in and covering the ground to our new temporary abode in quick time. That was just for starters. Camp was reached with a few faces looking drawn. Perhaps a gentle introduction had been expected. Achnacarry was a typical Scottish baronial mansion belonging to Campbell Cameron of Lochiel. Quarters, however, for all, irrespective of rank, were Nissen huts.

Sleeping arrangements were rather primitive: two hard 'biscuits' resting on low tressled planks of wood. Three Army blankets, of course. Pillow – your problem. Battle-order small pack, as like as not. After check-in it was on parade with an outline of the training programme in store.

A typical day at Achnacarry was a long one, and the programme did not stop for weekends. Part of the daily routine was always the same, including the assault course. But there was also time to learn other new skills, including abseiling, a popular sport today but then a novelty to the Commandos. They also learned such essential skills as living off the land.

Able Seaman Lofty Lucas, G Commando

A typical day at Achnacarry – up at 05.30 in the morning, shorts, no vest, physical training for half an hour. Then breakfast, or they might take you for a ten-mile run first. Then we had our lectures: how to live off the country if you got cut off, different grasses you could eat. The different shellfish you could find on the beach. You could break your knife getting some of the shells off the rocks.

Fieldcraft was an equally important part of the training programme. Realism was the name of game at Achnacarry, so that the Commandos would be as battle-experienced as possible before they ever got to the battlefield. A vital part of this was learning how to turn the sounds of the battlefield to their own advantage.

Captain James Dunning, Fieldcraft Instructor, Combined Basic Training Centre Achnacarry

An important demonstration was the Crack and Thump one. The main object was to show how an enemy position could be located by listening for the origin of the firing, and a secondary object was to familiarise the intake with distinctive sounds of our own weapons and those of the enemy.

The trainees were brought at a steady double – normal practice when moving from one place of work to another – to a piece of ground just outside the camp. There, once in the viewing position,

I said they were all in the weapons sights of the enemy and most of them were only 150 to 250 yards to the front.

'Try and spot them,' I challenged.

I didn't get many takers, and those I did get were mistaken. It was surprising how a clump of heather could be mistaken for the head and shoulders of a man lying in the firing position. While they were still looking I passed on some tips on searching the ground: how to search systematically, bit by bit, and to look hard at features that don't seem to blend or fit into the background or surroundings. We also passed around binoculars to help them, but to no avail. After a while I got the individual enemy to fire over the heads of the watching trainees.

Before they started to fire, I explained the importance and sequence of crack and thump. When a shot is fired at one, the first thing one notices – if it hasn't got your number on it – is the distinctive crack, like that of a whip, as the bullet flies overhead or to a flank. Then, as the bullet moves quicker than the speed of sound, it is followed by the thump (sound) of the actual discharge of the round in the weapon, and it is this thump they had to try and locate. Forget the crack, it's missed you and gone for ever . . .

Apart from learning specific skills, the Royal Naval Commandos were set tasks designed to help them to use their own initiative. Given the nature of Commando operations, it was vital that each Commando could think for himself if the occasion demanded it.

Leading Seaman Ray Bromley, N Commando

One part of our training was to be taken out at night a certain distance from the camp and abandoned. We had to find our own way back by the 08.00 parade using our own initiative. I heard the lorries had to be inspected, and all hands had to move away from the lorries. I dived into the bushes near the lorries. The drivers reported the lorries empty and prepared to move off. I made my move in the dark. I darted for the rear one as the drivers were climbing in to drive away, with the result that I was in camp in no time at all and had a good night's kip.

One of the highlights of all this training was an overnight bivouac for the Royal Naval Commandos, designed to test their ability to function together as a real Commando unit and to make sure that no enemies could get anywhere near them. N Commando's rations for the night were a piece of raw meat each, two potatoes and two slices of bread, which they cooked before the inevitable attack from the Achnacarry instructors. N Commando were ready and waiting.

Leading Seaman Ray Bromley, N Commando

When the meal was finished, we put out the fires and built the bivouacs over where we had been; believe me it was warm inside. Taking up defensive positions, we waited for the attack from the training instructors. It was not long in coming, and thunder-flashes rained down on our positions. We replied with blanks from our .303s but a few live rounds saved from the rifle range the previous day soon put the instructors to flight.

For those Royal Naval Commandos who finished their training at Achnacarry, the final passing-out parade was the moment they received their coveted green beret and Commando knife from Colonel Vaughan. They had made it through one of the toughest training regimes in the history of warfare.

Able Seaman Lofty Lucas, G Commando

At the end you got your beret and your knife. If you failed, they told you what you failed on and they gave you a chance to go back and do it again. You'd see tears on the faces of anyone who'd failed.

But not all the Commandos received their beret and knife at the passing-out parade. Unusually, N Commando had not received theirs at Achnacarry. Instead, they were to be given them just before embarking on the voyage to Sicily for their first operation. But even without them they looked the part.

Leading Seaman Ray Bromley, N Commando

We were dressed in khaki battledress with green belt and gaiters, a red plaited lanyard around the left shoulder and tucked into the left pocket. The Naval cap was still worn, and the beret and knife were being withheld until such time as we were ready to leave on the assault ship *Glengyle* for Italy. Why they were not given to us on passing out at Achnacarry I do not know. The Petty Officers and officers wore shirts and ties. We also carried a large pack and a small pack, a different type of gas mask, sealed against the water if we should have to wade ashore in deep water. On our shoulders were the flashes of the RN Commando, below this we wore our rank and gunnery badges and stripes, and in red under the shoulder flash was the Combined Operations badge.

For the newly qualified Royal Naval Commandos, fresh from either HMS *Armadillo* or Achnacarry or both, it was time to put all their training into practice.

CHAPTER 3

The Mediterranean (1)

In the Autumn of 1942, the men of Royal Naval Beach Commando G for George were distinctly unhappy. Training was one thing and they had done lots of that, but with North Africa on the cards and secrecy the order of the day they found themselves locked in a local school in Greenock. It was a situation they did not like one little bit.

Able Seaman Albert Cattell, G Commando

We climbed over the railings and went home for the weekend and when we came back to the station all the military police were waiting for us.

'Desertion in the face of the enemy.'

'Don't be so daft, where's the enemy?' We were fed up locked in this infants school. They threatened to hang me from the highest yardarm in the Royal Navy. We never thought we were deserting, we only took a weekend down the line. After climbing the railings some passing girls gave us a lift to the station and we jumped the train, no one had money for tickets and I got off before I reached my station because the military police and RTO [Regulating Transport Officers] fellows were there. They didn't punish us. They said, 'When you get back off this invasion you'll get your punishment.'

On return from their unauthorised leave G Commando were immediately put on board HMS *Karanja*, where all their identification was removed as North Africa was to be an all-American operation. Christened Operation Torch, North Africa was the one place where the Allies believed they could undertake successful amphibious landings in 1942.

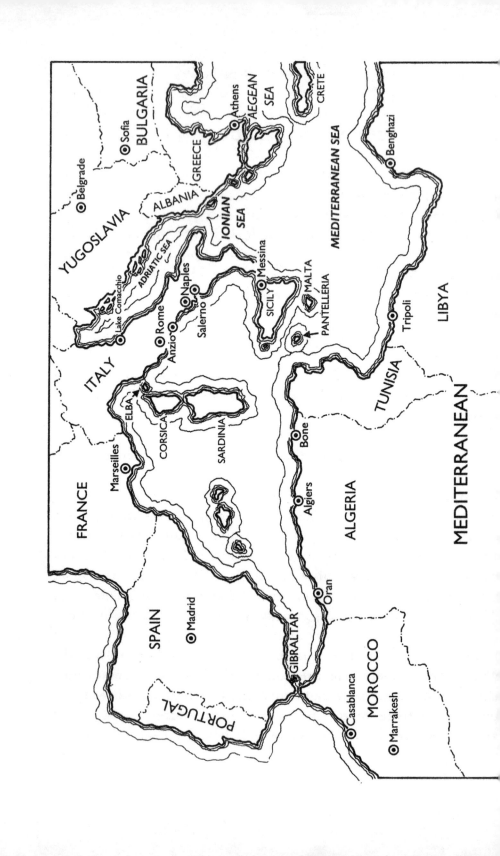

The Commandos landed with two of the three task forces, the Eastern Task Force which landed at Algiers and the Centre Task Force which landed at Oran. The Western Task Force landed at Casablanca and was entirely an American affair.

For this operation six Commandos were required, E Commando, F Commando, G Commando, C Commando as well as the newly formed H Commando (or How in the phonetic alphabet of the time) and J (for Jig) Commando.

The Task Force passed Gibraltar in the first week of November 1942, but with weather conditions unfavourable the landings looked like they might have to be postponed. However the night of 7th November 1942 was much less windy and the landings went ahead.

As with Dieppe the North African beaches were split up and given names. The Eastern Task Force landed at Algiers where the beaches were A (Apple) to the west, B (Bear) in the centre where the town was, and C (Charlie) to the east. G Commando were landed at Apple Beach.

Able Seaman Albert Cattell, G Commando

I was first ashore with my Lieutenant two hours before the invasion actually started. There was a beach, a sandy track leading off it, and an orange grove and a tiny village. We all landed, the Beachmaster was in the middle and it was dead quiet. No opposition at all. Got out of the craft and flung ourselves down in the jungle on the edge and waited and listened. Nothing. My job was to protect my officer while he patrolled the beach with a big pole. This is the daftest idea I've ever heard. He stripped off naked and went in the water probing for mines – if he hit one, Bang! As he walked up the beach the other two were coming down towards us, the Beachmaster in the middle. I was there to protect him from the enemy while he was prodding about. Thank God he never found any mines! That took some courage, I thought. Damm glad I hadn't got that job. He dressed himself wet – got nothing to wipe himself on.

Meanwhile the Centre Task Force was making its landings at Oran to the west of Algiers. Again the beaches were given names, from east to west: Z Beach, which was near Arzeu, Y Beach and X Beach, where there was known to be a sandbar between the ships and the beach.

Petty Officer Telegraphist John Savory, Royal Naval Beach Signals Section No. B7

I had stopped worrying about the amount of phosphorence we were creating and had time to wonder if we would ground on the bar said to lie off the landing beach.

We were all jammed together standing on the deck of the landing craft. I had the wireless set on my back with only two of the eighteen aerial rods jointed on when I found that contact with the wire cutters carried by the GI in front of me restored full signal strength. Then the craft touched on the bar, slowed, then lifted forward on the slight swell. Ahead a dog barked, otherwise all was quiet. The craft door went down, and to my surprise, presently breast deep in the water, buoyed up by my inflated lifebelt, I was gently lifted off my feet despite 30-plus lb of wireless and gear, 10 lb of spare battery, revolver and ammunition, entrenching tool, small pack and water bottle, plus a hundred rounds of ammunition for the rifle. Once ashore our party of four settled in at the top of the beach. I with all eighteen rods of aerial rising skyward from the set.

I noted there was a light on a building behind the beach and was interested to hear a Beachmaster Lieutenant send first an AB (Able Seaman) and then a Leading Hand to put it out. I decided I would check on the light still showing bright as ever.

I found a well-organised pub with the Leading Hand trying to get sand out of his stripped Lewis (a task which kept him occupied all the while we were ashore). The Able Seaman was on a stool at the bar so I joined him there, acquired a glass of wine and started to chat to the proprietor. He gave me a graphic description of what it was like to be wakened in the dead of night to find an alien army on his doorstep. The local Arabs wouldn't give any trouble but there was the Foreign Legion stationed somewhere near.

At this point the Lieutenant came in, took in the situation in a flash and joined the party at the bar.

Rumours of the French Foreign Legion were also troubling E Commando, who had landed at Arzeu and linked up with the American Rangers. But in the event it was not the Foreign Legion which posed the greatest danger to the Commandos.

Petty Officer Henry Clark, E Commando

When we landed in the Naval base we joined up with a troop of Rangers, supposed to be their Commandos. They were trigger-happy. The password was 'Heigh Ho Silver', and the answer was 'Away'. In the dark if we were challenged we dropped flat and shouted 'Away'. Then the bullets flew overhead. One of the Rangers opened fire on one of the cranes, he said there was a sniper up there. The body that hit the deck was a Ranger. He had been sent up to use it as an observation post.

Back on Apple Beach G Commando had also suffered a disaster although they had yet to find out about it. Several days after the landings their ship, HMS *Karanja*, was hit by dive bombers when she was sailing towards Algiers to pick them up. All their kit was on board.

The landings had been successful, but the Task Force was not quite done. The Eastern Task Force had unfinished business in capturing the ports of Bougie and Djidjelli, which were further east along the coast. But the Germans were increasing their air attacks on the invading forces and the landings at Djidjelli were abandoned in favour of a successful landing at Bougie by G Commando.

Having successfully got the Allied forces into North Africa it was time for the Commandos and Signallers to return home. But the U-boats, which had been absent for the outward journey were hunting the convoys with a vengeance. On the way home HMS *Ettrick* was found by U-boat *U155* about seventy miles from Gibraltar. It was just after 3 a.m. on 15th November.

Signalman Norman Weston, Royal Navy Beach Signals Section No. B5

I remember being tipped out of my hammock clothed in just a vest and a pair of pants and almost immediately being plunged into darkness and having to struggle over broken glass and debris which had been a glass side-panelled stairway to the next deck. Fortunately the boat was not overcrowded as it had been on the outward journey. Otherwise I hate to think what might have been the loss of life. Apparently the torpedo struck the crews' quarters, which was a deck below ours, and I recall the figure of twenty-one lives lost. I believe our Beach Section all survived. I and several others abandoned ship before it sank and were picked up by a Norwegian-manned destroyer whose crew quickly took us down below decks where we were given plenty to drink to take our minds away from what had happened.

They returned to Gibraltar and were put on another ship bound for Great Britain. No one slept below decks after that. G Commando hitched a lift on HMS *Keren* without any of their kit and made it home safely.

With North Africa safely in Allied hands the way was open for the invasion of Italy, a process which started with Operation Husky – the invasion of Sicily. Although North Africa had been a success, the military planners in Combined Operations wanted to improve the way that landings were organised for the future.

The Royal Naval Commandos were in charge on the beaches. That would not change. But the way the Army organised itself to move men and material through the beaches and to evacuate casualties would change.

Until and including North Africa, Army units and individuals were thrown together in military 'Beach Bricks' for specific operations, a system which was found to be inadequate in practice and also difficult to administer. Royal Naval Commandos trained alongside their allotted Beach Bricks prior to operations.

In November 1942 Mountbatten set out the new arrangements which would now involve permanent Beach Groups.

Memo dated 20th November 1942 referenced 3926/BRV/16 and signed Louis Mountbatten, Chief of Combined Operations

FUNCTION OF THE BEACH GROUP

Briefly the function of the Beach Group is, in conjunction with the Royal Navy, to:
(a) Arrange and control the movement of all personnel and vehicles from ships and landing craft to assembly areas inland.
(b) Move stores form ships' holds and crafts to dumps in the Beach Maintenance Area.
(c) Develop and organise the beaches and Beach Maintenance Area as regards defence, movement and administration, including evacuation of casualties and recovery of vehicles.
(d) Provide a Beach Signal Organisation.

There would be one Beach Group per Army brigade, and the Commander of the Beach Group would be the Army equivalent of the Principal Beachmaster in the Naval Commandos. As with the Beach Bricks the Commandos would need to work closely with the new Beach Groups.

The Principal Beachmaster reported to the Senior Naval Officer Landing (SNOL) or to his deputy (DSNOL). The SNOL was usually a Royal Navy Captain, the deputy usually a Royal Navy Commander. They would work alongside the Army Brigade Commander and the Principal Military Landing Officer (PMLO).

These new arrangements took some months to filter through but by summer 1943 the Commandos were training alongside the new Beach Groups. After their training at HMS *Armadillo* and other Naval centres, R Commando was allocated to their Beach Group at Strathpeffer in the Scottish Highlands where good working relationships were soon being forged.

Able Seaman Ken Barry, R Commando

We joined No. 6 Beach Group. I did not know then that a Beach Group was a mixture of units to enable a beach to operate smoothly. The largest unit was the Oxfordshire and Buckinghamshire Light Infantry. Everyone was billeted in hotels, as this was an old spa town. We messed in with this regiment and mustered on parade with them. It was here I got myself into a bit of trouble as I heaved a snowball at their RSM and hit him in the neck. I was put under close arrest and got fourteen days cells, which meant being confined to your room, but I did miss a couple of wet landings, which was a blessing.

Back at HMS *Armadillo* the training of new Commandos was in full swing. There was room there to train three Commando units, and the boiler rooms were kept busy drying out the khaki serge, wool and cotton which soaked up the Scottish rain.

C Commando were in training for Sicily at Bickley in south-west England. Albert Cattell, who had been transferred in from his mates in G Commando against his wishes, was crossing an assault course when a pain in his leg put paid to his career with the Commandos. It turned out to be a blood clot.

Although Albert Cattell had been transferred without any option, officers could and did transfer on request. The weekly dispositions of HMS *Armadillo* are full of officers moving between Commandos. And throughout late 1942 and early 1943 there were more Commandos for them to choose from.

They included K Commando (or King in the phonetic alphabet of the time), L (Love) Commando and M (Mike Commando), which was the first to be actually formed at HMS *Armadillo* itself in November 1942. Prior to that the individual Commandos had been formed at Coulport House, across Loch Long from HMS *Armadillo*, or at Inverary.

After M Commando came N (Nan) Commando, O (Oboe) Commando, P (Peter) Commando, Q (Queen) Commando and R (Roger) Commando in June 1943. Later in 1943 came S (Sugar) Commando, T (Tare) Commando, U (Uncle) Commando and V

(Victor) Commando. Finally there was the all-Canadian Commando W (William).

The invasion of Sicily was a bigger operation than North Africa and required no fewer than seven Royal Naval Commandos. These were C, E, F, G, K, M and N Commandos.

Before the invasion of Sicily could take place it was vital that the Island of Pantelleria was captured. This is a small island which lies between Sicily and Tunisia. Not only did its air base pose a significant threat to the Allied invasion of Sicily but it was needed itself for Allied use against the Germans and the Italians during the invasion.

The job was entrusted to D Commando, which was an unusual group because it did not train at HMS *Armadillo*. For some time there had been a Mobile Beach Party which had followed the 8th Army along the North African coast, supplying it with food and water.

In 1943 this was expanded into a full Commando, absorbing along the way another unit called No. 5 Beach Party which was also called the Saunders Beach Party. It became D Commando as most of the original members of Beach Party D had been killed at Dieppe.

Training took place at HMS *Saunders* on the banks of the Suez canal. Instead of route marches in the Scottish rain the Commandos marched through the soft sand of the desert.

Pantelleria itself is a volcanic Island and is surrounded by cliffs. The main assault on 11th June 1943 was through the small artificial harbour at the north end of the island, a job made easier by a massive aerial and naval bombardment. As always the Navy wanted to make sure its ships suffered as little damage as possible.

Signalman Reg Nadin, Royal Naval Beach Signals Section No. 8

As the armada assembled a general signal was sent out to say that every effort must be made to protect the command ship, HMS *Largs*, from getting hit by enemy air attack. This vessel had been someone's luxury yacht in better days. I will leave it to your imagination to guess what 'Jack' said about such a signal, but pulling up the ladder came into it. For the assault we transferred to an LCM (chipslicer, because of the ramp). The idea was to sail into the harbour at noon, which we did. As we reached the harbour entrance the craft's engine stopped and I well recall the Army Captain in command leaping to his feet, waving his revolver and shouting, 'Good God – Royal Navy, don't let us down at a time like this!' The Royal Navy came up trumps as usual. The harbour was very small and under regular Stuka attack, and the water supply became critical as the enemy had poisoned the island's wells.

Lieutenant Hugh Birley RNVR, Assistant Beachmaster D Commando

The harbour area had been thoroughly plastered with bombs over several days. There were few Germans on the Island and the Italians were for the most part deep in their air-raid shelters – tunnels in the soft volcanic rock. Our only serious discomfort came from the Focke-Wolf 190s which came skimming over the sea from Sicily bombing and strafing us several times a day while the '100 percent air cover' promised us by General Spaatz of the US Air Force was droning round in circles high overhead.

Although the defenders had not put up any resistance the air raids were a constant menace during the Commandos' stay. The harbour where the Commandos had landed and were helping with the subsequent invasion and accompanying supplies was a natural target.

Able Seaman William Woods, D Commando

One bomb hit and completely demolished the Military Police HQ which had been set up right on the quay. As we tried to do what we could, climbing on top of the ruins, I saw a hand protruding. I grasped it and found myself holding a man's arm. No body. Very sorrowful!

Further south at a small cove two enemy F-lighters had been captured. These were similar to the British tank landing craft and Hugh Birley was ordered to sail one to Sousse in North Africa, a journey which nearly ended in disaster when the heavy seas threatened to make it through the damaged bow doors. Also in his crew was Signalman Reg Nadin. However, they made it safely.

With Pantelleria safely in Allied hands the way was clear for the invasion of Sicily one month later on 10th July 1943. Sicily had been the subject of much debate between the Admirals and the Generals. Originally the plan had been for three American Army divisions to land on the north-west coast and to make for Palermo while the four British Army divisions landed on the south-east corner of the island and made for the ports of Syracuse and Catania.

The Naval Commander of the Eastern Task Force, which contained British and Canadian forces, was Vice-Admiral Sir Bertram Ramsay, and to him fell the task of planning the invasion. He was immediately unhappy with the original plan, as was General Montgomery. Ramsay thought the Allied forces were too spread out and he wanted all forces to concentrate on the south-east corner of the island where the strategically important airfields were located.

This was the plan which was adopted and all the Allied forces would land on a seventy-five mile stretch of coastline. Ramsay's Eastern Task Force would land in three separate Task Groups, each of which would land at an Assault Sector. Each sector would be under the control of a Senior Naval Landing Officer (SNOL) and his Royal Naval Commandos.

The sectors were, from north to south, Acid, which ran from just south of Syracuse to Vendicari Island, Bark East to the Pachino peninsula and Bark West to Cape Passero. After this point the American beaches began.

These sectors were further divided into areas. Acid had G, H and J which contained the individual beaches. These beaches were each called Green, Amber and Red. Bark East sector had Amber,

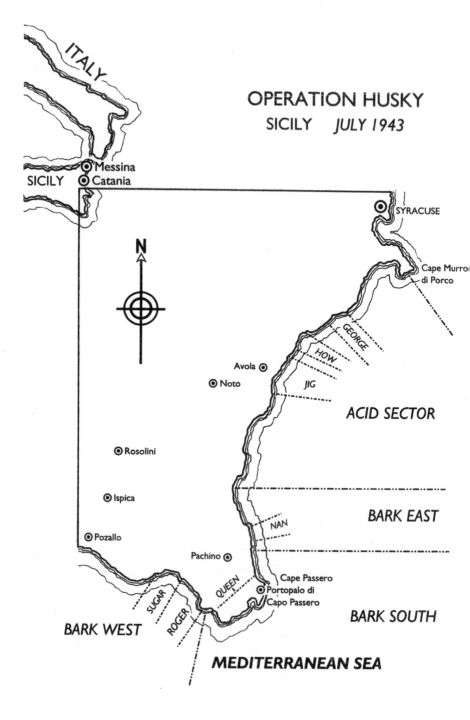

Red and Red Scramble beaches, and Bark South had Q, S and R areas, again divided into Green, Amber and Red beaches.

Before the invasion the beaches had been surveyed by the Combined Operations Pilotage Parties, which suffered heavy casualties in their task of coming in from small craft to reconnoitre the beaches in order to ensure that there were no surprises when the landings took place.

While the planning and reconnaissance were taking place the Commandos were making their way south from Scotland and England. Although M Commando went to Sicily via North Africa, which was now in Allied hands, most of the troop ships went south around Africa before heading north for the Suez Canal and the Mediterranean. F Commando sailed south in March 1943 in a convoy of twelve assault ships and twenty ordinary ships. At Suez all the troops were disembarked and F Commando took part in a number of exercises with the Durham Light Infantry. Shortly before embarking again for the invasion of Sicily, General Montgomery reviewed the assembled troops which included the Royal Naval Commandos.

Sub Lieutenant Derek Whitehorn RNVR, Assistant Beachmaster F Commando

Doing his rounds in a jeep General Montgomery pulled up and asked me, 'Who are the sailors and where do they come from?' He made a few remarks directly to us, emphasising our importance and how we must not let down the folks at home. Later I was ordered to attend an oration by Monty to all the officers involved in the initial thirty-minute phase of the forthcoming assault. This was most inspiring and for the very first time gave me tremendous confidence in what we were about to undertake.

There was still another voyage to endure before arriving in Sicily, although it turned out to be a pleasant cruise through the Mediterranean. Enemy aircraft spotted the invasion fleet some four days before it arrived off Sicily but no attack was made.

N Commando were also on their way to Sicily but in different ships to the journey from Scotland. N1 sailed in HMS *Glengyle* and N3 in the *Derbyshire*. N2 were in the care of Captain H. W. Hettema of the Dutch assault ship *Marnix van Sinte Aldegonde*, where there was time for a last drink the evening before the assault. It was 9th July 1943.

Lieutenant Commander Maurice Vernon Redshaw RNVR, Beach-master N Commando, later Principal Beachmaster Q Commando and K Commando

The last night on board Captain Hettema invited me to his cabin for a final drink and we talked about what lay ahead. He said how much he wished he could accompany me ashore in the dawn and he gave me a pistol to enable me, on his behalf, to shoot the first German I saw! We looked at the chart and I offered to hoist the Netherlands ensign as soon as we landed so he could be with us in spirit; he sent for a new ensign, which he gave me. He also pointed out that the Netherlands in London had overlooked to declare war on Italy but he and I would do it for them – he would ask their approval on his return to London!

H-Hour was 03.30 hours on 10th July 1943. By midnight on 9th July the invasion force was assembled just off Sicily. F Commando, as per their orders, we sent in to land in Acid Sector, area J near the town of Avola.

Able Seaman Ken Oakley, F Commando

After a good meal we donned our equipment and manned the assault boats. I was sitting right in the stern of the boat and spent some time making myself comfortable. At last the order came, 'Lower Boats,' and we were away, the sea was rough and our boat was thrown against the parent ship. Crash! Away went the two-inch mortar, swept over the side by the hook of the boats' falls. 'It's time they supplied us with umbrellas,' said one soldier, as another great sea swept over us.

Now came that very trying time between ship and shore when one wonders if he will survive the unknown that lies ahead. The boats were tossed all over the ocean and all the soldiers were seasick, but they had cardboard boxes to vomit into and this helped them a lot.

Suddenly a flare burst above us and surprise was lost, when we still had about a mile to go. The formations split up and began to make for their own landing places, with fire from enemy machine guns passing over them.

Tat-tat-tat-tat. Bren guns began to speak and then, Crunch, 'Down door,' and we were there. A Sapper began to cry, plead and cling to the floorboards, swearing he would not move. We left him (his nerve was gone) and dived into about three feet of water to wade fifty yards to the shore. The shrill whine of bullets speeded us on and at last we went to earth at the water's edge. Bren guns engaged the enemy machine guns and we began to take our bearings. We had landed in almost exactly the right place and so it did not take us long to set up our lights and call in the second flight. We then waded out along the length of the beach to find the best landing places. These were marked and the Assistant Beachmaster and myself proceeded to find the Beachmaster. By this time the enemy MGs had been silenced but we could not find the Beachmaster. I was detailed to find him and make the report, so off I went towards the Marina d'Avola. I joined up with four more Beach Commandos but could not find the Beachmaster.

We were approaching the marina tower when a sniper opened fire at us. We took cover and replied as best we could. Our cover was a ledge towards the top of a small cliff, and to regain the beach we had to cross a lot of open ground.

The Assistant Beachmaster, Derek Whitehorn, was coming in the opposite direction to Ken Oakley and his group of Commandos. As Assistant Beachmaster it fell to him to carry out a reconnaissance of the smaller side beaches, looking for obstacles in the water and on the beaches as well as exit points for possible use later on. As he came towards Ken Oakley the bullets from the sniper's rifle started to kick up the sand a couple of feet in front of him.

Not only was the sniper a problem but the shells from a British destroyer were falling short and endangering the Commandos. Derek Whitehorn was totally exposed on the beach with only a loaded revolver to defend himself against a high-powered sniper's rifle. He decided to pretend to be hit.

Able Seaman Ken Oakley, F Commando

We had decided to make a dash for it when one of our destroyers, HMS *Tartar*, opened fire at the tower. The situation became sticky. *Tartar*'s shells fell short and were too close for comfort. I decided to make a run for it when the sniper opened up again at a man coming from our beach. This man appeared to be hit for he rolled in the water and floated away. (However we found out later that it was the Assistant Beachmaster and he was just playing possum).

A little while later we made a run for it and regained our beach safely. No other Beach Commandos had landed and the Beachmaster had not appeared so we did our best getting the craft in and directing the avalanche of men ashore. It was about this time, nearly an hour after H-Hour, that a battery in the hills began to shell us. A landing craft carrying about 250 men was the target. It was beached and the men were pouring off down two ladders, but near misses and one hit were making things hot. I waded out and told the men to jump for it as the water was not very deep. A few jumped and I steadied them as they fell, and then it came. A terrific explosion and I felt myself fading away into oblivion. I came to under the water. I felt numb and shocked, had I been wounded? Or maybe some limbs were missing? I could not tell and then I felt someone catch my legs and drag me down again. I lost my reason and kicked like mad until I was free and shot to the surface. A body floated by, its limbs still kicking, it must have been the man who clutched me. The water had become a sea of blood and limbs, the remains of once grand fighting men who would never be identified.

I staggered though all this to the water's edge and then looked dazedly around. My comrades were fleeing for cover and in the water were men crying for help. I went in the water again to fetch a man whose arm was hanging on by a few bits of cloth and flesh. He cried, 'My arm! Look, it's hit me!' I said nothing but managed to get him to the beach and lay him down. I then collapsed, exhausted, and still those shells came down far too close for comfort. I rose again to see a man sitting on the ladder of the landing craft crying, 'Help me, oh help!' I went and goodness knows how I got him to the beach. He was hit all over his body and was a dead weight with shattered legs dragging in the water. I shall never forget how he thanked me as I lay there almost sobbing at such terrible sights; so this was war!

By this time the cruiser supporting us had silenced the batteries and I had time to look around. The landing craft had been hit directly above where I was standing at the time of the explosion. How did I get away with it? A man or his remains lay splattered over the side of the landing craft.

With the beach working and the Assistant Beachmaster ashore the next wave of landing craft started to arrive. Conventional Commando practice meant that the Beachmaster and the Principal Beachmaster landed in subsequent waves even though they might be needed on the beaches earlier.

Able Seaman Ken Oakley, F Commando

At about H plus four hours the Beachmaster turned up, and it was about this time that we had a calamity. An LCI had beached some distance from the shore and the men were ordered to disembark. At once they were up to their necks with full equipment on and it looked serious.

I went out to give a hand and was swept off my feet by the receding tide. I caught hold of one soldier and tried to get him ashore but I discovered that my boots and tin helmet were pulling me down. I was forced to release the soldier and had to fight for my own life as the tide was taking me out and under. I struggled desperately but it was no use. I threw away my tin hat and tried again. Twice I went under and I had almost given up when I saw a boat coming along picking soldiers up. I hailed it with what little breath I had left and they threw me a line, which I missed. So I was left until they had picked up the two soldiers and then they threw me a life belt and towed me to the beach, where I collapsed again.

I came to and swilled out my mouth with fresh water, for I felt as if I had swallowed half the Med. In the mean time a lifeline had been passed to the LCI and I hung onto that and assisted soldiers to get ashore. All visible signs of enemy resistance had now disappeared and our troops and equipment were pouring ashore.

For his actions at Sicily, Ken Oakley was Mentioned in Dispatches. Not too far from him E Commando had also landed in Acid Sector. F Commando were in J area, E Commando were in G area. They too had come through the Suez Canal and the Middle East. Ahead of E Commando glider troops had been dispatched as advance-assault soldiers. E Commando saw them on their way to the beach.

Petty Officer Henry Clark, E Commando

When we got in the boats to go ashore it was heartbreaking to pass glider troops in the water, they were shouting, 'Go on Commandos, knock hell out of the Eyeties!' The inexperienced American pilots had slipped them too far out against an offshore wind. We were overloaded. So we couldn't help. I later learned that a lot drowned. When we hit the beach I knew it was the wrong beach, I had been studying the models for days, I told the cox'n to go back out and go to our beach on the right. This young Lieutenant in the Green Howards said, 'Is this Sicily?' I said, 'Yes,' and he promptly jumped ashore saying to his men, 'Come on, this'll do us!' We went back out to sea and approached the beach to our right. Before we hit the beach a machine gun opened fire from a pillbox, and because the LCA (assault landing craft) are made of plywood we started to take in water. I lifted the cover over the engines and said to the stoker, 'Can you go any faster? We are under fire.'

He looked at me and said, 'Is this where all this bloody water's coming from?' He was sat in between the two engines and was up to his knees in water. After a bit of juggling he coaxed more speed and we hit the beach. My objective was the pillbox on the right. As I ran towards it a huge steel door opened and four men ran out and ran up a lane along the side of the river. At the top of this lane was a bridge over the road to Syracuse. We chased after them and caught up to them sat on boxes of explosives which they were supposed to explode. Fortunately they changed their minds. We took them prisoner and later handed them over to the Military Police. When I looked in the pillbox there was a machine gun pointing down the beach, and when I looked through the sights it was aimed at the ramp mark in the sand. All it wanted was firing. We would have had many casualties.

Further south in the Bark West sector, just to the west of Cape Passero, N Commando were landing with the Canadians. As in the other sectors, each sub-unit of N Commando had their own beach to attack. Apart from the practicalities of getting ashore N2 Commando were also carrying the Netherlands ensign, given to their Beachmaster the night before by Captain H. W. Hettema.

Lieutenant Commander Maurice Vernon Redshaw RNVR, Beach-master N Commando, later Principal Beachmaster Q Commando and K Commando

We landed in the assault and his ensign was hoisted where we had agreed on the chart; he told me after the war that the news had got round the ship and when it went into the inshore position after the assault landing all hands seemed to have binoculars and were looking at the ensign. The run into the beach was without incident although the barrage from our warships firing over our heads was a little unnerving; unfortunately our landing craft hit a false beach in the half-light and we had to swim a little way. The weather was warm and a swim would have been welcome but for the fact that we were in battle order and rather weighed down (I carried a tommy gun, a Smith & Wesson .45, four hand grenades, binoculars, compass and a great deal of ammunition and twenty-four-hour ration pack). We landed against light opposition.

Further north at Pachino, N1 Commando had their own beach to capture. They landed under the fire of the shore batteries which were dealt with by the shells of the British battleships. But although the battleships had taken out the big guns of the batteries there was still an Italian machine-gun post which tried to defeat the invaders.

Leading Seaman Ray Bromley, N Commando

We landed at Pachino and came under fire from the German howitzer guns on our way in. At first we thought the shells were from one of our cruisers falling short and only later learned that they were firing at the howitzers that were firing at us. On leaving the assault ship and on our way in Able Seaman Perry of our Commandos wanted to go to the toilet real bad and was promptly told to sit over the stern to the amusement of all, including the LCA crews. This, while shells were dropping all round us! It should never be forgotten that the LCA crews had to brave whatever befell us. The Canadians were the troops who landed in this sector with us, and on the whole it was a peaceful landing except for a troublesome Italian machine-gun pit situated by the side of a small hut. We were pinned down for a while until I was called forward with my stripped Lewis gun to return fire. Able Seaman Dodds, my number two, took up position among some grape vines and Lieutenant Harrison took up position on my right to direct my fire. We opened up on the hut and spotted the machine-gun post to the right, which was duly attended to. On completion of the return fire Petty Officer Letby, Leading Seaman Lamb and Able Seaman Pete Lightfoot charged from the left as Lieutenant Russell and Leading Seaman Sam Gregory came in from the right.

Further south at Cape Passero, M Commando had landed with the Black Watch. They landed on Green and Amber beaches although Green Beach was later found to be unsuitable for landing the tank landing craft.

Petty Officer Maurice Pascall, M Commando

The darkness of the early morning of D-Day shrouding a huge armada of ships held a certain expectant stillness, a stillness broken now by the manning of the LCAs forming up with precision for the landings. A little lop on the sea as we slipped and headed for the shore of Cape Passero. Dawn now, swiftly and surely we had landed, accurately, quietly and keyed up for the battle we were expecting but did not meet. Success so early and establishing a beachhead with efficiency was a sweet reward for many months of training. Troops ashore, vehicles and equipment soon followed.

It was still dark but first light revealed all and our Scottish unit moved forward. The battle was about to erupt. The enemy had a rude awakening and the Scots simply lined up and with a bloodcurdling yell and skirl of the bagpipes took up the challenge.

Although the soldiers were moving inland, life for the Commandos on the beaches started to become more dangerous rather than less. Despite the fact that the prospect of further ground fighting had receded the danger now was from beneath the Commandos' feet where the Germans and the Italians had left booby traps and mines, and from the frequent air attacks.

Extract from the Sicily diary of Petty Officer Ken Harvey, E Commando

July 11th 1943. At approximately 02.30 enemy aircraft sink our hospital ship. It took 20 minutes to sink, about 300 people saved. Raid again 06.30 plane shot down and I see 2 pilots from other planes bale out. MT ship hit and burns considerably before sinking, survivors all taken off by the invasion craft. The sky for miles is covered in black smoke, about 200 Italian prisoners build a road off the beach.

July 12th 1943. We are attacked once again this morning at 06.30. We get down as far as possible in our slit trench. One more transport ship hit and after 2 great explosions she goes down in half an hour.

Sub Lieutenant Derek Whitehorn RNVR, Assistant Beachmaster F Commando

On Sunday, about noon, I was shot up by an enemy aircraft strafing the beach. On regaining consciousness after being worked on in the casualty clearing station I was alarmed to find a picture of Mussolini on the wall and an Italian on the stretchers each side of me, but all was well.

For all the Commandos the daily hazard of mines and booby traps was a constant threat to life and limb. The retreating Axis forces had not only mined the beaches and the surrounding areas but they had also turned innocent daily objects into potential death traps. G Commando had landed further south than E Commando but the hazards were just the same.

Able Seaman Lofty Lucas, G Commando

We did mine clearance with a bayonet. We had to be careful with barbed wire because of booby traps – we never cut the strands because as soon as you did the whole thing went up. We would get a jeep, put a rope on it and then get well away, then half the beach would go up. Red devils were hand grenades which the Italians armed and put in the sand. If you stood on one of them you stopped and the demolition Army blokes would come along and put a pin in it so you could take your foot off. They were full of ball bearings.

Petty Officer Henry Clark, E Commando

In greenhouses, among the tomatoes were red devices shaped like tomatoes. If you weren't careful they blew your hand off. In houses if you used the toilet and pulled the chain, Bang! Pictures that weren't straight, once straightened, Bang! S-mines had green prongs amongst the grass, if you stood on them, when you removed your foot they sprang into the air and exploded.

One day two sailors came ashore with baskets and asked where they could get some grapes for the ship. I pointed out the vineyards and also said they had to cross a minefield. At that moment I saw a Royal Engineer Sapper walking across with a Polish mine detector, I told these two lads to follow him. They did so and after crossing half the distance he turned to me and said, 'Don't rely on me too much, this thing isn't working.' These RE chaps were the greatest, they crossed minefields by sheer instinct.

Meanwhile further down the coast at Cape Passero M Commando had settled into the routine of life on the beach. M2 Commando had landed on Green Beach, but shallow water and other hazards meant that after a while they were ordered west to Amber Beach to assist with the constant traffic.

Here the Americans were unloading their DUKWs, the amphibious trucks which were useful in being able to drive through the water as well as on land. But the fact that they were amphibious led to some false assumptions about their abilities. On Amber Beach one of the landing craft had run aground on a bank with its bow hanging over deep water.

Sub Lieutenant Joe Bramble RNVR, Assistant Beachmaster M Commando

The luckless driver of the first DUKW was given the order, 'Drive Off!' and proceeded to the ramp, driving straight into the water and immediately sank. The poor fellow was drowned as he was wearing heavy gear and could not swim. Before anyone could do anything it was too late and a salutary lesson was learned – once again too late.

Despite the dangers vehicles were a useful addition to any Commando on the beaches. Occasionally a DUKW might be made available or there might be a chance to borrow a jeep. Of course the Americans and the Canadians had both the best kit and the best vehicles but occasionally there was a chance to acquire a set of wheels.

Sub Lieutenant Joe Bramble RNVR, Assistant Beachmaster M Commando

On duty on Amber Beach, M2 Commando was calling in an LST with Canadian troops aboard. The last vehicle, a three-ton lorry, was being driven off the ramp when a seaman appeared wheeling a motorcycle. 'Hey!' He shouted, 'They've forgotten this!' I immediately shouted to the Canadian Sergeant leaning over the back of the lorry, 'You've left a motorbike!'

'Nothing to do with me, we can't wait,' he shouted in reply. With that the lorry roared up the beach, we never saw it again. I beckoned to the seaman to bring the machine down the ramp and went to meet him. 'Right,' I said, using my most authoritative Assistant Beachmaster voice, 'I'll take charge of this now.'

'Aye, aye, Sir,' he said and ran back to the LST.

Shortly after, the LST heaved in her kedge and disappeared over the horizon. I studied the motorcycle. It was obviously a fairly new machine, a Norton 500 cc covered in Canadian Army insignia, including a prominent maple leaf. It was painted khaki of course. It took me two minutes to make a decision.

More craft were heading into the beach. I did not have much time. I called out to Able Seaman Johnny Power, a lorry driver in peacetime. I knew he was able to ride a motorcycle. 'Take this to the back of the beach, somewhere, anywhere, as long as it's out of sight. The next time I see it, I want to see it painted black with RN painted on the tank.'

'Aye, aye, Sir,' said the grinning Power. He jumped on the Norton and drove it away.

About thirty-six hours later, Able Seaman Power appeared riding the Norton. He was obviously very proud of his paint job. It certainly looked very professional with the black paint gleaming and the large letters RN on each side of the tank. 'Fantastic,' I said, 'Well done!' I did not ask him where he obtained the paint and he never told me.

After one to two weeks ashore the Commandos had finished and were taken off. F Commando went via Syracuse to Malta and from there back to the United Kingdom leaving behind Assistant Beachmaster Derek Whitehorn, who was sent to hospital in Cairo where he underwent three operations. It was the end of his Royal Naval Commando service. E Commando and N Commando both went to Malta where they went their separate ways.

M Commando returned to North Africa, still in proud possession of their newly acquired motorcycle. There they camped at a small town called Zuwarah, some sixty miles west of Tripoli, where they engaged in more exercises with the Army. One day the Principal Beachmaster, Lieutenant Commander P. U. Bayly RN borrowed Joe Bramble's Norton motorcycle to attend a conference in Sicily. On the way back he was involved in an accident and the bike was a write-off.

Sub Lieutenant Joe Bramble RNVR, Assistant Beachmaster M Commando

I visited him in hospital and he was a sorry sight, trussed up in bandages. He managed a grin as he muttered, 'Sorry about the bike, Bramble.' What could I say?

During the two weeks the Commandos had been on the beaches in Sicily the British, Canadian and American troops spread out through the island. Palermo was taken on 22nd July, Catania on 5th August. The advance was hindered by the nature of the Sicilian countryside, with its narrow winding roads being the only route through the rugged terrain.

Shortly afterwards the Germans and Italians started on their own Dunkirk-style operation to bring all their forces back to the Italian mainland from the Island of Sicily. Although the Allies had received high-level intelligence about the German plans, they made few efforts to interfere.

In the first two weeks of August just over 100,000 German and Italian troops crossed the Straits of Messina with their heavy equipment. The last left Sicily just before the Allies entered the town of Messina on 16th August 1943.

Now that the Axis forces had been pushed out of Italy it was inevitable that the Allies would follow them onto the mainland of Italy itself. The Royal Naval Commandos would be needed again very soon.

CHAPTER 4

The Mediterranean (2)

Part of the established tactics of warfare up to and even beyond Napoleonic times was the infantry square. Once the foot soldiers closed ranks in the form of a square it was very difficult for the cavalry to break them up, whereas the cavalry could and did smash through rows of infantry lined up to meet them.

In August 1943 the Royal Naval Commandos proved that there was still a place in modern warfare for the traditional infantry square. With Sicily in Allied hands N Commando had been sent to Malta from where N2 Commando was sent to the beach at Oued Marsa near Bougie in North Africa where they lived under canvas with the British 4th Division. When not on active duty it was the task of the Commando officers to arrange the training for their Commandos as they saw fit.

Lieutenant Commander Maurice Vernon Redshaw RNVR, Beach-master N Commando, later Principal Beachmaster Q Commando and K Commando

One day I had the bright idea to have a route march to help us clear the beer and blowflies. There were some hills at the back of Oued Marsa and these we ascended in battle order in line abreast carrying weapons. We had been going well over an hour when ahead of us we saw a great number of apes barring our way. They were bigger than us and greatly outnumbered us. They appeared definitely hostile, but there was nothing in the drill book to tell me what action to take under the circumstances. I halted the Commando and as the apes were advancing from many directions I gave the order to my Petty Officer to 'Form Square!' He looked at me as though I was suffering from heat stroke or gin but managed to get everyone into a rough square. We had weapons and ammunition with us, so after asking if anyone knew anything about apes

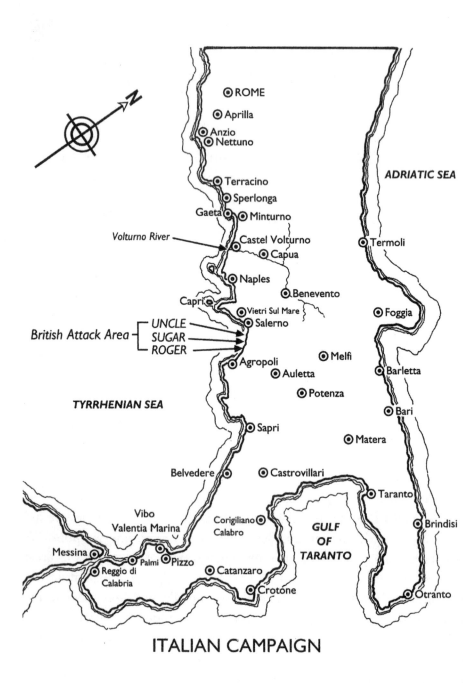

ITALIAN CAMPAIGN

I gave the order to load. I then fired a short burst over the heads of the apes. While they stood and watched from a distance of about twenty yards, we retreated down the hillside in single file, my bodyguard and myself taking position at the rear of the column and firing an occasional burst over the heads of the apes whenever they approached too closely.

The shortest way for the Allies to approach Italy was across the straits between Messina on the Sicilian side to Reggio di Calabria on the Italian mainland. Reggio di Calabria is right at the point of the toe on the map of Italy. But the move to the mainland did not happen immediately. There was some haggling over the issue of whether the Italian peace terms were in accordance with the principle of unconditional surrender agreed by the Allies at the Casablanca Conference. The Germans took advantage of this delay to move more men, comprising some sixteen Army divisions, into Italy.

Along with the landings at Reggio di Calabria, the Allied plan was for another landing further up the east coast of Italy at Salerno Bay, and for the two invasion forces to link up for the advance north. The landings at Reggio di Calabria were codenamed Operation Baytown and were carried out by N Commando and G Commando. On the night of 2nd September 1943 N Commando were in Messina ready for the crossing.

Leading Seaman Ray Bromley, N Commando

We mustered on the beach. The LCAs came in to pick us up and away we went. The Cameronians were the second wave, with their bagpipes going like hell trying to drown the noise of the shells from the heavy barrage laid down by Montgomery's guns.

Lieutenant Commander Maurice Vernon Redshaw RNVR, Beach-master N Commando, later Principal Beachmaster Q Commando and K Commando

My bodyguard and myself embarked in a motor launch which was to lead the assault and show the LCAs towards the right beach.

Our target was Gallico Marina, just north of Reggio di Calabria. The straits were about four miles just there, and a strong current played havoc with our navigation. In addition to Montgomery's barrage, our gunners were firing tracers on fixed lines over our heads for us to steer by. In Sicily two searchlights were pointing skywards to assist us to make a fair course. Both ideas were very good, but we found that all was soon obscured by smoke from the guns. We learned later that opposition was light, but, judging from the amount of stuff falling in the water around us, quite a few of our guns must have been firing short. H-Hour was 04.30 September 3rd 1943, and we landed at that time on How Green Beach and settled down to controlling our end of the ferry service carrying the follow-up troops.

Leading Seaman Ray Bromley, N Commando

We set up our camp close to a stone wall and dug slit trenches, and that was where we were to stay for the next two to three weeks. Able Seaman Pete Lightfoot decided to cook for the party, and as was practice a slit trench was always nearby to put away all the slops and leftovers. However, we came under attack from three Messerschmitts. We dived for our slit trenches and Able Seaman Lightfoot made the fatal mistake of diving into the wrong slit trench and dived into the slop trench, much to the amusement of all! Monty came and gave us a pep talk on the beach, although we still had trouble with snipers. We suspected that one or two civilians had rifles hidden which they brought out now and again, fired one or two shots, and then hid them again.

With a toehold in Italy established, the Allies wanted to land troops further north. The Germans and Italians had not defended Reggio and were now retreating northwards. Hot on their heels was the Eighth Army which had landed in a massive shuttle service between Sicily and the mainland.

Leapfrogging along the coast were the Royal Naval Commandos. G Commando landed at Vibo Valentia Marina where the Eighth Army was to attack the retreating Germans in order to prevent them from blowing up bridges. Vibo Valentia Marina has a small harbour with a sandy beach. Things were complicated by the fact that the German Army was retreating along the road which ran by the shore.

Able Seaman Lofty Lucas, G Commando

We landed from an LCA at 4 a.m. We were about two or three miles from the beach in the harbour so we ran along the road. There were 88-mm guns there and Tiger tanks only about a mile away. The first LST in was knocked out. We were bringing the craft in when I was hit by a shell from a six-inch mortar. When these things land you stay still because they land in a circle. It was like being thumped on the back, then there was a burning sensation. I was blown over the wall, but I got up and went back to the beach. One of the lads said to me, 'God Lofty, half your back's gone!' I went up to the Casualty Clearing Station, which was later hit itself.

Further up the coast N Commando landed by mistake at a place called Sapri. It was an error because they were in the wrong place, but also because the Eighth Army was behind them instead of being with them.

Leading Seaman Ray Bromley, N Commando

It was not long before we were off again, this time to land up the coast, only to be landed at the wrong place. A slight navigational error (not the Royal Naval Commandos). The place was Sapri and it was situated right bang in the middle of the British and German lines. Receiving no opposition from the shore we just strolled up the beach to the road. One always has a comedian in every company, and we had one. He called out at the top of his voice, 'Anybody at home?' We took up a defensive position in a couple of houses by the side of the road. Next day British tanks came round a corner at the end of the bay and it was not until later that the Sappers came and cleared S-mines from the very beach we walked up the day before. We were informed by a Sapper that the reason the mines never went off was because they had been laid on a pebble beach and not a sandy one, where the tale would have been different.

North from Sapri is the Bay of Salerno. Here there are almost twenty miles of beaches which were visited secretly by the Combined Operations Pilotage Parties at the end of August 1943. They were canoeists and landed from a submarine which had slipped north through the mines off the Italian coast. The canoeists brought back invaluable information about the beaches where the landings would take place. They noted gradients, bearings and other essentials, such as likely beach exits.

The Allied landings at the Bay of Salerno were christened Operation Avalanche and were in line with the now established military doctrine that landings had to take place on beaches near to ports. The Bay of Salerno was chosen for its proximity to Naples, which could be attacked from land rather than from the sea.

On 8th September news of the Italian surrender was announced. Although this removed the threat of opposition from Italian troops, the Germans had not surrendered and they moved into Italian positions in the Bay of Salerno as the Italians moved out.

Although the news of the Italian surrender caused some to relax, M Commando were not put off their guard.

Sub Lieutenant Joe Bramble RNVR, Assistant Beachmaster M Commando

We were all more apprehensive about the forthcoming landing at Salerno than we had been in Sicily. We were convinced that this was not going to be easy and that we could expect fierce resistance from the Germans. We knew now just how exposed the Beach Landing Parties were during the initial assault, and that confusion and

ncertainty was the rule of the day. Very few landings ever went
ccording to plan.

With the Eighth Army moving north to meet the troops
anding at Salerno, the Germans realised they had to throw the
llies back into the sea if they were to stand any chance of
ictory in southern Italy. They very nearly did.

The town of Salerno lies at the northern end of the Bay of Salerno.
o the south were the main landing beaches. The Americans landed
n the Southern Attack Area, the British in the Northern Attack
rea. This Anglo-American Force was under the command of an
merican General, Lieutenant General Mark Clark.

In the British area there were three sectors, from the south,
oger, then Sugar and then Uncle, which included the Picento
iver. These sectors were split into beaches, each sector having a
reen Beach and an Amber Beach.

To the North of Uncle Sector was the town of Salerno itself, and
eyond that the smaller settlement of Vietri Sul Mare. This was
where D Commando landed. On the main landing beaches to the
outh K and M Commandos spearheaded the assaults. The landing
leet sailed from North Africa. D Commando sailed from Palermo
n Sicily with 41 Royal Marine Commando under Brigadier
aycock. It was dawn on 9th September 1943.

*ieutenant Hugh Birley RNVR, Assistant Beachmaster D
ommando*

e travelled from Palermo in an ex-Belgian cross-Channel steamer,
ow an LSI. Sitting in the smoking room, we listened to Eisen-
ower's broadcast telling of the Italian surrender. The Prime Minister's
on Randolph Churchill was there, being attached to Laycock's
Q, and he obviously had some foreknowledge of the surrender. We
ere wisely assured that we must still expect plenty of opposition
rom the Germans, which proved only too true.

Our landing took place in pitch darkness. As usual the two
ssistant Beachmasters were in the two wing boats of the first

assault. We then turned right and left towards each other, hoping to meet somewhere in the middle.

I, from the left-hand LCA, walked to my right but saw no sign o my colleague Sub Lieutenant Stevens from the right-hand boat. I wa challenged, stood stock still in the darkness, and was relieved to hea footsteps retreating up the beach. Next day revealed a pos containing a large Breda machine gun, one of several the Italian abandoned without firing a shot.

I soon located Stevens. His LCA must have beached a few minutes later than mine. We had been landed in exactly the right spo and soon set up our lights to bring in the later waves of landing craft

Able Seaman William Woods, D Commando

Even before we set off for the landing I was having trouble with my left arm. It had swelled up so much I couldn't use it, but of course we had to go and as I was carrying a rifle and a great big wireless on my back you can imagine how I felt. I managed to stagger ashore We spread out and when we tried to get the radio going it jus wouldn't work. Later on as it got light I discovered the reason - there was a great big hole in it. Whether it was a bullet or shrapnel it must have saved my life.

The Marine Commandos under Brigadier Laycock soor advanced inland and Brigade HQ was established in Vietri. Bu soon another problem emerged for the Marines. Their equipmen had not been sent to the right beach.

Lieutenant Hugh Birley RNVR, Assistant Beachmaster D Commando

As it got light we soon realised that the soldiers had no penetrated very far. The beach came under intense mortar fire an we were clearly under observation, as the mortars followec remorselessly whichever end of the beach we chose to bring in th next lot of landing craft. However there was not much to brin ashore. The Commando Brigade had been allocated only one LC1 which brought a few anti-tank guns towed by Bren-gun carriers etc. and a few jeeps.

Fortunately for the Marine Commandos, they were reunited with their vehicles and equipment which had been sent by mistake to the main landing areas further south. Meanwhile on the beach all the troops had been landed.

Lieutenant Hugh Birley RNVR, Assistant Beachmaster D Commando

When all the troops were ashore we were left with one LCI stuck on the beach. She had received several mortar hits round the bows and some of her for'ard compartments were flooded, making it impossible for her to drag herself off the beach under her own power. Her crew joined us ashore while her Captain rowed out into deep water in a borrowed dinghy and dumped all his codebooks and marked charts over the side. This perhaps was prompted by an order to our small party to set up an ambush on a minor coast road owing to a threatened visit by some enemy tanks. To our relief no such visit occurred.

Eventually the Commandos, the prisoners, the wounded and the landing-craft crew were taken off in the stranded LCI by a US Navy salvage tug. Because all the marked charts had been thrown overboard, the voyage back to Palermo was in a straight line despite the danger from mines. Back in Palermo William Woods had to have an operation on his arm.

Meanwhile, 41 Commando Royal Marines were pushing inland. But the Navy was still with them. Crucial to the success of the invasion were the roving observation units which combined sailors from the Navy and bombardiers from the Royal Artillery and which called in the fire from the ships out at sea onto German targets from their Observation Posts (OPs) using Morse Code.

Leading Telegraphist Leonard Lloyd, Combined Operations Bombardment Unit, also known as FOB Party (Forward Observer Bombardment)

WIRELESS TRANSMISSION ROUTINE

Ashore, having established an OP and a target selected, the following W/T procedure was used:

1. Call sign of ship from call sign of FOB. Typically F1 – *dididadit ditdadadada*.
2. Map reference of target transmitted by abbreviation in the form of a six-figure map reference.
3. Description of target transmitted by abbreviated code letters such as INF for infantry – *didit dadit dididadit*.
4. On firing the first ranging round, the ship would transmit KT – *dadida da*.
5. On observing the fall of shot the FOB would transmit T – *da* – and then proceed to transmit corrections (up 100 yards, down 100 yards or whatever correction was required).
6. When target had been bracketed the FOB would ask for salvoes to be fired, i.e. SSS – *dididit dididit dididit* – until hopefully the target had been destroyed.

The above was standard procedure although other messages, ad lib and ad hoc, were sometimes transmitted such as 'Good shooting', or on occasion 'Enemy getting too close – will have to move OP – stand by for later contact'. Other ad libs will not be repeated!

During this operation my four-man party was supplied with a Jeep. I recall that we stopped in a tiny village when proceeding to a forward observation post, and one of the villagers invited us into his cellar for a glass of wine. We accepted gratefully, but, whilst taking advantage of this hospitality, the Germans targeted the village with a 'Moaning Minnie', i.e. a six-barrel mortar. When we eventually emerged from the cellar we found that our Jeep had been hit and was a complete write-off. I have never refused a glass of wine since.

Further south the main landing areas were also running into difficulties. The Italian surrender had lifted the hopes of the assault troops, only to have them dashed when they found the Germans waiting for them.

Extract from the diary of Telegraphist Eric Dove, Royal Naval Beach Signals Section No. B9

September 9th. Two hours before 'Zero' we are informed that the Italian forces have surrendered. Everyone cheers in anticipation of an easy landing.

2.00 a.m. Check all weapons are in working order, our portable wireless sets are tuned into correct frequency, a final briefing with maps and aerial photographs of our beach sector, all ships' interior lights are switched to red in order that we can adjust to the darkness outside.

3.00 a.m. Zero hour. We feel our way along the ship's deck and climb down the scrambling nets and into the assault craft waiting below. A moderate swell, our twelve assault craft leave the mother ship and head for the beach. As we close the beach the German coastal batteries open fire on our task force. Their batteries soon ranged on our task force and claimed a hit on an LCT (landing craft tank) setting it on fire. We charge up the beach and head for the sand dunes where we dig in. Set up advanced signal station, the German guns are only about forty metres in front of us with four 88-mm guns. Beach criss-crossed with red, green and blue tracer, troops continue to land on the beach, casualties start to mount up. British warship closes the beach and engages the coastal batteries, knocking out two of them. One of the other batteries scores a direct hit on the bridge of the warship.

6.30 a.m. Dawn is breaking and we are able to observe the carnage around us. Several ships are on fire in the bay, our tanks and infantry drive the enemy form the bridgehead, wounded are being brought down from the front line. About sixty prisoners are under guard only a few yards from our dugout.

Mid-morning. Enemy tries to counter-attack to push us back into the sea. It's touch and go but the attack fails.

In Roger Sector, M Commando had also heard the news of the Italian surrender, and, as they neared the coast of Italy, they could see the night sky lit up with the fires on the island of Capri, which had been attacked by Allied bombers the previous night. The weather was perfect, but the flotilla of landing craft had a problem.

Sub Lieutenant Joe Bramble RNVR, Assistant Beachmaster M Commando

An Army Major sought permission to be towed ashore by one of the LCAs in his amphibious Jeep, as there was not room for it aboard the LCMs. I do not know what this officer's function was, but I do recall he was being towed behind the LCA that my Assistant Beachmaster's party was embarked in for the landing. Incidentally, we would never have advised this course of action, having had some experience of Jeeps in a seaway. All went well for a while, until the LCA flotilla was ordered to speed up to keep to the timetable. Soon there were cries from astern, 'Help! Help! We're sinking!' The tow rope was immediately let go and, fortunately for the Major and his driver, the LCA returned to rescue the two soldiers who climbed thankfully aboard the LCA. We soon caught up with the flotilla but this foolish act could have ended in tragedy. The LCA coxwain put the troops aboard his craft in jeopardy when he broke formation to retrieve the luckless soldiers.

However, there was still a problem. Were they at the right beach? M Commando were due to land on Amber Beach, which is where most of them landed, but one small group found themselves on Green Beach instead, where things were uncannily quiet. It was not to last.

Sub Lieutenant Joe Bramble RNVR, Assistant Beachmaster M Commando

As the first assault group approached the beach it was eerily quiet. Only the noise of the LCA's engines, which were remarkably quiet petrol engines, could be heard as we spoke in whispers. This was always the moment of uncertainty and apprehension as no one ever knew whether we would land on the designated beach. This was something that was out of the hands of the Beachmasters. The officer in charge of the LCA flotilla was responsible for navigating the flotilla and landing on the correct beach.

Our responsibilities started as soon as we stepped ashore. We still did not know whether we were on the correct beach but the Assistant Beachmaster's assault group did not have time to consider the niceties of location. Our job was to facilitate the subsequent landings and at all times *to keep the beach clear*. There was no sign of any activity ashore, let alone enemy fire. It was ominously still in fact. My ALMO (Assistant Military Landing Officer) was alongside me and we both thought that the situation must change; we could not believe there was no enemy reception.

In the mean time we set about setting up our transit lights and calling in the next wave of craft. We were fortunate that there was ample water on this beach, with no hazards for the larger craft. The second wave always included an LCM carrying an amoured bulldozer which was essential for forcing an exit from the beach. There was no enemy fire during the first wave of landing craft.

The German machine guns opened up as the second wave began to hit the shore, and those of us on the beach were caught in a hail of gunfire. Before we had time to lie flat the AMLO who was standing alongside me disappeared. I never saw him again.

Fortunately for those of us in the vicinity, the bulldozer began rumbling up the beach from the LCM, and this was to be the saviour of many of the Beach Party and those soldiers not yet taking cover at the top of the beach. We rushed to shelter behind the bulldozer and remained there until the machine-gun nests were eliminated.

Reports later revealed that the very accurate gunfire from the destroyers was an important element in securing many of the beachheads and eliminating the opposition. It is almost impossible for a Beachmaster to have any idea of exactly what is taking place behind his beach.

Further north at Amber Beach the rest of M Commando had landed, including the Principal Beachmaster, Acting Lieutenant Commander P. U. Bayly RN, whose arm was still in a sling after his accident with the Norton motorcycle. Here there were German 88-mm guns sited on high ground beyond the beach.

Petty Officer Arthur Hollands, M Commando

In the early hours, we embarked on our assault landing craft and quickly made our way towards the beach. As we neared the beach we encountered heavy fire from the batteries of German 88-mm guns, which, we later discovered, had only been sited the day before. In addition to this the Germans had heavy artillery installed in tunnels in a mountain range a few miles inland, which could come out and fire at the beach and ships and then return into the tunnels on rails. One of the destroyers came in almost to the beach with her guns on full depression and silenced one of the 88-mm guns on the beach by blowing up its ammunition dump.

Petty Officer Maurice Pascall, M Commando

We were ashore, but only just, and whoomph, the bombardment opened up and in the crossfire we were pinned down. Eighty-eight millimetre German guns. They were less than a few hundred yards away, entrenched on the high ground. They fired over our heads, attacking the landing craft awaiting our signals to come in. The sky was lit up with flames and flashes of heavy gunfire from capital ships silhouetted against the horizon. Orders were given to attack the gun positions, but small-arms fire put us down quickly and with some early casualties.

The 88-mm guns could not train low enough to blow us off the beach, and only the small-arms fire was effective when attacks were made. After some hours of tension and waiting the assault troops attacked – a unified effort by the soldiers assisted by the sailors of M Commando made a dent in the formidable German defences.

Lieutenant Commander Bayly RN quickly made his way from Amber Beach to Green Beach. Joe Bramble then moved his beach organisation north to Amber Beach where the landings continued. One day a flotilla of landing craft appeared with a contingent of American troops with a rather unusual cargo.

Sub Lieutenant Joe Bramble RNVR, Assistant Beachmaster M Commando

In due course the last vehicle was heading up the beach when there was some frantic activity on the LST's ramp. Sailors were waving their arms about and shouting, 'Tell them to stop!' We managed to stop the US truck and by this time a group of sailors was struggling down the ramp with a piano!

The truck reversed and the piano was carefully loaded on the back amid shouts of, 'Gee, thanks fellers!' The truck roared off up the beach and the last LST kedged off to disappear over the horizon. We were left shaking our heads and smiling to ourselves. However, we had not seen the last of the US soldiers.

Two hours later we saw another flotilla of LSTs approaching, requesting permission to land. Once permission was given the first craft arrived on the beach and the ramps and the doors opened up but there were no troops or vehicles in the LST. We approached the First Lieutenant of one craft. 'What are you doing here?' we asked.

'We've come to pick up the troops we landed an hour ago,' he told us. We shook our heads in disbelief again, but sure enough we could see clouds of dust from behind the beach as the US troops returned. 'What's the problem?' we asked the officer in the first vehicle to appear on the beach. 'Wrong beach,' was the laconic reply as if this were an everyday occurrence. Presumably the soldiers' piano was also reloaded and subsequently delivered onto the correct beach!

Meanwhile in Sugar Sector, K Commando were having difficulties of their own. The landing troops were all clustered together because of the mines which had been laid right up to the tide mark and the fact that the exits out of the beaches were jammed. K Commando also had to deal with the paraphanalia of a modern media war. War correspondents and film crews all wanted to get themselves, or their footage, back to Sicily. Not only that, but there was a feeling that some landing craft were relying on asking the Commandos where to go rather than reading their own orders. Acting Commander Arthur Havers RN, Principal Beachmaster, was not entirely happy about how things were going.

Although both Vietri and Salerno were captured quickly on 12th September the Germans launched a counter-attack. The situation became perilous. Plans were formulated to evacuate the beaches. In Roger Sector the advancing troops were pushed right back to the beach. Even the Pioneers were given rifles and fifty rounds of ammunition to help defend the beaches. Finally the use of airborne troops from the 82nd US Airborne Division as well as the appearance of two extra British battleships turned imminent defeat into victory.

The Royal Naval Commandos were still on the beaches. For the hard-working Commandos there were the delights of compo rations as well as the joys of fresh bread delivered from the ship's bakers aboard HMS *Hilary*. Any other delicacies they had to find themselves, and fortunately because it was early autumn there were plenty of peaches, almonds and various other fruit and nuts.

By 16th September the Germans were retreating and the Allied forces at Salerno were able to link up with the Eighth Army moving north from Reggio. The Allies entered Naples on 1st October.

For the Royal Naval Commandos it was time to clear up after another successful operation in getting the Allied Forces ashore and off the beachhead at Salerno. But Arthur Hollands was on his way to hospital after sustaining a fractured skull on the beach.

There were valuable lessons to be learned for the future, and the lull between this operation and the next would be a good opportunity to put some ideas down on paper.

CHAPTER 5

Later Operations

The job of a Principal Beachmaster could be both rewarding and frustrating. Rewarding, because the Principal Beachmaster was the Commanding Officer of his own Commando and was in charge on the beaches when they carried out an operation.

Frustrating, because Combined Operations did not always see things from the same operational perspective as the Principal Beachmaster.

Memo dated 18th November 1943, reference P.O.G/17

From: *Commanding Officer K Beach Commando (Naval Party 803), c/o Naval Officer in Charge, Bougie*

To: *The Commander-in-Chief, Mediterranean Fleet through the Director of Landing Craft, Algiers*

Copy to: Chief of Combined Operations

Subject: Chain of Command in Beach Commandos

. . . [2] It is proposed that the officer next senior to the Principal Beachmaster should be known as the Deputy Principal Beachmaster and should not be encumbered with the duties of a Beachmaster. This would enable him to land in assaults on a different beach to the Principal Beachmaster, assess the situation there, then rendezvous with the Principal Beachmaster and report the state of affairs.

[3] It has been found in 'Husky' and 'Avalanche' and also in training exercises that it is impossible for the Principal Beachmaster to get a rapid and accurate idea of the state of affairs on two beaches immediately after landing by means of V/S, W/T or by walking along a crowded foreshore from one beach to the other. This is particularly so when beaches are a mile or more apart as on 'Avalanche' and certain of the training exercises.

It is submitted, therefore, for consideration as a matter of policy and future Beach Commando organisation that the officer next senior to the Principal Beachmaster should be referred to as Deputy Principal Beachmaster. The appointment of and title of an Assistant Principal Beachmaster should not be made or used.

(Signed) A. A. Havers,
Lieutenant Commander RN, Acting Commander

Letter dated 20th December 1943, reference C.R.12638/43 and addressed to Commanding Officer HMS Armadillo, c/o Post Office, Ardentinny, Argyll

Your remarks are requested on the attached copy of Commanding Officer K Beach Commando, observing that it is very unlikely that any extra Officers will be available.

(Signed) J. H. Unwin
For Chief of Combined Operations

Memo dated 27th December 1943, reference 2862/21D

From: Commanding Officer HMS Armadillo, c/o Post Office, Ardentinny, Argyll
To: Chief of Combined Operations
Subject: Chain of Command in Royal Naval Beach Commandos

The following remarks are submitted in accordance with your letter C.R. 12638/43 of 20th December 1943 . . .

(b) Paragraphs 2 and 3
I do not agree with the remarks of the Commanding Officer 'K' Beach Commando, in these two paragraphs. The duties of the Principal Beachmaster are to assess the situation on all beaches in the sector. This will now be greatly facilitated by the use of an LCA, specially fitted, or an amphibious vehicle. To have two officers doing this would, to my mind, cause confusion. The

eachmasters, who are carefully trained with a view to assessing he situation on their own particular beach, are in direct ommunication with the local Naval Commander, and in view of he current development of the 'I' method of ordering craft in to eaches it is considered that a Beachmaster should not be ithdrawn from this most important work.

(Signed) E. A. Davis
Commander in Command

The autumn of 1943 had been a somewhat stressful one at HMS *Armadillo*. U Commando had been formed in September nd partly filled with General Service (i.e. regular Navy) ratings ho resented having to leave the ships they had come from. he Royal Navy's policy of filling the Commandos with a nixture of volunteers and Naval personnel who were to all ntents and purposes press-ganged into joining the Commandos had backfired.

However, the unhappy ratings were duly weeded out and lispatched back to the mainstream Navy. In direct contrast V Commando, which was formed at the same time, had none of his mixture and the HMS *Armadillo* officers were pleased to ote that 'This unit proved exceptionally smart and keen as here were no GS [General Service] Able Seamen or other nalcontents from big ships'.

Also in residence in HMS *Armadillo* in the autumn of 1943 vas J Commando. Once they had recovered from their shock t the training they were being put through they turned their ttention to making sure they enjoyed their stay there.

ble Seaman Alexander Hutton, J Commando

little light relief was gained by an evening out in Dunoon. This vas achieved by a lift into town on the back of a lorry. As closing ime at the pub was 9 p.m., the Pavilion Dance Hall would refuse dmission after 9 p.m. We therefore posted one of our party in

the dance hall and he would position himself in the WC to ope
the window after 9 p.m. We would shin up the drain pipe and clim
along the parapet to gain access to the dance hall. This worke
successfully until it came to the notice of the management. On ou
next visit we found the access had been heavily greased making ou
mission impossible!

Just after the Salerno landings, the Royal Nav:
Commandos were in action on the other side of Italy. On th
heel of Italy there are three ports which were quickl
captured. G Commando were sent in to help capture Taranto
which was taken on 9th September, followed by Brindisi o
11th September and Bari on 14th September.

Back on the Western side of Italy the Army had move
northwards following the Salerno landings and the capture o
Naples. By 12th October the combined American and Britis
forces were at the Volturno river.

Crossing the river was vital to the Italian campaign, and i
fell to M1 Commando, who, having taken part in the mai
Salerno landings, were sent north to get the Army across th
Volturno river and into northern Italy. So, instead of thei
usual task of opening a beachhead from the sea, th
Commandos were asked to get the Army from one side of
river to the other. In charge of the operation was th
Principal Beachmaster of M Commando, Acting Lieutenan
Commander Patrick Bayly RN.

Vice Admiral Sir Patrick Bayly KBE CB DSC and two bars

And so to Naples where at some headquarters they told me tha
the Army was to cross the Volturno that night and that we wer
needed to land tanks on the beach north of the river. They ha
few details and time was short, so on I sped through th
suburbs, the orchards and then the marshes reclaimed by th
labour of centuries and flooded for the moment's advantage b
the retreating Hun.

The road being as ruinous and crowded as every road in Italy then was, it was well into the afternoon before I reported to an infantry brigade HQ near the mouth of the Volturno. There the staff explained that the river was too wide, deep and fast flowing for tanks to ford (even though waterproofed to wade through six feet of water). It had therefore been decided to embark the tanks in landing craft at Naples and beach them on the north side of the river. My party was to cross the river in the wake of the assaulting infantry and find a landing place for the tanks. This was a good straightforward plan and I could foresee few difficulties; so while waiting for my party I passed my time studying maps and aerial photographs in brigade HQ.

My party arrived as darkness was falling. The plan was quickly explained, the essential gear selected and stowed in the truck for the two-mile journey to the river crossing. The infantry around us had already moved off into the darkness by the time we were ready. Our directions for reaching the crossing were simple. 'Up the road until you come to a turning on the left by a canal; de-bus and carry your gear the last mile following the canal.' So off we set up the long straight Roman road towards the river. The darkness was absolute, but soon the moon came from behind clouds and we could see from the raised embankment on which the road ran the flat and quiet countryside. There were no floods here, no life, nor was there a canal. When we guessed we had covered more than two miles I was getting mildly anxious, for I had seen no signs of soldierly activity and we knew we must be getting near the river.

Suddenly, the battle started. Our artillery opened behind us with a roar and the Germans replied in good measure. In a flash we saw where we were. The river ran here, at Castel Volturno, in a sharp loop to the north, and our road actually ran into this loop and although we were on the south bank of the river, we were to the north of the Germans on our flanks. To add to our discomfiture there was no room on our embankment to turn the truck and an 88-mm gun with its unmistakable flat trajectory started firing tracer shells straight down our road, fortunately well above our heads.

We debussed hurriedly and, risking minefields, plunged down the embankment into a field. The truck disappeared down the road at high speed in reverse, sped on its way by the frequent flash of the shells passing overhead. We plodded under the safety of the embankment Southward carrying beach signs, wireless sets and the other paraphanalia of our trade, until we came to a dry canal but no sign of the turning we had expected. However, that placed us on the map again and we struck down the canal towards the sea.

Presently we arrived amidst our infantry brigade and made our way to the river crossing, over an hour late. We had not been missed and no one seemed in the least keen to see us. There was trouble afoot and sailors were superfluous for the moment. By mischance of planning, the Army assault boat crews had been trained rather hurriedly in the flooded marshes and were now faced with ferrying the brigade over a river in spate some hundred yards wide. The intention was that on its initial crossing, each boat should tow behind it a light rope, paid out from the near shore. On arriving at the further bank the rope was to be secured to a bush and the boat would then cross to and fro by hauling on the rope. The idea was excellent – for a lake – but translated to a wide and swift flowing river on a dark night, under fire and with boat loads of eager but unskilled soldiers the results were catastrophic.

The floating ropes being paid out from the shore soon formed huge bights behind each boat and the paddlers found themselves struggling against not only the current but the pull of a hundred yards of rope which was being swept downstream at six knots. The only Army crews which reached the far bank were those who realised what was happening and cast off the ropes. The other boats were swept downstream dangling on the end of their ropes until they returned willy-nilly to the bank they had started from, but a hundred yards further downstream.

The scheme had been for two men in each boat to secure the rope on the far bank and to haul the boat back to the starting point. But now the few boats that arrived at the far side had no ropes and the two men were quite incapable of paddling the unwieldy craft back across the river. The platoons they had landed disappeared into the dark. As if that was not enough, the heavy-footed infantry managed to punch large holes in the thin sides of many of the boats with their boots.

This then was the situation an hour after the battle had started. A company or so was across the river instead of a battalion. I found the brigade Major in a field pervaded by the smell of a dead herd of cattle. He was on a wireless set urgently demanding amphibians from some higher authority. Ad hoc arrangements were being made to provide paddlers for the few serviceable boats. He wasn't interested in me and my problems apart from saying that I couldn't use a boat to take my party across. However, as the control of these goings-on seemed rather loose, I thought something might be done.

On inspecting various damaged boats which the soldiers had discarded I found one with a neat four-inch hole from someone's toe near the bow and below the waterline. By stuffing the rent with socks and sitting in the stern to lift the hole above water we could make the craft quite riverworthy for eight men. The embarkation officer intimated that he had no objections to us trying to drown ourselves so we loaded and shoved off.

On the way across an idea occurred to us. Seeing that as only a company or so had landed it was unlikely they had yet reached the beach, half a mile away on the left flank. That being so, to be hung up behind these few soldiers might delay us unduly. We therefore sent half our party of eight by land as planned and the four downriver by boat, out into the sea and so to land on the beach from seaward. I went by water and sent my excellent South African Sub Lieutenant, Sam Ellman, in charge of the land party. The battle had died down on this stretch of the river and the fireworks upstream gave a wonderful background. No one challenged us as we swept through the narrow entrance at high speed and out into the calm Mediterranean. Hard paddling by three while the others wielded a sounding pole took us slowly back to shore against the current, and with excitement we realised that at the first try we had hit a place on this shallow coast where tank landing craft could disembark their loads.

It was only afterwards that we realised our good fortune, for later surveys of the coast for more than a mile northwards of the river found nowhere that was not obstructed by off-lying sandbars outside and deep intervening runnels with some eight feet of water in them.

While we were occupied in marking the position of our landing place and checking our surroundings a group of figures appeared on the dark skyline a hundred yards away. After a few moments of tension we recognised each other as the other half of the Beach Party. We set to work erecting leading lights for the landing craft while our wireless operator made abortive attempts to get in touch with our main party beyond the river.

Presently, I realised that as our wireless would not work the brigade would have no idea that we were across the river and that we had found a landing place for the tanks. Leaving Ellman in charge, I therefore took one man with me and walked back the way the overland party had come to try to contact a headquarters of some sort, leaving the remainder of the party to call in the landing craft when they should appear. Our way led through marshy scrub with thorny bushes waist high and occasional open drains small enough to be jumped.

Just as we were poised to jump across one of these drains a voice from the far side said, 'Give the password,' Now, it had never occurred to me that I would need the password and I had not thought to ask for it, so I replied, 'I'm Royal Navy and I don't know your beastly password.' After more argument, I persuaded the voice to let us jump the ditch one at a time so he could examine us more closely. The examination apparently satisfied him for he reluctantly told us to go on wherever we were going to. I said, 'Anyway, what is this password?'

'Windsor Castle,' he said, 'but don't say I told you.'

Finding no headquarters on the north bank of the river we crossed in a boat to the south side where we found that DUKWs were just arriving and a pontoon ferry was nearly ready. Work was being hampered by a good deal of enemy mortar fire from multiple throwers known as 'moaning minnies' which I had not heard before. We made our way to brigade HQ, lying in the ditch whenever we heard the hiss of a descending mortar salvo. Some bursts came close, but by running between salvoes we went quite fast down the half-mile or so of road. I delivered my message to the brigade Major who was relieved but thought I was a bloody fool to run the gauntlet of mortars. Ignorance was certainly bliss for with the brigade Major's opinion in our minds we took four times as long to get back to the riverbank.

By the time we regained the beach dawn was breaking, although my watch still showed a comfortable 03.00. In the flurry of the evening's work I had forgotten to wind it, and I thought there was still two hours to go before the tanks were due to land. But as I arrived, the first LCT grounded on the beach, and against the frantic protests of my assistant out rolled a brand new Sherman tank onto the sandbank and into eight feet of water between the sandbank and the shore, The LCT had beached thirty yards to the northward of the marks. The tank faltered, stopped and drowned.

The crew climbed disconsolately onto the turret. With the drowned tank as a mark we persuaded the subsequent tanks to turn sharp right on leaving the LCT, run thirty yards along the submerged sandbank and then turn a sharp left and come into the beach through steadily shoaling water. Two more LCTs beached successfully and all their tanks rumbled ashore before it was light enough for the enemy in the hills across the plain to see what was going on.

Then, when the last LCT was starting to withdraw, a salvo of shells arrived very close. The LCT backed off astern quickly and left our boat from which I happened to be talking to her Captain as the only object of interest in view. It was a hundred yards to shore but the sailors paddled the boat ashore as if there were an outboard motor attached. We made a dive for our slit trenches and waited for the shooting to stop. Unfortunately the only tanks in sight were on either side of us. One drowned, and one bogged in the marsh behind the beach. The shooting was irregular and erratic at a range of about five miles but constant enough to make life very uncertain. Sometimes it was one gun and sometimes four but it was kept up all day with occasional salvoes at night just to keep us awake.

With the Army across the Volturno, M Commando returned home to *Armadillo,* finally arriving in early December. But the journey home was not entirely without incident. En route to England, M2 Commando, in its own LCI, stopped in Gibraltar for a week.

Sub Lieutenant Joe Bramble RNVR, Assistant Beachmaster M Commando

During our stay there I narrowly missed being 'logged' aboard the LCI for insubordination. This procedure allowed the CO to make an adverse report in the ship's log concerning an officer's performance. Most days the wardroom bar was open early, and by mid-afternoon one day the CO, by now approaching an advanced state of inebriation, began ordering a series of exercises for the ship's company. 'Your men will have to take part, of course,' he said to me.

'Aye, aye, Sir,' I replied, assuming this would be a series of essential drills in readiness for an emergency. I alerted Petty Officer Todd and we awaited the next order. They came thick and fast.

The ship's company and the Beach Party started to run around the vessel in response to shouted commands from the wardroom of 'Abandon ship!' 'Fire in the engine room!' 'Man overboard!' 'Action Stations!' And many more in quick succession. There was no time to complete one before the next one was given. As PO Todd led the perspiring M2 Commandos past the wardroom he gave me some meaningful glances. The situation did not improve during the next half-hour.

At last I shouted, 'M2 Beach Party, stand fast!' There was an ominous silence in the wardroom. The Midshipman shuffled his feet and looked embarrassed. The CO of the LCI glared at me, 'I'm going to log you, Bramble!'

'Aye, aye, Sir,' I said, 'but the Beach Party is not going to perform any more evolutions!' Nothing more was said and I was left trying to decide whether I had done the right thing. I knew that if proven guilty the Navy could literally throw the book at me. But I heard nothing more about the incident.

Back in Italy during the autumn of 1943 the other Royal Naval Commandos, having concluded their activities after the landings at Salerno and on the Italian east coast, gradually made their way across the Mediterranean to North Africa and the Middle East.

After their mistaken landing at Sapri, N Commando went first to Corsica, where a small group was installed in the lighthouse at Ajaccio to prevent any Germans landing on the island. Next, they made their way to Bougie in North Africa. Here, there was no camp for them to move into so they had to make their own, a process with its own special routines.

Leading Seaman Ray Bromley, N Commando

We had to make our own camp, and with tents borrowed from the Army the camp started to take shape. Our first task was the building of latrines. These were built with rolls of hessian and seven-foot poles which surrounded a twelve-foot-long, three-foot-wide trench. At each end was a box on which a long pole was rested. A tall lad was already seated on the pole when in came the smallest lad in the Commando. He tried to heave himself onto the pole but, alas, instead of alighting onto the pole he hit it. The result was that the pole came off the box, and the two came off the pole and landed in the trench. Nobody would go near them for days. Now the second latrine was for the Petty Officers and officers. This was a trench but had wooden boxes over them with lids covered with hessian. To keep out the flies a rating had already gone in to the latrine and poured a small drop of petrol in. He had then gone to get a match because he was a non-smoker. In the mean time in came a Petty Officer smoking. He lifted the lid to drop in his fag end – the results go without saying!

After Bougie, N Commando then made their way to Malta and onto HMS *Saunders* at Kabrit, where they spent Christmas Day 1943 in the desert. Just after Christmas D Commando also arrived in HMS *Saunders*. Because N Commando were not up to full strength and with another big operation looming several officers were transferred from D Commando to N Commando at thirty-five minutes' notice.

Lieutenant Hugh Birley RNVR, Beachmaster N Commando

My switch from D Commando to N Commando was done at such short notice that there was no time to collect one of my two blue uniforms from a tailor where it was being promoted by having the Midshipman's patches replaced by the single wavy stripe of a Sub Lieutenant. I never saw it again.

On New Year's Eve 1943 N Commando were embarked on HMS *Phoebe* for the return journey to Italy. There they camped in a small orchard outside Naples, near to other units preparing for the Anzio landings, codenamed Operation Shingle, on 22nd January 1944. Also on their way to Naples was A Commando, who had been in India.

Petty Officer Gordon Holwill, A Commando

During the voyage we had been issued with battledress to replace the tropical kit we had been wearing. With the battledress were shoulder flashes which were to be sewn on. However, we were told that this was not compulsory as some members of an RN Commando had been captured at Salerno and executed (Hitler had issued a directive that any special forces that were captured were to be executed without trial). I still have my flashes in the same condition as when they were issued.

Hitler's infamous Kommando Befehl (Commando Order) of November 1942 had certainly resulted in the deaths of some Commandos, and it is possible that the Royal Naval Commandos themselves might have been directly affected. During training, the Royal Naval Commandos were warned about the dire consequences of being caught because of Hitler's Order. Given the secrecy surrounding executions under this order the full facts about its use may never emerge.

There were to be two sectors at Anzio, a small town with its own port north of Naples and south-west of Rome. To the north the British would land – their sector was called Peter Sector. The Americans would attack Anzio itself and the area to the south – this was called X-Ray Sector. US Major General John Lucas's 6th Corps would land at Anzio. They were part of the US 5th Army under Lieutenant General Mark Clark.

A, K and N Commandos were used for the Anzio landings, with O Commando being held in reserve. The landings took place in the early hours on 22nd January 1944. The Royal Naval Beach Signals went with the Americans into Anzio itself.

Signalman Reg Nadin, Royal Naval Beach Signals Section No. B8

We ate a hearty breakfast at midnight. As I was the junior Signalman I was put into one of the advance parties. The LCA crew were trying to make as silent approach as possible but the Americans were very noisy, calling to each other or banging their equipment. Our target was to capture the harbour ready for the follow-up troops to land once the beachhead had been made secure. It did not take the Germans long to awaken to the fact that we were on their doorstep. We came under continuous gunfire from what I was told were 88-mm shells, many of which burst in the air giving the effect of hailstones.

The Royal Naval Commandos landed further north on Peter Beach. As with A Commando, N Commando had intended to land in assault landing craft, but the presence of a sandbar in their area meant that plans had to be hastily revised. N Commando therefore landed in DUKWs, which could make it over the sandbars. But this was not the only improvisation that the Commandos had to cope with.

Leading Seaman Ray Bromley, N Commando

The landings were successful, except for a mine belt which ran along the length of the beach. Seeing the Sappers had landed on the wrong beach we had to clear a path through the minefield. This we did by probing the sand with our knives, and we were able to make a pathway. Digging in for the defence of the beachhead, we could not go too deep, owing to the trench filling with water. The nights were spent huddled up in our greatcoats, and many was the time I felt movements in my pockets and discovered rats after any bits of food that might be in them.

Petty Officer Gordon Holwill, A Commando

At Anzio we encountered another development in assault landings – rockets. These were designed to destroy minefields and also to make the defence force take cover. As we approached the beach, the LCAs stopped and suddenly hundred of rockets passed overhead, turning the darkness into light and destroying our night vision. When we landed we encountered another hazard – a lot of unexploded rockets which we could not see in the darkness.

Lieutenant Hugh Birley RNVR, Beachmaster N Commando

The beaches were only used for a few days. There followed a gale which wrecked a number of landing craft and also the floating pier which we hoped to use for LSTs to overcome the rather gentle gradient. However the Americans did a fine job in erecting 'hards' in the small harbour of Anzio from the rubble of bombed houses. Three LSTs could berth at once and achieved a very quick turnround by arriving from Naples full of loaded trucks and doing the return journey full of empty ones.

All appeared to be going very well. Although the Germans had responded to the landings with air attacks and motor-boat attacks, they had not caused a delay. On the beaches, N Commando were supervising the tank landing craft which brought in the stores, while K Commando were running the landing of the bigger ships' loads of vehicles. The day after the landings there was even time for a walk to take in the surroundings.

Telegraphist Malcolm Robinson, Royal Naval Beach Signals Section No. B5

On the morning after the initial landings, several of us walked in as far as the coast road running from Anzio and eventually linking up with the major route to Rome. It was eerie. At that time all seemed to be quiet, and, whilst there must have been some activity not too far away, we were not conscious of it. With Rome only twenty miles distant, it seemed incredible that no effort appeared to be taking place to send, at the very least, a mobile scouting party to the city.

The key question for the Allied Commanders was, should they push straight inland while the way was clear or should they consolidate their position? The British favoured a rapid advance inland but the Americans decided to stay and consolidate their position before moving out of the beachhead. It was a mistake the British had made nearly thirty years earlier at Gallipoli. Bad weather slowed down the Allied build-up, and by the time Major General Lucas decided to move his troops out it was too late. Field Marshal Albert Kesselring, the German Commander-in-Chief, had reacted with speed, and by 26th January he had six divisions surrounding the Anzio perimeter. In the days and weeks that followed the initial landings, attack and counter-attack with the usual bombardments marked the Anzio campaign. The Naval bombardments were an important part of the Allied strategy, and the Royal Naval Commandos were called upon to assist.

Petty Officer Gordon Holwill, A Commando

Germans shells started to hit ships lying off the beach waiting to unload. Spotter planes had failed to find the position of the German guns, so I, together with seven men, a Forward Observation Officer and a Signalman carrying a receiving-and-transmitting radio, were sent out.

Our job was to locate the guns and to send their position back to HMS *Spartan*, a cruiser lying off the beach and supporting the landing. After moving through a line held by the Americans, we came to a low hill which overlooked a plain beyond.

Here, we saw some German tanks beside what looked like aircraft hangers which were obviously responsible for the shelling. The Forward Observation Officer started to relay the position of the tanks, and shells started to fall around them. After a few minutes we saw Germans making for our position – needless to say we did not stop to argue. The shelling was not resumed. Shortly after this HMS *Spartan* itself was sunk by a bomb which was guided to its target by a high-flying aircraft.

The German shelling continued to torment the Allied forces in Anzio. Shortly after the landings N Commando had left the beaches and moved into Anzio itself, where one of the big German guns soon sought them out.

Leading Seaman Ray Bromley, N Commando

We were constantly under attack from 'Anzio Annie', a big gun back in the hills firing into the port area. This, plus the air raids, meant that life was never dull. We managed to dodge 'Anzio Annie' although her shells had fallen many times around us, and a number of times we had gone to help others, but 'Anzio Annie' was going to have the last word with us in the end.

The house we had taken over and fortified had the front door on one street and the back door on the street below because the place was built on the hillside. I was returning to the billet from the port area, when one of her shells landed yards away. I was blown to the ground, and, on getting up, noticed a Tommy lying on the pavement. Seeing no movement I went to help him. He had got a lump of shrapnel in the back and out of the front pushing his guts out. He was alive, so all I could do was to press them back and put the field dressing around his middle to hold them in (we all carried field dressings in our large trouser pocket). A passing Jeep took him to the First Aid Dressing Station and I heard later that he died soon after arriving.

With the troops in the Anzio beachhead going nowhere fast, life settled down in a pattern reminiscent of the static campaigns of World War I. Also in Anzio was Beach Signals Section No. B8, which had been in residence since the landings on 22nd January. They had a key role in communicating between the sea and the land, a job made harder by the shells from the 88-mm guns and the aerial bombing by the Stukas. Sometimes there were additional dangers.

Signalman Reg Nadin, Royal Naval Beach Signals Section No. B8

We were being shot at by a sniper, and even the tolerance of RN ratings can run out, so a-hunting we went. Near to the harbour were some shops and we found two snipers. One was an arrogant young Nazi, and his comrade was probably in his late thirties and to us an old man. He was very small in very baggy trousers and seemed delighted to have been captured. Being daft as the British are, we gave them cigarettes, food and drink before handing them over to the Military Police.

Apart from snipers, there was the constant threat from enemy aircraft in Anzio. As well as the familiar whine of the Stukas with their bombs, the machine guns of the fighters could also inflict casualties. But it was not just with bombs and bullets that the Germans tried to harass the Allies.

One German tactic was to turn out civilians into no man's land during the night in the hope of confusing the Allied armies. They would be brought down to the harbour the next morning for onward passage to Naples. Apart from the outgoing traffic, the beaches were constantly busy with the unloading of stores and ammunition. But although N Commando spent much of their time on the shore at Anzio, trouble was never very far away.

Leading Seaman Ray Bromley, N Commando

A convoy of American lorries carrying ammo from the LSTs to the front got as far as our billets when an air raid started and 'Anzio Annie' joined in for the fun of it. The drivers were off into the wood, leaving the convoy. The front lorry was hit, and the fire started to creep back along the convoy, for the drivers had left them nose to tail. Leading Seaman Lamb received a Mention in Dispatches for taking the second lorry away from the burning one and getting it clear. In the mean time hell was breaking loose. Ammo was being thrown up by the explosions and then going off again. Everyone turned out and managed to get the remaining lorries to safety – all this was going on in the smokescreen that was laid down by the Army during the air raids.

It was very difficult to see where we were backing the lorries, but any space would do as long as we could get them off the road. I was guiding Lieutenant Russell back when I saw an opening and directed him back into it. The smoke really came down and I could not see my hand in front of me when there was an almighty Bang! I thought we had been hit by a bomb, but we had run into a brick wall. However, the convoy was saved, which was one up for us. We all suffered from the 'Anzio stoop'; wherever we went we went bent from the waist to duck the shells. In fact we gave new words to the song 'The Lambeth Walk'. It went something like this – 'When you get down Anzio way, any evening, any day, you'll find them all doing the Anzio stoop.'

But 'Anzio Annie' had not finished with N Commando. They were coming to the end of their three-month stay in Anzio when the shelling started again.

Leading Seaman Ray Bromley, N Commando

Two Army lorries came to pick up our gear. The two drivers were outside having a smoke, and the lads were up and down the steps with ammo and gear loading up the lorries to embark on an LST at the harbour for Naples. Petty Officer Letby, Leading Seaman Lamb, Leading Seaman Gregory, Able Seaman Brown and myself were taking boxes of ammo up the steps to the front door when suddenly there was an almighty Bang! Dust was everywhere, the plaster on the ceiling came down on us, and the blast blew us into one big heap at the bottom of the marble stairs. The hand grenades were rolling down the steps with us and all over the floor. The havoc outside was worse. The shell from 'Anzio Annie' had landed right in the middle of the two lorries, killing the two drivers and taking arms and legs off some of our shipmates.

One of the casualties was Lieutenant John Russell DSC RN, one of the N Commando Beachmasters who lost a leg. Later he was awarded a bar to the DSC which he had originally won on destroyers. He was evacuated back home to Britain via Naples and North Africa. N Commando returned to Naples, and from there crossed to the Adriatic coast, keeping a look out for British POWs on the run.

Leading Seaman Ray Bromley, N Commando

The whole unit moved to Rimini and the small port of Berchi ne Porto. Our first duty on arrival was to clear the small harbour of mines. Getting hold of a generator and a long cable we ran it around the sides of the harbour. Starting up the generator and throwing the switch produced no results, but the next try was much more rewarding for there was a terrific roar and water was thrown into the air, drenching us.

Italy was to be the last operation for N Commando, and they made their way slowly home to Liverpool and from there to Scotland again in time for Christmas 1944. But the Navy was still active in the Adriatic as well as further south in the Greek Islands. There was a number of different clandestine Naval organisations and special flotillas operating in these areas to give assistance to the Allied regular and special forces as well as to the Yugoslav Partisans.

Leading Seaman James Trotter

We were towed by three MTBs, and there were three landing craft to each MTB. We were towed at night and arrived at the island of Vis in the morning. Vis was to be our base for eighteen months. We were working with Tito's Partisans, killing Germans. The Partisans never took any prisoners. If any were taken, they were shot in the field at the end of the road. Our job was to support the troops in any action, pick up the wounded; mostly feet blown off by booby traps on other islands. Jerry always made booby traps and left souvenirs for our boys to pick up when they left their bases, like knives, helmets, caps, tin mugs, anything to keep us on the look-out and not get killed. We used to pick up fliers from B17s coming back from raids. Most of them jumped out and parachuted down into the bay when there was trouble. Another job was to take secret agents into Yugoslavia and call back at a certain time in the dark.

Wireless Telegraphist Leonard Rowland DSM, Levant Schooner Flotilla, No. 3 Caique

Lieutenant Robert Ballantine DSC, skipper of No. 3 Caique (a small coastal vessel) – was losing his wireless telegraphist due to hospitalisation and I was his replacement. That afternoon, our skipper was called to a conference with Lieutenant Commander Adrian Seligman DSC on the HQ schooner. When he returned to No. 3 Caique he looked very worried. Our stoker mechanic asked our skipper, 'Where to this time, Sir?'

'Kos,' was the quick reply.

'Damn that!' said the stoker. 'We were shot at the last occasion we raided it!'

The SAS soldiers arrived on board with their inflatable dinghy, stores and weapons. We cast off and the skipper set the compass bearing for the Greek island of Kos. We were due to make landfall in the bay at approximately 23.00 hours. With fair winds and calm seas we made good progress and arrived in the bay on time, having lowered the sails and mast about seven miles from the coast to minimise our silhouette.

The soldiers inflated the dinghy and put it over the port side of the caique. They pulled away steadily on their paddles, setting a steady pace. The stoker manned the quick-firing Solothern gun in the bows. Our coxwain manned the starboard Lewis gun positioned just aft of the mast. I sat on the transom manning the port Lewis gun. The skipper had the tiller about two feet behind me. We watched the soldiers in the dinghy land on the beach. When we were about to leave there was a short burst of gunfire from the shore. I jumped up to shield our skipper from the gunfire. He said, 'Sit down Sparks, I cannot see where I am going!' I returned to my gun position covering the shore party in case they were attacked. The skipper steered the caique away from the shore then asked me, 'Why did you stand up?'

'It was to shield you from the gunfire. If you are hit no one on board can navigate us back to this beach tomorrow for the pick-up. The patrol of soldiers would be stranded and in danger of being captured. After all I am only a Sparker and I am expendable.' He turned and said, 'Thanks Sparks, but we are all expendable.'

Apparently one of the soldiers had picked up a machine gun with the safety catch not set correctly in the 'on' position. We found out about this when we returned from our daytime hideaway creek in Turkey the following night when we picked up the patrol after their successful mission which was to contact the Greek guerilla forces and obtain intelligence about the disposition and strength of enemy forces.

The Royal Naval Commandos had also been in action in Burma, where the Allies were fighting to clear the Japanese and to prevent any incursion into India.

The dense jungle meant that travel was slow, so that roads and especially rivers assumed great significance for both sides. But even the rivers were not ideal.

Report on Rivers and Lakes of Burma published by General HQ, New Delhi 15.07.43

They rise in the hills with dense jungle where there are no roads and tracks are few. The survey maps indicate villages and tracks but the villages move from time to time so that it often happens that they are some miles away from the place shown on the map, while some have disappeared altogether. Others have come into being since the survey. In the hills the rivers are mountain torrents.

In the summer of 1943 H Commando had good reason to be less than happy with their lot. Having been kitted out in khaki at HMS *Armadillo* they were on their way to the tropics, where they could reasonably expect to be issued with smart tropical uniforms. However, they were to be disappointed.

Able Seaman George Fagence, H Commando

Whilst in Durban, we were issued with tropical kit, shorts and bush shirts, which were coloured orange! These were stores left over from the Boer War and a right lot of fairies we looked disembarking at Bombay.

Apart from the uniform H Commando also had to endure the hardships peculiar to long voyages on troopships destined for the Far East.

Sub Lieutenant Clifford Claughton, Assistant Beachmaster H Commando

When doing the rounds of the mess deck and asking, 'Any complaints?' there was not a murmur in response. It was sufficient to see strung across the mess table, as though a line of washing across a north-country street, several cabbage leaves, all of which must have been ten inches square. The silence said it all.

Able Seaman George Fagence, H Commando

The mindless morons at the War Office advocated all men on convoy ships should receive one Mae West lifebelt and emergency rations consisting of a tobacco-sized tin of solid chocolate, the eating of which was punishable by death. At the end of the voyage every tin was empty! The same morons devised 'Tea Compo' rations consisting of tea, sugar and powdered milk in an Oxo-sized tin. One took one spoonful out and added hot water (instant tea). But the suns that shine in the tropics are greater than the eggheads supposed, which accounts for the powdered milk congealing and turning into cheese. So if you were gasping for a cuppa it was Cheddar or Gorgonzola.

Eventually the troopship *Highland Chieftain* arrived in Bombay, where H Commando duly embarked upon a voyage in *dhows* northwards up the coast looking for other *dhows* which were supplying fuel oil to the Japanese submarines.

In crystal-clear seas the Commando set off to the north

and the Portuguese island of Diu. Keen to see if any sharks were around, they tossed the smallest Commando, Mick Lowry, overboard as bait. The subsequent appearance of the ominous fins meant a rapid reappearance on board the *dhow*. In the event they did not find the Japanese. But they did find pirates.

Able Seaman George Fagence, H Commando

When they came, we were ordered to put a salvo above their heads when a flare was lit. They sailed silently alongside and, Bingo! all hell broke loose as twenty-odd rifles went off above their heads. That boat turned about so fast it nearly tied a knot in its foremast. I was all for putting a shot up their shirt tails – the glare of the light had caught the flashes of the knives and swords that the murderous bastards had.

On arrival at Diu, there was a chance to sample the local culture. Despite the apparent lack of danger, sightseeing was a process which had its own perils.

Able Seaman George Fagence, H Commando

We were strolling down this track alongside a drystone wall when we heard singing, 'I belong to Glasgow.' I looked at Yorky and he said,

That man has got to be pissed!

'Where did he get it?' We very soon located the source of our constipation, there sitting behind the wall was a Lascar. We called, 'Where did you get the giggling juice?'

'Come along with me,' he said and off we marched to a little *basha* just outside the village. We went down this ladder, it was an earth cellar stocked to the walls with five-gallon jars of whatever! We speculated that the original Portuguese galleon went aground some years before and this was part of the salvage. Me and Yorky got stoned out of our minds, and in returning back aboard I stepped off the eight-foot jetty and landed fair and square on my bonce and the bruises glowed in the dark.

Arriving back in Bombay, H Commando had a new Principal Beachmaster, Lieutenant Commander Anthony Cobham GC RN. He had won his George Cross in 1929 on the cruiser HMS *Devonshire* for his actions in dealing with an explosion in one of the gun turrets during practice firing.

H Commando was in Bombay with two other Commandos, A and O. However, these were both recalled to Europe (A Commando for the Anzio landings) and sub-units of both Commandos took part in the landings at Elba in 1944. Early in 1944 H Commando was dispatched north to Chittagong via Poona and Calcutta, where they boarded the troopship *Jalapadna*. Once more H Commando was at the mercy of Naval rations.

Able Seaman George Fagence, H Commando

The evening meal aboard the *Jalapadna* convoy ship to Chittagong was tinned steak-and-kidney pudding. The vessel sailed at first light, by which time every toilet was permanently manned. The ship's side had the best coloured camouflage you have ever seen and the smell kept us in the clear.

H Commando were being sent to the Arakan in Burma to land Allied forces in an attempt to expel the Japanese. Operation Screwdriver was planned to get troops ashore at landing points up and down the coast. The first Operation Screwdriver was not considered to be a military success despite the landings passing without incident. Having returned with the soldiers, H Commando were then involved in the planning of Screwdriver II . This was a landing on the Arakan coast in March 1944 when the Army and Marine Commandos were to be landed with the West African troops of General Christison's XV Corps. The idea was to divert the Japanese from the land-fighting on the strategically important road from Maungdaw to Buthidaung and the Razabil crossroads.

Able Seaman George Fagence, H Commando

We went by sea down the coast to another strip of beach below Maungdaw in company with 42 Royal Marine Commando and No. 3 Special Service Brigade who took off inland while we took up the rearguard in a concrete shelter and listened to the ruckus of small arms up the kuds. A party recced up the trail and came back with several walking wounded.

Sub Lieutenant Clifford Claughton, Assistant Beachmaster H Commando

As the heavily laden LCA pulled away from the beach with its cargo of wounded, dying and relieved, there was a frightening moment. The engine stalled. The boat wallowed, bobbing up and down on a calm but gently undulating sea. A time, if ever there was one, to be spotted. And so we were. A time for the Japanese to do their worst. Thankfully it was their worst. It could have been with an unfamiliar 25-pounder 'borrowed' from XVth Corps or one of their own. Whichever, the result was uncomfortably close, with the familiar plumes rising from the sea as missiles struck the water. The few minutes seemed like hours with that feeling of 'sitting ducks'. Arms waving, much shouting from all and sundry in the hope of attracting a neighbouring craft. Then the relief. The engine sprang to life and we were on our way. It was just that feeling of helplessness.

Able Seaman George Fagence, H Commando

Then onto Alethangaw by landing craft. We took up patrols in this area. We encountered the African native troops who put the fear of God up the Japanese with their assegais, and our mates the

Gurkhas who were ever ready to tear into them. After several sorties and feeding the leeches, we were shipped away to Akyab and spread out in the woods doing the usual skirmishes. In this area, the Japanese were getting nasty and shouting abuse. During a lull my oppo Dixie Dean had his optics on a pair of dead Japanese's boots who was lying down on the slope in front of us. He slithered down to relieve him of them but in tugging them off one of his legs came off with the boot. Exit one very sick squaddie.

With Screwdriver II having achieved its objectives of diverting the Japanese from the main land battle, H Commando returned to Bombay where their troopship the *Jalapadna* was blown up during a fire at the docks. But some of the Commandos had also fallen by the wayside due to tropical illness, including George Fagence.

With their mission in the Far East over, H Commando were sent back to Europe for the final operations in Italy. Ahead of them, A and O Commandos had already returned for the landing at Elba. But before they got there, the Royal Naval Commandos had taken part in the greatest amphibious assault of the war, D-Day.

CHAPTER 6

D-Day (1)

Extract from the D-Day diary of Able Seaman Edward Blench, Q Commando

TUESDAY 6TH JUNE, 'D'-DAY

06.30 Sighted French Coast.
08.30 Landings commenced. Shore battery firing on landing craft. First wave of assault troops had heavy casualties walking up beach under machine-gun fire.
09.30 Beach commences working. Sappers still in action. Many vehicles drowned. Fighting in village (Le Hamel). Prisoners begin to come in. Lieutenant Crammond and Petty Officer Williams wounded.
p.m. Village taken – fighting continues about six miles inland.
23.00 Air raids. First enemy planes sighted. Beaches now cleared of most obstacles.

The problem of clearing the obstacles laid by the Germans to prevent an invasion on the Normandy coast had exercised the planners' minds considerably. It was why the first units to land on D-Day were the Landing Craft Obstacle Clearance Units (LCOCU) and it was why they had one of the most difficult and dangerous tasks of any that day – mine clearance. The obstacles were also one reason why H-Hour was different in each of the Assault Areas, Gold, Juno and Sword. At its earliest, H-Hour was 06.30 on 6th June 1944, at its latest it was up to an hour and a half later, and the tide was rising all the time.

Able Seaman Andrew Henderson, Landing Craft Obstacle Clearance Unit

The Germans erected obstacles at low tide, approximately ten metres from the beach with a Teller mine on top of each. These obstacles were two pieces of steel in the shape of a diagonal cross with an upright pole to stabilise them. The Teller mines were attached to the diagonals.

Of course, these obstacles were hidden at high tide and would be devastating to landing craft. Our equipment for the job was a two-piece Dunlop wetsuit, flippers, weights, a belt of TNT and cortex fuses and detonators. We had the Davis escape apparatus for breathing, this consisted of an oxygen tank for one hour, an emergency oxlet for ten minutes, and a buoyancy oxlet. We were taken to the beach one hour before H-Hour on D-Day in an assault landing craft near the mouth of the River Orne, followed closely by the Royal Naval Commandos.

The ramp went down. Because we were breathing pure oxygen we had to get all the air out of our chests before we connected to the Davis apparatus.

We went straight out into twelve to fifteen feet of water. It was pitch darkness under the water and it was impossible to see. I had a watch with a light to tell me when the hour was up. After fifteen to twenty minutes, I found my first obstacle. I could feel along it to find the Teller mine. I attached the TNT from my belt to the mine with a cortex fuse and then swam on. I found eight obstacles before my time was up, the whole unit found a hundred mines.

The most difficult part as a frogman was the feeling of loneliness and isolation. You were in complete darkness and on your own, handling your own fate. After the charges were in position you had two places to go, back to your landing craft or onto the beach. As far as I know, most of us made it back to the landing craft where we detonated all the fuses and the obstacles exploded with a muffled bang.

The Germans had still not reacted to the invasion, and the LCOCU units were able to carry out their tasks without

GERMAN BEACH OBSTACLE WITH TELLER MINE

coming under fire. But what they were doing was dangerous enough. Further West in the Sword Assault Area the LCOCU were blowing up the obstacles as they ran up the beach from their landing craft.

Able Seaman Colin Harding, Landing Craft Obstacle Clearance Unit No. 3

We were frogmen for underwater obstacle clearance. We were force marched from Appledore to Ilfracombe to the swimming pool where we had training on diving with submarine escape apparatus with oxygen (forty minutes each dive). I must have done one hundred hours on oxygen.

The first landing on D-Day was on Sword Beach at 06.30 hours. We had awakened at 03.00 hours, breakfasted and got into wetsuits. To get into wetsuits you have to get your body through a hole about four to five inches across, which was made of elastic rubber that stretched for you to get into the suit (feet were included in the suit). We had cruised around for a bit to let the Americans bomb the beach. We were about half a mile offshore when the bombs dropped. We blew the obstacles as the tide came in. Where we landed was a house three stories high, and there was not a slate missing or a window glass broken. So much for the bombing.

We had worked for about two hours when the troops and the tanks came in. As no one had been to the house to see if any Germans were in occupation we were called off the beach. The landing craft were coming in where the beach had not been cleared. Suddenly, a tank exploded between our group of divers and the house. We watched three tanks explode – there was an 88-mm gun in the bottom of the house, facing along the beach.

Later, the Germans must have seen us on the beach, because they opened up with shrapnel shells that exploded in the air. I was standing with my mate Michael Austin about four feet away from him when we heard a shell come in and we dived for the sand. When the shelling stopped I got up but my mate was dead in front of me. He was from Newfoundland and had just got married in London.

133

Behind the LCOCU were the main body of the Royal Naval Commandos who were leading in the main assault forces of troops and tanks onto the Normandy Beaches. But even as they did so the Navy was already behind the German lines. The Combined Operations Bombardment units had dropped by parachute on the night of 5th–6th June into occupied France.

Telegraphist Wilf Fortune, No. 1 Combined Operations Bombardment Unit (also known as FOB Party – Forward Observer Bombardment Party)

We went to Normandy with A Company of the 7th Battalion, the Parachute Regiment. We flew from Fairford airfield in Gloucestershire. The FOB party was split up – the Captain and the Leading Telegraphist went in with one plane and me and the leading Bombardier went in another plane in case of accidents.

I had a No. 18 wireless set strapped to my leg on ten to twelve feet of rope. As I parachuted out the idea was that I pulled a cord and the wireless released and landed before me. Royal Artillery Captain Vere Hodge and Leading Telegraphist Alex Boomer landed in the one place, myself and Bombardier Ted Eley in another.

We set off at 10 p.m. on 5th June in an RAF Stirling. We jumped just after midnight from 600 feet. We could see the tracer fire. Some didn't make it. I landed, but when I released my cord the wireless just disappeared and I was left with just a piece of rope. But Alex had his radio. We landed in a cornfield at Ranville. I looked for Ted but couldn't find him so I went to the rendezvous point, a green light. I found Alex and Vere and then Ted Eley joined us, but he had caught his arm in the rigging lines of his chute and it had pulled his shoulder out.

Captain F. Vere Hodge MC RA, No. 1 Combined Operations Bombardment Unit

Our plane was caught in searchlights before we dropped and there was a good deal of tracer flying about. When my parachute opened I looked around; quite a lot was happening. I saw one parachute on fire and bullets started coming my way. I don't remember landing. I must have been knocked out for a few seconds because I found myself being dragged along the ground, the canopy still being filled with the stiff breeze. That was probably lucky for me; the chap firing at me probably thought he'd got me as I didn't get up.

I caught the rigging lines, pulled them, collapsed the canopy, twisted the quick release box on my chest and threw off the harness. I had lost my helmet, surprisingly, as it was firmly strapped on with a chin piece as well as a strap. I put on my red beret. I found later that my dagger, strapped in its leather scabbard on my right leg, had pierced the leather and my trousers and made a small but annoying hole in my leg.

There was no one near me but I sussed out where I thought I was and made towards what I hoped would be the prearranged rendezvous (RV) for my party along with part of 7 Para. I had a torch with a green light to identify myself as on 'our' side if necessary, and as I got near the RV there were some green guiding lights. At the RV I found Alex, then Wilf arrived (dropping down into a fresh cowpat) and finally Ted.

Telegraphist Wilf Fortune, No. 1 Combined Operations Bombardment Unit

We all moved towards Bénouville, crossing Pegasus Bridge where we found A Company in an orchard. When dawn broke, we found a house on the outskirts which would make a good Observation Post, tried the door. Locked. Round the back there were some steps down. Vere went down and this door was also locked, so he took his revolver out and shot the lock off. We burst in – the owner of the house was there with his two daughters. Vere explained in French that we were British but they would have none of it, saying, *'Allemands'* – 'Germans.'

We went upstairs into the front bedroom from where we could see right across the fields. Alex got the radio out and we used a window on the landing. One of these ladies came up and took out the fur coats from the wardrobe, which made us laugh. Vere took his binoculars out for viewing the area. Then we saw the Germans coming very quickly towards A Company. I said to Vere, 'They're on bikes Sir.' He said, 'No, they're running Wilfred.' I couldn't see their legs! Vere decided we had to warn the other lads so he told me and Ted to run and let them know. The attack happened shortly afterwards.

Captain F. Vere Hodge MC RA, No. 1 Combined Operations Bombardment Unit

Alex continued trying to get a ship without success. There was a knock on the front door and the occupants spoke with a German soldier. Alex and I held our breath but they didn't give us away and the soldier left.

The battle rolled past us and everything went quiet and I decided it was time to try and refind the platoon who had been forced to withdraw. Calling on my French again I told the household, 'If I don't find my friends we will return here – *ici*.' They nodded but no one spoke. They were terrified, poor things. I've always been very appreciative of that family's courage; had the Germans caught them sheltering us they would have been shot on the spot.

As Alex and I left the house everything was uncannily silent. There were one or two dead men lying in the road, and one of our Airborne helmets lying by itself, which I put on, and a German bandolier of ammunition, both of which I picked up. I then led the way over the road to a hedge and started to walk cautiously along it towards where I estimated A Company might be, Alex following me. I hoped they would not shoot us. After some minutes of cautious progress I saw them and they saw me. They told us that Wilf had taken Ted on to find the First Aid Post.

Telegraphist Wilf Fortune, No. 1 Combined Operations Bombardment Unit

One Sergeant was giving us a hard time because Ted was so slow in climbing a wall, so I said, 'Can't you see my mate's injured?' He said to me, 'Sonny, we are the only ones left.' Ted was a big lad, but that did not seem to matter lifting him up and over the wall. I took Ted to the First Aid post by the bridge and left him there. Ted was was eventually taken home.

By then I thought that Vere and Alex must have been captured, so I found another Forward Observation Unit under Captain Ritchie. I joined them and we went to do a shoot. Tosh Monks, the Telegraphist, was listening and he picked up a signal from Alex. I said, 'It looks like Captain Hodge is alright,' then the Captain said, 'What do you want to do?' I said, 'I think I should go back to them'

I crossed the bridge just as the seaborne troops crossed, and the Paras pointed them out in a wood across this cornfield, but they warned me about snipers. I zig-zagged across expecting a sniper's bullet at any time, but I made it and found Vere and Alex. Alex was signalling to the ships by Morse Code to send the shells over. We had our position and the position of the enemy and we telegraphed that to the ship by Morse. Then the officer would give his 'Fall of Shot'. This was a reference to the target which is at the centre of the clock face, the FOB is at six o'clock. Then 'Direction of Fall of Shot Landing', A equals 100 yards, B equals 200 yards etc.

Captain Vere Hodge got a call that there were German 88-mm guns firing at the landing craft from Frenchville Plage, and we were sent to put it out of action. At first we wanted to use the top of a church tower – I remember that going up to the tower, we walked part of the way between the walls and a service was going on.

Vere thought the lighthouse would be better so we used that. Alex was driving the jeep which we had the use of. A photographer rolled up, noticed Alec's Royal Navy badge and

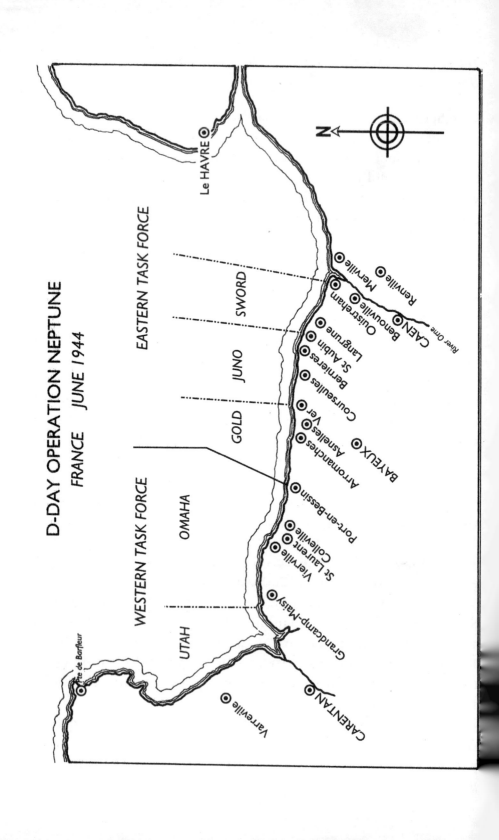

parachute wings and took a picture of the four of us in front of the lighthouse. The 88-mm guns were 800 yards away and we used letters for each 100 yards, so H was 800 yards and the direction was given as one o'clock, two o'clock etc. from our position. The ship had an artillery officer on board, but the ship also had to get itself in position for the shot so it might be ten minutes before anything happened. Then there would be the call from the ship, 'Fire for effect,' and the ranging shells would come over.

A couple of days after we used the lighthouse the Germans shot the top off.

For his part in this operation Wilf Fortune was Mentioned in Dispatches. It is interesting that as parachutists the Naval Telegraphists could and did wear the red beret of the Parachute Regiment. As Commando Signallers they could and did wear the green beret of the Commandos. And some, like Wilf Fortune, chose instead to wear an ordinary black French beret.

While the Bombardment units had been at Fairford airfield the Royal Naval Commandos were at various locations on the south coast. This was the biggest landing of the war, and it required no fewer than nine Royal Naval Commandos. These were F, J, L, P, Q, R, S and T Commandos, as well as the all-Canadian W Commando.

Each of the Commandos were attached to individual Naval Forces for the Normandy landings. These Naval Forces were given the same letters as the first letter of the Assault Force Area in which they were to land. Thus Force S was to land in Sword Area, Force J in Juno Area, and Force G in Gold Area.

In overall charge was Admiral Bertram Ramsay, Allied Naval Commander-in-Chief. Missing from the Royal Naval Commandos was one of their more experienced Beachmasters, Lieutenant Commander P. U. Bayly RN, who had left M Commando and become Cable Officer on board HMS *Mauritius* on D-Day. When Admiral Ramsey met him he exclaimed, 'Not *the* Bayly?'

Sword Area was furthest east and covered the area from the River Orne westwards. Juno covered the area in front of Bernières-sur-Mer and Courseulles, while Gold was the western part of the British and Canadian landings and extended west to Port en Bessin.

Forces O (Omaha Assault Area) and U (Utah Assault Area), covering the area west of Port en Bessin, were the American landing areas. The whole landing front was some fifty miles across; the British and Canadian forces landing on a thirty-mile front, with the Americans landing on a twenty-mile front.

F Commando had returned to HMS *Armadillo* from Sicily at the end of July 1943 and was attached to Force S together with R Commando for the assault on the Sword Area. R Commando had distinguished itself so much at HMS *Armadillo* that it was placed on official record: 'Thanks to the keenness of the officers, the loyal and hardworking co-operation of the Petty Officers and Leading Seamen, and above all to the absence of the disturbing older hands from barracks, this unit set about its work with great zest.'

J, Q and T Commandos went into Gold with Force G, while S, P, L and later W Commandos went into Juno with Force J. Of all of the Commandos destined for Normandy only F Commando had been in action before. However, Q Commando had been on exercise at Slapton Sands in Devon where the training exercise had gone tragically wrong.

Petty Officer Eric Gear, Q Commando

On one particular exercise the landing craft carrying instructors and thunderflashes blew up, killing most of them. The job of cleaning up the mess was supervised by my CO Petty Officer Paddy Bell in Q Commando. Not a very pleasant job.

Because of the scale of the Allied landings, two new appointments were made within each Assault Area. Firstly there would be a Beach Naval Officer in Charge (NOIC) in Sword, Juno and Gold. These were senior Naval officers and they ruled each area where there would be several Royal Naval Commandos and several Principal Beachmasters. In each Assault Area there would also be a Senior Officer Ferry Craft (SOFC). These officers would work closely with the Principal Beachmasters and Beach Group Commanders to control the ferry craft in an area.

Gold, Juno and Sword Assault Areas were further sub-divided into sectors. In Sword these sectors were, from east to west, Roger, Queen, Peter and Oboe Sectors. In Juno these sectors were, from east to west, Nan, Mike and Love Sectors. In Gold these were, from east to west, King, Jig, Item and How Sectors. Each of these sectors contained the landing beaches which were designated Red, Green and White.

Operation Overlord was the name given to the overall invasion of Europe through Normandy, but the Naval operation to get the troops and tanks across the Channel and onto the beaches was codenamed Operation Neptune.

The Naval Forces were assembled on the south coast ready for departure at the end of April 1944. Force S was based in Portsmouth, Force G in Southampton and Force J on the Isle of Wight. With all the Assault Forces assembled, it was decided that a visit by King George VI would boost morale.

Telegraphist Eric Dove, Royal Naval Beach Signals Section No. 9

We stood for two hours in the heat of the day, armed to the teeth, waiting for the King. The whole episode was a typical British farce. It was only by chance that we stood to attention facing the sea and that we saw the King flash by across the bay in a motor launch doing about forty knots. It looked no larger than a matchbox held at arm's length. We all had a good grumble that day. To add insult to injury we were asked to cheer the King as he went by.

Initially, D-Day had been planned for 5th June but bad weather caused a delay. With the forecast bad for an indefinite period apart from the 6th June itself General Eisenhower took the momentous decision on the 5th to set D-Day as 6th June at 04.00 hours.

At 09.00 hours on 5th June, the first groups of landing craft sailed from the Portsmouth area, and this marked the beginning of the voyage of the D-Day forces. Heavy weather added to the complications caused by so many craft all making their way towards France. Accidents were bound to happen.

Telegraphist Eric Dove, Royal Naval Beach Signals Section No. 9

Our craft was just clearing Southampton harbour when we were rammed by an LST (landing ship tank) which was three times the size of our craft and which was designed to carry forty lorries and tanks on its two decks. Our LCT (landing craft tank) was a flat-bottomed barge designed to carry four tanks.

On impact, our craft turned turtle, we were thrown into the sea and lost most of our gear. We were rescued by a French tug. The crew wrapped us in blankets, and took us down to the boiler room to dry out. We were also given half a mug of neat rum to drink. Everyone had to wear an inflated lifebelt, which saved many lives that day; there was more than one collision. The minor landing craft were skippered by very junior officers who had no sea experience. Our clothes were still wet when we were landed back at the jetty, but the rum had started to have its effect and the three of us were in a very happy mood. We asked if we would get survivor's leave. Not a bit of it. We got a kick up the backside and put on another landing craft.

Others were not so lucky. Fellow signaller Lionel Pitts had been involved in a similar accident, but he was not picked up for more than six hours through that night. He watched as the silhouettes of the landing craft slid past him, and his cries for help were lost in the wind. Finally at dawn he was rescued and taken to hospital.

However, the majority made their way slowly across the Channel to the coast of France. En route through the night breakfast was served. But anyone expecting a gourmet feast was to be disappointed.

Captain W. F. N. Gregory-Smith DSO and bar, DSC and bar RN, then Principal Beachmaster T Commando

In all our previous exercises with the Merchant Navy breakfast had always included bacon and eggs, a real wartime luxury. Anticipating a repetition, I was shocked to be served with liver and onions, a horrible mixture to offer at 2 a.m. to men who would be eating their last decent meal for days, if not for ever.

If breakfast was not going to provide the anticipated distraction from what lay ahead, there were other ways for the Commandos and troops to pass the time during the night before D-Day.

Lieutenant Commander Jack D'Arcy RNVR, Principal Beachmaster R Commando

One of my Beachmasters, 'Polly' Perkins, had shared with me a predilection for crossword puzzles, especially the cryptic skeleton ones. In our many hours of spare time, we had got around to compiling our own puzzles for the other to solve. As it happened, 'Polly' was embarked on the vessel steaming right alongside mine, and it was close enough for us signal in semaphore to each other with our arms. He had been in the process of solving one of my efforts before we embarked and he was now checking his answers with me as we went along.

Leading Telegraphist Paul Elliott, Forward Observer Bombardment Party No. 70 (FOB 70)

Below decks on the night before D-Day, some Canadians of the Regiment de la Chaudière on our deck were playing a game they called craps. It is played with two dice. A large pile of money soon appeared and was probably all they had. It was won by one of them. I said to the Canadian next to me, 'What are you going to do for money when we get over the other side?' 'What the hell, we will all be dead in the morning,' he replied.

Signalman Bernard Stone, Royal Naval Beach Signals Section No. B5

The weather had deteriorated and the sea was choppy. It was then that my little hell hole began to show itself. The throb and smell of the diesel from the engines was sickening and we had hardly started yet. We took our station at the head of a large flotilla carrying 48 Royal Marine Commando and the Canadian divisions which we were to lead into the beachhead for the first assault. As we progressed, the sea became much rougher. A landing craft is not the most favourable vessel in a choppy sea, and with the smell and noise of the engines I became violently ill. Seasickness does have one advantage. You are too ill to be scared. I had to keep the hatch open to get air, and as we approached the French harbour of Courseulles in Juno Sector, our landing point, we passed under the guns of HMS *Warspite*, about a mile offshore, firing at designated targets. She had been firing since 04.30 and it was now about 07.00. Over two and a half hours. The roar of her fifteen-inch guns, firing broadsides, was ear shattering, and yet comforting to think what damage she was causing on the land. As we neared the shore, her shells passing overhead caused a vacuum in my tiny cabin as the air was sucked out.

Able Seaman Jim Watson, F Commando

We were stood to, awaiting to board the landing craft, when there was a huge flash off the port bow of the ship followed by an explosion, and we then watched the Norwegian destroyer *Svenner* go down after an attack by a German torpedo boat. We were just stood, unable to comprehend the sight. As we watched three torpedo tracks crossed our quarter, and it happened so unexpectedly that it did not sink in until we were in the landing craft.

The landing craft were now approaching the beaches in their designated sectors. The wind was Force 4 and was west northwest, which did not make for calm seas. It also meant that the landing craft would not find it easy to realign themselves after they had come all the way from England at night.

Some of the landing craft also had with them the supposedly secret DD tanks (Duplex Drive amphibious tanks). Although a closely guarded secret amongst the Allied forces, captured documents later revealed that the Germans knew more about them than most of the Allied forces did.

The first H-Hour came at 06.30 in the American Assault Areas, Utah and Omaha. Utah was a largely unopposed landing, but troops landing in Omaha faced heavy opposition and heavy losses. H-Hour for the British and Canadian Assault Areas came an hour to an hour and a half after the American landings.

H-Hour came first for Gold at 07.25. This Assault Area covered the area from Port en Bessin where Omaha started to the mouth of the River de Provence. J, Q and T Commandos were the designated Royal Naval Commandos for this area, and they were first in. T Commando landed furthest east in Gold, in front of La Rivière. From here west to Arromanches the golden sands ran up to the sand dunes at the back of the beach.

Captain W. F. N. Gregory-Smith DSO and bar, DSC and bar RN, then Principal Beachmaster T Commando

After breakfast we mustered alongside our landing craft, the RN Commando being split up among several of these. It was a dark silent night except for the drone of aircraft overhead. Far to the eastward silent gun flashes flickered along the horizon.

The LSIs anchored about seven miles off the Normandy coast and the assault waves embarked in their landing craft. As each man went over the side, he was handed anti-seasick pills and a vomit bag, which seemed a curious contradiction. But the planner responsible obviously knew his pills, because the bags were in constant use during our slow wet passage through a choppy sea which was rougher than it had looked from the high decks of a large ship.

Able Seaman Fred Simpson, T Commando

We got shelled during the night, two of our Commandos were wounded, two Royal Marine gunboats were alongside, and all were killed from the shelling by the German shore batteries. We boarded the LCM with all our gear, flag poles, loud hailers and batteries, and landed on the beaches in a panic.

Captain W. F. N. Gregory-Smith DSO and bar, DSC and bar RN, then Principal Beachmaster T Commando

A number of badly wounded were clinging weakly to beach obstacles against which the flood tide was brutally battering them. Closer inshore several dead men were lying in the shadows, their bodies rolling back and forth as the waves advanced and receded over them. Higher up the beach, little mounds, which from a distance looked like piles of sand, proved to be khaki-clad casualties of the initial assault. Of the living there was no sign. The several hundred men who had just landed had vanished into the dunes as if the sand had swallowed them. Only the rattle of small-arms fire gave them away.

It was shortly after 07.30 when we waded ashore. Mitchell, the Beachmaster, turned left and I turned east to ensure that the Commandos were acting according to plan. I ran along the half-tide mark looking for runnels and other obstructions. To my right the battle among the dunes was still continuing, although it was barely audible amid the general noise of aircraft, Naval guns, landing craft engines and shouting men.

With the Commandos now ashore, the tides immediately became a problem again. Although the approach of high water meant that the obstacles which had not been destroyed were now out of harm's way in deep water, the plain fact was that it was 07.30 hours, the sea was filled with hundreds of landing craft which were heading into Gold, and they needed to offload their vehicles and men before the tide started to go out again.

Captain W F N Gregory-Smith DSO and bar, DSC and bar RN, then Principal Beachmaster T Commando

More than 400 vehicles were now ashore or wading towards it. But, owing to casualties among the assault vehicles, only a few exits had been cleared and the planned flow of tanks, guns and trucks into the open countryside had dwindled to a mere trickle. Conditions offshore were just as bad, and the shallows were now blocked by wrecks and empty craft trying to back off the beach in the teeth of a strong westerly wind. Prudence clearly demanded that the third wave of vehicle carriers must defer beaching for a time.

'Tell the flotilla to wait offshore for ten minutes,' I told the Yeoman. Signals were semaphored, lamps flashed and the R/T chattered. But they might have been sending their message to the moon for all the good it did, and the third wave of LCTs bulldozed their way through the flotsam and discharged another 200 vehicles which came to a grinding halt behind the waiting queue.

Eventually, a combination of high tide and the success of the Royal Engineers in clearing the beach freed up the traffic jam and the beach started moving again. But by now the German defenders had woken up to the fact that there was an invasion taking place and resistance increased.

Captain W. F. N. Gregory-Smith DSO and bar, DSC and bar RN, then Principal Beachmaster T Commando

It seemed only prudent to dig in the control post, so we borrowed pick and shovels. One of the Commandos swung his pick into the ground. Immediately there followed a blinding flash and my brain went blank until I found myself lying on the ground among the gruesome bits and pieces which had once been a human being.

Meanwhile, further west in Gold, Q Commando landed in the Le Hamel area. Not all of them landed in the right place, but they were all grateful to the sand dunes for providing essential cover from the German fire.

Able Seaman Ken Green, Q Commando

We hit the beach, down came the ramp, but the officer and I got off by jumping over the side. That was good thinking for coming out the front was risky. One poor chap was badly wounded and asked to be pulled out of the sea. He was in a very bad state, an 88-mm shell must have gone off near him. The officer asked, should he shoot him, but I said let's pull him to the beach. We left him there, but I don't think he lived very long. We had a long walk to meet up with the rest of the Commandos. Thank God there were sand dunes, which gave us plenty of cover.

Petty Officer Eric Gear, Q Commando

It was a very windy day, and the sea was quite rough. We unloaded into assault craft off the French coast and began our run in. The noise was deafening, rocket firing craft, gunfire from a Royal Navy destroyer, and a good deal of gun and rifle fire coming from the beach. The whole length of the beach was covered in smoke, with the beach below the waterline filled with great iron obstacles. We had a fairly dry landing and we were only wet to the knee. Getting ashore was fairly comfortable. The beach in front of us was completely filled with tank traps and it was difficult to see where we were going, what with the smoke and the continuing noise.

A few men around me were falling over and staggering to get on their feet. It didn't take us long to get to the back of the beach, and it took an even shorter time to realise we were in the wrong place. We also realised that we were under fire from positions along the end of the beach. We returned the fire, but I did not have a clear target as we could not make out where the fire was coming from.

It was then that I saw Petty Officers Williams and Hodgetts returning from their encounter with an enemy pillbox. Hodgetts was carrying Williams, who was wounded. They were both from Q1 Commando, and we heard later that one had provided covering fire as the other jumped on top of the pillbox and threw grenades through the slits. We then made our way along the coast through Le Hamel. There we came face to face with a couple of Jerries in a trench. I was with two other blokes and when we ran towards them they surrendered. By the time we got to where we were supposed to be the whole beach was an organised shambles with abandoned craft, further craft coming in, and some vehicles stuck in the sand. There were the injured, the wounded and a few prisoners.

However, our signs were soon in place and the exits clearly marked. We were still under fire from points at the back and the ends of the beach. At one point a Royal Navy Seafire came down on the beach, the pilot parachuted down, landing on his feet on the beach – he was worrying about getting back as he had a date that evening! By this time some of us were realising how hungry we were. We cadged some bread and jam from an LST – I was standing in the water up to my waist eating bread and jam, and another craft gave us a sack of potatoes.

Also landing in the Gold Assault Area were J1 and J3 Commandos, who were scheduled to look after the area around

Arromanches, on the edge of Gold and next to the American Assault Areas. J2 Commando followed several days later.

Able Seaman Alexander Hutton, J Commando

I was sorry to see some of the lads aboard, as it was still rough and a lot were seasick. As we got nearer the beach the noise of gunfire from the big ships was overwhelming, and seeing men struggling in the water from craft that had been hit was very frightening.

Sub Lieutenant Jack Gaster RNVR, Assistant Beachmaster J Commando

What an amazing sight met our eyes when we eventually came on deck on that morning of 6th June. The initial landings had already gone in. We could hear the bombardment long before we arrived in the holding area. I watched as the heavy guns of the monitor *Roberts* fired its shells weighing some ton apiece over the landing area; it was possible to watch their flight over the beaches. We could see the wreckage of damaged landing craft where they had hit beach obstructions that had mines attached to them as we approached the landing site. It then struck me that we were coming in on the wrong beach as far as J Commando was concerned. This was King Beach in the Courselles area. As soon as we cleared the LST, I arranged with the Beachmaster for a lift with an LCM Mk 1, the British version, to ferry us along to Item Green Beach at Le Hamel.

I was upset to see quite a few bodies of those young Canadian soldiers in the shallow waters off King Beach. They had never made it ashore to be able to use those grenades that they were priming and tossing to one another like toys just a few days before.

Our Coxswain laid offshore a bit as we passed the sanatorium by Le Hamel, as there was still quite a bit of activity and firing in that corner. But he brought us round, dodging between obstacles onto the beach near the western end, where a chalk cliff separated us from Arromanches. We quickly scrambled ashore, where we were met by our colleagues from J Commando who had landed with the assault wave. They had already established a sheltered position for the Beachmasters' HQ. It was sited on a sand ridge running along the top of the beach beyond which lay a flooded area surrounded by barbed wire and with signs proclaiming *Achtung Minen!* Looking along the base of the wire, we could see strands of fine wire disappearing into the sand along its length, these were attached to Teller mines, as we did not wish to cross the wire at that point we left them very much alone.

Members of the Landing Craft Obstacle Clearance Units were busy doing their dangerous work making the beaches safe for the landing craft, who were coming in an endless stream to disgorge the military hardwear onto the beaches. In the mean time the Royal Engineers beach-recovery tanks and bulldozers were clearing the hedgehog obstacles away from the beaching areas. Other tanks fitted with flails were busy clearing a path through the field that lay to the right of the beach and continued uphill to a point where it joined a road through to Arromanches. These were closely followed by another tank with a roll of Sommerfelt Tracking that unrolled as it went uphill, making a steel-mesh roadway as it progressed. Meanwhile, as the sounds of battle receded away from the beach area we took stock of our position. A bivouac area close to a drystone wall that had been checked for mines by members of the Royal Engineers was chosen for a tented site.

With the Commandos dug in on Gold, there was time to look back at the events of the day. But even now they were destined to have little peace and quiet.

Sub Lieutenant Keith Andrew RNVR, Assistant Beachmaster T Commando

I remember the lack of enemy aircraft on D-Day, but at dusk they came over and strafed the beach. When they appeared, the whole invasion fleet opened up with tracer fire so there were fireworks everywhere.

Captain W. F. N. Gregory-Smith DSO and bar, DSC and bar RN, then Principal Beachmaster T Commando

Some time after midnight, after confirming that the wounded were now being smoothly evacuated, I scraped a hole in the mud. During the past twenty-two hours I had been in and out of the water, and had eaten only a bar of chocolate. So I was cold, wet and hungry, and badly in need of alcoholic refreshment. But having none I lay shivering in my foxhole.

The lack of enemy air strikes had been a notable feature of D-Day, and was a testament to Allied control of the air. In the Gold Assault Area one of the key objectives for the troops landing there had been Le Hamel. This was given to the Hampshire Regiment to assault, but due to enemy resistance it was only captured in the late afternoon. Similarly No. 47 Royal Marine Commando captured Port en Bessin after landing at 09.30. Although Gold had been the Assault Area with the earliest H-Hour of the British and Canadian beaches on D-Day, the landings in the Juno and Sword Assault Areas were not far behind.

CHAPTER 7

D-Day (2)

East of the Gold Assault Area was Juno, where the tides had given the planners particular problems. Juno covered Bernières-sur-Mer and Courseulles-sur-Mer, a coast known for its outlying rocks. In order for the landing craft to clear these rocks the tide would have to be just that much higher than for the other Assault Areas.

Therefore H-Hour was slightly later for Juno than it had been for the Gold and Sword Assault Areas. For the assault, Force J was divided into two. J1 landed in the area next to Gold, while J2 landed in the area next to Sword. Owing to the heavy weather, and confusion among the defined shipping lanes, the official H-Hour had been put back by ten minutes so that H-Hour for Force J1 was 07.45, and for Force J2 it was 07.55.

But this opened up new problems because of the obstacles. The original plan had been for the landing craft to beach just short of the obstacles, but now, with a rising tide, the landing craft would land right in amongst them. Casualties were inevitable.

Signalman Bernard Stone, Royal Naval Beach Signals Section No. B5

We had only taken on a few Commandos for the first assault, as our main job was to guide the boats in and then go back for other flotillas awaiting guidance to their particular sectors. We were now getting shells falling around from the German batteries and, closing in, heavy machine-gun and mortar fire. Pressing on, we had landing craft hit around us but we were still lucky. Our turn was to come. Because we were about fifteen minutes late in reaching the beach the tide was now on the ebb and we were drawing too much water to cross over the mined barriers. I poked my head up to see what the conditions were like. We were still in water too deep for heavily laden troops to get ashore. The beach was littered with sunken craft, drowned tanks and vehicles, and machine-gun fire was coming in now. A long low wall ran alongside the promenade at Courseulles. Because of the heavy machine-gun crossfire sweeping the beach, troops were sheltering behind this, waiting for the tanks to clear a way through the town so that they could fight their way inland. Buildings on the seafront were shattered and on fire and the place was an inferno.

We could now see the tips of the tripods which had been set in the water with the mines on top. The Beachmaster yelled at us through the loudhailer. We would have to put out to sea again and head east towards Sword Sector, where there was a possibility of getting in closer. With all the craft that were heading to the beach, this meant that we would have to go out about half a mile to get round them. Once again we started our run in and came under fire from a German battery of 88s that were situated in or near the churchyard in Courseulles. The church tower was being used as a spotting point, and as the land was flat and low lying we were in full view of their guns. HMS *Warspite* was firing at them, trying to give us cover and to take them out. I went down behind the hatch cover to check on an incoming message when it happened. There was a loud thump. I thought that we had hit another craft, so poked my head out to see. Half the boat was gone. The deck was at right angles, poking into the air and the water was on fire.

No one was left that I could see. I climbed out from my cubby hole and stood on all that was left of the boat, the stern, and the rest was going down pretty quickly. I remember a destroyer coming in very fast with its siren whooping and being whipped aboard, wrapped in a blanket and drinking something hot. With the fore part of the boat completely destroyed, the crew and the Commandos must have disappeared in the explosion.

Two Canadian infantry brigades and 48 Royal Marine Commando were to be landed in the Juno Assault Area in front of Bernières and Courseulles. Ahead of them were the Royal Naval Commandos, and it was down to P, L and S Commandos to lead the way in on Juno, with W Commando relieving P Commando later. P Commando was destined for the beaches in front of Courseulles. Not all of them made it there straightaway.

Petty Officer Ron McKinlay CGM, P Commando

All of our equipment was lashed on top of a DD tank; these were special floating type tanks which were to land and go to designated positions at the back area of the beach, to give covering fire to the landings and also to help secure vital positions. We were to land sitting on top of the tanks. As they left the water and proceeded up the beach, we were to cut our equipment off and abandon the tank the best way we could. This was the plan, but on the approach to the beach the LCT landing craft tank we were in was hit up forward and the ramp which was partly lowered just dropped and hung underneath the bows of the craft, this making the only way to get underway astern.

This was when I can first remember any feelings. I was bloody mad, to think that after all my training day and night, weeks on windswept beaches from Scotland to the south coast, Berwick to Land's End, I was suddenly going to be denied my finest hour. Frustration was the greatest feeling. Here we were, a sitting target, just wallowing around like a sick elephant. We were slowly taken by the tide and it must have been an hour or so later – I cannot say how long – when we finally managed to hail an LCV(P) and persuade the Coxwain to take our party ashore, which he did, straight into the beach. By this time we had drifted out of the landing area, and our landing was our own little invasion with all odds and sods. We were under fire as we hit the beach, and we all made for cover at the top of the beach and sort of consolidated our positions.

When we sorted ourselves out as best we could, there seemed to be quite a number of soldiers in this area with their officers. My boss was a Lieutenant RNVR. I remember a Major and a number of junior officers; our only other personnel on this beach were dead. I vividly remember their bodies on the shoreline being washed in and out with the waves – they just rolled in and out, in and out. I still at this time had no feelings of fear or regret: I seemed to feel guilty that I had not landed where I should have done and not made my contribution at the right time.

I knew that my destination was the Courseulles area and I was near Cabourg. The only thing was to start walking. I don't remember anyone giving orders but off we started to amble. Although enemy fire was still coming from inland and along the beach, I never felt it was aimed at me. Before we could start our country walk we were blocked by two large gun emplacements with some of the other side inside. I was near the senior Army officer and asked if I could go ahead and put three grenades in each. On their detonation the rest could advance and take the emplacements.

I remember him saying, 'How many grenades have you in your pouches?'

'Sir,' I said, 'in one pouch I have my boot-cleaning gear and in the other my soap and towel.' It was then he first discovered I was a sailor and not a soldier. Anyway, I obtained the necessary grenades and, with these distributed about my person in pockets and down my jacket, I went over the top for glory. Honestly, I still cannot remember seeing any danger in this, and at no time did it seem other than what I had to do. I suppose it was about fifty to one hundred yards across the beach to get there. I started weaving in and out of sand dunes; my first face-to-face encounter then came with the enemy. As I rounded one dune there was this large German pointing his rifle at me. At the time he looked ten feet tall. He lowered his rifle and I lifted mine. I was not afraid of him nor did I have any feeling to kill. I took his rifle, searched him and directed him to carry on around the dune and back to our lines.

Then something happened that I will never be able to account for and which made me feel very ashamed. As he continued to walk around the dune, a single shot rang out and he fell clutching his hands to his stomach, he half turned and came to rest in a sitting position up against the dune. As I got to him the blood was coming through his fingers which were still clutched to his belly. He looked up at me, and I can assure you I will never forget that look as long as I live; it was as if to say, 'You bastard!'

I found myself saying to him, 'I'm bloody sorry, it wasn't me.' But inside at that time I was really angry; there was this man surrendering with his hands in the air just shot. My anger then doubled when I realised if he had been missed I could have been shot in the back from our own lines. Anyway I propped him up and carried on.

When I got as close as possible to the first gun I lobbed three grenades in one, then three in the other. I then up and charged like the gallant 'six hundred', but became aware that there was only me leading the charge and only me in it. God knows what happened. I suddenly felt, is there no one else here to help? Anyway this lot was sorted out.

The Conspicuous Gallantry Medal from the 'London Gazette' of 29th August 1944. Awarded to Petty Officer Ronald Harry George McKinlay P/JX 245579 for gallantry, skill, determination and undaunted devotion to duty during the initial landings of Allied forces on the coast of Normandy.

Petty Officer McKinlay was put ashore between noon and 14.00 hours on 6th June. Finding himself at some distance from his pre-arranged destination, he made his way along the beach and took charge of a party of Naval ratings and Army ranks who were bound for the same point. Single-handed, he silenced two enemy strong points on the way with hand grenades.

Later, on an open stretch of sand which was under fire from enemy snipers, he went to the rescue of a wounded man and brought him safely to cover.

Further east at Bernières-sur-Mer, the main body of S, P and L Commando and their Beach Signals Sections were landed on a beach which was shrinking due to the rising tide, and on which space was even more limited by the German flooding of the ground near the back of the beach. Here there was an opportunity to take the fight to the Germans in their pillboxes.

Ordinary Seaman Mick Richmond, S Commando

When D-Day came, very early that morning, we were called on deck for launching in the landing boats. I was nineteen and my artillery was a Lanchester sub-machine gun and a .45 revolver. We could see the flashes of guns and heard the explosions, I thought, 'Here we go into the unknown.' Good job I was carrying a clean pair of trousers. When our craft reached the shore the boat next to us hit one of the underwater obstacles, the iron tripod with high explosive on top. Hate to think about it; there were bodies and wounded all along the beach. I tried to patch up two Canadians. One was a de la Chaudière and the other a Queen's Own Cameron Highlander of Ottawa. One was wounded in the chest. I undid his jacket, put a thick padded dressing over the bullet hole, told him to keep it pressed tight so the blood congealed. I saved his life until the medics got there. I did the same for the other one. They were both gasping for a smoke. I lit them a cigarette each, they asked my name and I told them it was Mick.

I left them and walked round the point of the concrete wall, keeping close to the wall which was twenty feet high. Round the point there was spasmodic machine-gun fire, firing on boats that were still arriving with troops. I passed underneath the machine gun. Where the concrete wall finished, it was a sandy grassy slope. It was a hard job to climb up to get on top (idiot that I was I should have known it was landmined all along and on the top. It hit me when I saw the snake-like footpath – one foot wide where the Germans patrolled the beachhead).

The German machine-gunner did not see me coming from the right. He was watching the left. I shouted at him, and he raised his hands and they were covered in blood. He was standing on a small concrete bunker; his leg was a mess. I took the machine gun and I was on the point of putting him out of his misery; then I thought, no, let him suffer.

I then went down into an underground command post. (By the way, I was the only one on the top.) I heard voices in the darkness, then I shouted, *'Raus! Raus!'* at the top of my voice. They all brushed past me – there were thirteen of them – and climbed out. I came out last, lined them up in single file, hands behind their heads, and marched them further down. We passed where our troops were making a passageway through the concrete wall for the Army tanks and vehicles to pass through. When we got to the beach everyone was surprised to see me on the end of the file.

For his bravery on D-Day, Mick Richmond was awarded the Croix de Guerre avec Étoile d'Argent (Croix de Guerre with silver star) and Mentioned in Dispatches.

Along with Signals Section B12, L Commando also went into the Juno Assault Area at Bernières. L Commando's Headquarters party had been hit immediately on landing by German fire with the loss of several officers and men. With the Germans advancing to repel the Allies within 800 metres of Bernières, L Commando were on hand to ensure they did not succeed.

Able Seaman George McAuliffe, L Commando

On 6th June 1944 we were well prepared for the job in hand, but most of us didn't have a clue where the landings would take place. All I knew was I had just turned eighteen years old, and we were headed towards France to fight the Germans.

We led the landings on Juno Beach and there was a lot of hellfire, both incoming and outgoing. I don't remember being scared. I think everyone was too concerned with getting the job done right. Although there was a lot of enemy fire, we reached the beach pretty much unscathed and took up position to prepare for the landing. Our first job was to reconnoitre and clear mines, traps and obstructions. We had mine detectors but they wouldn't work underwater, so ten men had to link arms (with the tallest furthest out into the sea) feeling their way as they went in areas off the beach – while under fire!

After that, it was a case of ensuring that the landings continued, and where a craft obstructed the landing area we had to clear it away. On one such occasion, I was ordered to free up an LCA that kept on circling off the beach and couldn't exit. I waded into the sea up to my chest and dived underneath the LCA to free the propeller which had become entangled with the webbing and equipment of a dead Canadian soldier. I untangled the propeller and the LCA moved off the landing area. I pulled the dead Canadian's body to shore so that he could be identified and buried. By this time there were plenty of wounded soldiers on the beach, but we could not stop to attend to them because our prime objective was to keep the landings going. Once we had sorted the LCAs we moved further along Juno Beach to deal with the landing of tanks and vehicles.

After several hours of continuous work, a sort of shift was organised where we spent four hours on duty, then four hours of rest. During my second rest, I was woken up and told to go to the village of Bernières where the Germans were counter-attacking and threatening to break through. We took up position in some old German trenches and fought off an attack by tanks and infantry with grenades, mortars and small-arms fire. I guess the Germans lost a lot of men because we forced the tanks to retire.

Signalman John Hall, Royal Naval Beach Signals Section No. B12

The Coxwain turned the LCA to shore and lined up an LCT that had been hit and was stuck on the beach. He headed straight for

G1 Commando, April 1942. In the back row, Lofty Lucas is second from the left and Albert Cattell second from the right. *Below*, Admiral Sir Dudley Pound inspecting Royal Naval Beach Party C before the Dieppe operation. Most of the men seen here did not return

Troops in a landing craft prepare to go ashore during Operation Jubilee, Dieppe, 19th August 1942. (*Photographer unknown/National Archives of Canada/PA-183767.*) *Below*, bodies of Canadian soldiers lying among the damaged landing craft and Churchill tanks of the Calgary Regiment following Operation Jubilee. (*Photographer unknown/National Archives of Canada/C-14160*)

Illustrations from this page to p. 168 are of F Commando training at HMS *Armadillo. Left*, Leading Seaman Gooding (left) and Petty Officer Howard. *Below*, raising the ensign on the quarterdeck

Setting up a beach marker. *Below*, digging in on the foreshore

Calling in craft with the signal 'G flag'. *Below*, officers in boat-handling training

Control section calling in a landing craft. *Below*, handling a landing craft to kilter it 90° to the beach

Cliff scaling with full pack, after which would follow a five-mile forced march. *Below*, exiting a bunker under fire

Under fire: *above*, a rope-walk crossing and, *below*, a single-rope bridge

US landing ship tank unloading British equipment at Red Beach near Salerno, Italy, 9th September 1943. (*NARA*.) *Below*, a general view of Roger and Sugar Beaches, the landing sites of units of the 1st Canadian Division during the invasion of Sicily, Pachino, 10th July 1943. A beach marker, as that shown on p. 164, is visible on the right. (*Frank Royal/ National Archives of Canada/PA-166751*)

Right, Petty Officer Telegraphist John Savory of Royal Naval Beach Signals No. B7 operating a heliograph near Le Hamel: 'I cannot conceive why we should have been issued with a heliograph for Operation Overlord . . . I don't think we had any success with it!' *Right*, ablutions after a patrol – H Commando in the jungle. George Fagence is on the far left. *Below*, under the watchful eye of a Royal Naval instructor, Canadian Commandos learn how to disarm an opponent attacking with a knife, Ardentinny, Scotland, February 1944. (*Gilbert Alexander Milne/National Archives of Canada/PA-183057*)

A group of Combined Operations Bombardment personnel with a local family somewhere in Normandy, June 1944. Telegraphist Wilf Fortune from No. 1 Unit is on the far left. Telegraphist Alec Boomer from the same unit is in the centre, leaning on the sofa

Above, a pile of underwater obstacles carrying explosive charges – the flag indicates that not all of the charges have been removed, 10th June 1944. (*Frank L. Dubervill/National Archives of Canada/PA-131541.*) *Right*, two frogmen of the Landing Craft Obstacle Clearance Unit (LCOCU) on exercise. The leading frogman is Petty Officer Ron McKinlay, CGM. *Below*, a group of LCOCU frogmen. Ron McKinlay is second from the right

Members of the 3rd Canadian Infantry Division disembarking from landing craft 299 of the 262nd Flotilla during Operation Overlord, Bernières-sur-Mer, 6th June 1944. (*Gilbert Alexander Milne/National Archives of Canada/PA-131506.*) *Below*, tanks roar along the hard sands of a Normandy beachhead manned by Canadian Royal Naval Commandos, 20th July 1944. (*Arless/National Archives of Canada/PA-138181*)

Troops of the French 9th Colonial Infantry Division, *above*, boarding landing craft in preparation of the invasion of Elba, 17th June 1944, and, *below*, disembarking at Elba. (*Both photographs NARA*)

The German flak lighter sunk at Marina di Campo during the invasion of Elba. (*Illustrated London News Picture Library*)

Right, Leading Seaman Ken Oakley F Commando – the author of this book's Preface – in early 1946. *Below*, No. 2 Combined Operations Bombardment Unit on the way to Sousse, North Africa, after the invasion of Elba. Ken Simmons is furthest on the right and George Gingell is crouching second from the left. Ken Simmons: 'By the time this photo was taken I was pretty much better after Elba. I remember it being a lovely trip, there were dolphins swimming and flying fish used to land on the deck of our landing craft'

her, and at the last minute he swung her around, and we were tight alongside the beach. The LCT had obviously detonated everything near it when it landed, and we were very grateful. Telegraphist Taylor and I were given two cases each to carry and assemble on shore.

Down went the ramp. We landed dry which was a blessing, and we ran up the beach to the sand dunes, before going over them. There was a Canadian soldier lying in a prone position looking towards the town, and he shouted, 'Do not go over the top until I tell you, there are some problems to sort out.' Apparently the town had not been cleared. As I lay on the sand, I looked back onto the beach and saw the devastation and the dead soldiers at the water's edge and on the sand. The Canadian said, 'Go now!' Over we went. On the other side of the sandbanks was a railway line that followed the coast to the next village, and on the shore side was a line of Canadian soldiers who were lying holding their rifles facing inland. They were all dead. The first one I saw just had a small hole in his forehead. I found out later that the Canadian soldier had stayed behind to look after his dead comrades. We set up a temporary station. Taylor and I put our four cases on top of one another, fastened the clips down on the sides, pulled out the telescopic aerial, plugged in a telephone, switched on and made immediate contact with HQ at sea. We handed it over and the NOIC was talking within half an hour of landing. It must have been the first version of the mobile phone.

We were told to scout around, but not to go too far in case we were required. We came to a concrete bunker, and, being careful, we went inside it – it had just been evacuated. There was a staircase which we climbed and we came to a room with a concrete roof with a large hole in the middle, and standing on a box looking out of it you could see the whole of the beach. On the floor were some photographs. I picked up two and put them in my pocket.

Also landing in Juno were the Combined Operations Bombardment Units. Whereas the Royal Naval Commandos and the Royal Naval Beach Signals were staying on the beach, these Naval Telegraphists were going to carry on through the beaches to call in the Naval shelling on targets inland.

Telegraphist Neil Gregory, No. 3 Bombardment Unit

Down the ramp, never thinking about the approach beforehand when being shelled and shot at. I spoke to a Marine Commando one minute, next he was dead, shot in the head. At nineteen I saw too much, enough to last a lifetime. On shore the Canadians took casualties. Here many asked us for aid. We couldn't get off the beach for a while and were having to bear what was being thrown at us. On the move to take up a position just outside the village of Saint Aubin-sur-Mer to start a bombardment called for by an officer of the Canadian division who were being shelled too much.

Leading Telegraphist Paul Elliott, Forward Observer Bombardment Party No. 70 (FOB 70)

We boarded out the LCA (part of FOB 70). Captain Kroyer, myself and Telegraphist Jock Collier (the other two members of our party landed separately with our Jeep). It was about three o'clock after a hearty meal. It was dark as the LCA was lowered lifeboat-fashion into a rough sea. When all the LCAs were in the water we set off accompanied by an ML with navigational equipment on board. I was informed by Captain Kroyer that we had seven miles to go. The brown sick bags were soon in use. I have never been so seasick in all my life and felt really grim. Some Canadians held the sick bags too long and the bottoms fell out, whilst others threw theirs over the side and the wind carried some of them back to the landing craft – what a mess.

There were about twelve LCAs in our little convoy. Half a mile to go and the ML wished us good luck. 'Your beach is right ahead.' As we approached the shore we stood up to see what was in store for us and saw a high sea wall with a blockhouse on the left-hand side. I did not see any of Rommel's obstacles, perhaps because of the state of the tide. The Queen's Rifles of Canada had landed just ahead of us. There were many dead and wounded lying on the beach. FOB 70 crossed the beach, seasickness all forgotten about, to the fifteen-foot-high sea wall. Captain Kroyer disappeared and found a hole in this sea wall.

We followed Captain Kroyer along a road and through part of the village of Bernières-sur-Mer and stopped in a field and made contact with HMS *Algonquin*, our bombarding ship. Our target was a GNF (Guns Now Firing). Captain Kroyer got the *Algonquin* to fire a good many shots and we sent a situation report back to our destroyer.

We spent the days searching out targets, sometimes with the infantry but most often on our own. By nightfall we were miles inland with the Nova Scotia Rifles and another Canadian infantry regiment. There were two FOB parties in a copse and a field, but we could not see the enemy well enough for a shoot. We were heavily mortared in this copse and there were quite a few casualties.

As night fell it was time to take stock. The Commandos were ashore and so was the Army, but the situation was still dangerous enough to require everyone to be dug in at night. With the Germans off the beaches some of the unsung work of the war could continue.

Lieutenant Fred Killick RNVR, Beachmaster L Commando

We soon realised how important air supremacy was to be, as no air attack happened. At the end of the day the Army had not advanced as far as hoped, so all beach personnel were in position in trenches (dug by the Germans) facing inland in case of counter-attack.

Telegraphist Eric Dove, Royal Naval Beach Signals Section No. 9

The Pioneer Corps were digging the graves just in front of our dugout. The dead were wrapped in Army blankets before they were dropped in a hole. The padre was having a busy time, and the little graveyard had filled up fast at the end of the day.

Juno and Gold Assault Areas had both been secured. Inland, the Canadians had advanced to a point beyond Creuilly, which meant that together the Canadians and British from Gold had created a large pocket of Allied control. However, between Juno and the eastern part of Sword there was a gap where the advance had been hampered. The beaches on Sword had also seen a busy day.

CHAPTER 8

D-Day (3)

word, the furthest east of all the Assault Areas on D-Day, had lready seen concentrated activity from the Landing Craft Obstacle Clearance Units. They had worked hard to clear the obstacles although the sheer number of them meant that they were still a danger to the landing craft. Apart from the dangers on the ground, Sword had also received the full attention of he Allied air forces because of its vulnerability to attack from he heavy batteries around Le Havre and from some of the hips in the port.

F and R Commandos were attached to Force S for the Sword andings. F would be the first in along with R1 Commando, with R2 and R3 Commandos as the reserve. F Commando had been in ction before, but for R Commando this was to be their first operation. The Sword Assault Area was slightly different to Juno nd Gold. In those two areas the assault was made on a two-brigade front, whereas on Sword the assault was made on a single brigade front. The assault was planned for Queen Sector, just to he north-east of Colleville-sur-Orne.

Crucial to the landings on Sword were the thirty-four DD amphibious tanks earmarked for this Assault Area. They were aunched at five thousand yards. Apart from two which sank traightaway, and one which was rammed by an LCT, the remaining hirty-one tanks reached dry land at 07.30 and promptly set about aking out the German 20-mm, 50-mm and 75-mm guns. They also ound time to give a hand to Royal Naval Commando F for Fox.

Able Seaman Ken Oakley, F Commando

Reveille was early, approximately 03.30, and the Beachmaster, Lieutenant John Church RNVR, and I boarded the LCA to run for our target: Lion-sur-Mer/Hermanville (codename Queen Red, Sword Sector) which was about five miles away. The sea was rough, and several of the soldiers were sick, but as we ploughed along I could see that all around us were landing craft and warships of all shapes and sizes.

Off to our port side an LCT(R) discharged a salvo of rockets in the direction of the Merville battery we had been briefed about. We evaded all the small-arms fire, but suddenly the dreaded steel stakes with mines or 56-lb shells attached loomed ahead of us.

Daylight was with us now and the Coxwain of our LCA did very well to miss a shell attached to a stake on our starboard side, and then we heard the order 'Down Ramp!' and our time had come. The Beachmaster and I were quickly out of the craft and running up the sandy beach as mortar and machine-gun fire sped us on our way. At the high-water mark we went to ground to take stock of the situation and to get our bearings. John said we had landed almost exactly in our scheduled area, but as the mortar fire became more intense we wriggled deeper into the sand. It seemed as if we were just outside the mortar-fire pattern and suddenly a DD tank loomed up behind us. The hatch opened and a voice called out, 'Where is the fire coming from?' I answered, 'A couple of hundred yards to the right at 45°.'

'OK,' he said. The hatch banged shut, then Bang! The shell screamed over our heads. It was no contest, the mortar fire ceased, the machine-gun fire subsided and just the occasional sniper shot rang out.

The DD tanks had suffered problems of their own. Some had flooded engines on reaching the beaches, but they kept on firing at targets, even though they were stranded, until the rising tide silenced their guns. Out of the thirty-four DD tanks which started the landings, some twenty-three survived the beach battle. On the beaches with F Commando was R1 Commando. Although they were destined for the same Assault Area as F Commando, they did not actually join up with them until they were physically on the beaches together. The process of making it to the shore was tricky for both R1 Commando and F Commando.

Sub Lieutenant George Walker RNVR, Assistant Beachmaster R1 Commando

We went in with F Commando, but whereas they went in on LCAs, for some reason we were stuck on the HQ ship so we went in on an LCP instead. The LCPs were like little launches, and we hung on the outside as we dodged between the obstacles on the way into the beach. We made it right onto the beach in our LCP and landed in only a foot of water. Then we found we were on the wrong beach and had landed as near to Ouistreham as we possibly could. However, it was only a short walk to our beach although we were under continual sniper and mortar fire. At one point we were attacked by a German plane which strafed the beach. There were three of us in our little group so we dived under a nearby vehicle, but the vehicle kept on moving so we had to crawl along after it.

Able Seaman Jim Watson, F Commando

The next thing was our craft ramming the quarter (stern) of the craft ahead, the crewman had failed to release the fall at the stern (a hook with a locking device which secured the landing craft to the ship and which was sometimes difficult to release in bad weather). Our Coxwain had not realised this and had gone full ahead! The impact dented our ramp and it was a case of man the pump. We eventually touched down after having lost much of the craft's steering way about fifty to seventy-five yards out, and how we avoided the obstacles is beyond me.

The landing craft were discharging their loads continually and there was clearly a need to keep the beaches moving. Controlling the beaches was an essential function of the Royal Naval Commandos and it was up to F and R1

Commando to take charge, despite the fact that they had landed at the peak of enemy small-arms and mortar fire. It was small consolation that their difficulties were appreciated at the very highest levels.

Naval Commander Force S Report, part of ANCXF (Allied Naval Commander in Chief, Expeditionary Force) Report Volume 2

The task that confronts Beachmasters on first landing is superhuman. The beaches are long and difficult to inspect quickly or easily at all. The Beach Parties are . . . extremely vulnerable. Things are happening very quickly on all sides. It must be accepted that craft are not flagged in, that beach signs are not immediately erected at this stage.

The man charged with taking on this superhuman task on the beach in Sword Area, Queen Sector, was the Principal Beachmaster of F Commando, Acting Lieutenant Commander Edward Gueritz RN.

Rear Admiral Edward Gueritz CB OBE DSC

My Army opposite number, the Beach Group Commander, Lieutenant Colonel D. V. H. Board, and I took passage in LCI 185, which was the flagship of Commander E. N. V. Currey, Deputy Senior Officer of the Assault Group S3 under Captain Eric Bush (who carried out his first assault landing at Gallipoli when he was fifteen). During the training period in Scotland they had been responsible for working up the Assault Group, and not the least the skills of the units which were to provide the close-in support for the assault troops.

We had distinguishing marks on our helmets for easy identification; as a Principal Beachmaster my helmet was painted blue. My own contribution was a red scarf and a walking stick.

The scene on a beach in the early stages of an assault landing is seldom encouraging. The situation on Red Beach, Queen

Sector of Sword Area, was therefore much as expected, not the least the fire from enemy guns, mortars and some small arms. Of two tank landing craft beached to give fire support on the eastern edge of Red Beach, one was one on fire, and some wounded were crawling up the beach.

A number of armoured vehicles were standing halfway up the beach, some firing; flail tanks were operating to explode beach mines; beach exits were jammed with vehicles impeded by the soft sand and mine explosions. The sharpest impression, as always, was created by the sight of bodies scattered on the beach from the water's edge. One of these turned out to be my immediate superior, Commander Rowley Nicholl, who was deputy Naval officer in charge of the Sword Assault Area; not dead but severely wounded, having insisted upon accompanying the leading Beach Parties. We had been right to expect casualties among the early landings of the Naval Beach Parties, and each of the first reconnaissance parties suffered losses. A little later a Beachmaster was killed when a mine exploded. As I stopped to talk to Commander Nicholl, Colonel Board went on. We did not see him again until we found his body in the evening, only a short distance along the beach lying beside his dead escort.

The task of No. 5 Beach Group and its associated Royal Naval Parties, including F Commando, was to bring order out of chaos, or at least to organise the chaos as far as possible. As soon as we landed we had to reconnoitre the beaches and set up signs to mark the beach limits, approach channels and navigational hazards. Landing Craft Obstruction Clearance Units (LCOCU) co-operated with Royal Engineers to clear beach obstacles, explode mines and booby traps, and mark potholes and quicksand. Landing Craft Recovery Units (LCRU) with waterproofed or amphibious vehicles brought help to damaged or stranded craft.

While this was going on the Beach Group, with its many specialised units, began marking the beach exits, carrying out mine clearance, laying beach roadway across the soft sand, recovering drowned or damaged vehicles, ministering to the wounded and directing the ever-increasing flow of traffic. We had to keep every-body moving: momentum had to be maintained. It was sometimes necessary to speak sharply to keep groups of men moving to clear the beach, even in one case some military policemen.

Able Seaman Ken Oakley, F Commando

More and more landing craft were beaching by now, and we were kept busy persuading Army personnel not to stay on the beach to brew their tea, but to go and chase those Germans who were still shelling us. The flail tanks and other 'funnies' had done a good job in clearing mines from the beach and we were getting good exit lanes marked down leading to a good road.

Rear Admiral Edward Gueritz CB OBE DSC

On Queen Sector, circumstances conspired to create very considerable congestion on the beach and just inland. Traffic congestion impeded the forward movement of the Intermediate Brigade, which came ashore hot on the heels of the assault brigade at about 9.30 a.m. This brigade had intended to press forward with the tanks of the Staffordshire Yeomanry to attack Caen. Also, 41 Royal Marine Commando had landed on Queen Green Beach to swing right towards the Canadian Sector, while 4 Commando of 1 Special Service Brigade, led by Lord Lovat, moved briskly over Red Beach to swing left and join 6 Airborne Division over the River Orne. Commandos were easily distinguished by their berets, whereas everyone else wore a steel helmet.

Able Seaman Ken Oakley, F Commando

Suddenly, the shrill scream of bagpipes could be heard along the beach, and on looking to my right I saw a piper emerging from an LCT and following him came Lord Lovat, then the remainder of the Commandos marched off as if they were on Horse Guards Parade. It was an incredible sight, I'll never forget it.

The fact that No. 4 Commando and their piper could march straight off the landing craft as if the beach were a parade ground was a testament to the work of the Royal Naval Commandos in clearing the beaches. But although the sound of the bagpipes had been a welcome distraction there was still much to be done.

Able Seaman Ken Oakley, F Commando

Harry Shaw, a member of our unit, had come to request aid in helping Sid Compston, who had been very badly wounded. Sid had landed with the Assistant Beachmaster Sid Willis to place the left-hand marker for the beach into position. I went down the beach a hundred yards or so and there was Sid; a cannon shell had torn along his back, exposing his kidneys. The Assistant Beachmaster had applied a first-aid dressing to the wound, and we were able to get him along to a First Aid Post which had just been established on the beach. In later years Sid asked me what happened to his mouth organ, a cherished instrument, that had just been repaired.

During the day we had occupied the basement of a large gabled house just off our beach. The Army came along to sweep it for booby traps and we never got back in there. We set up our HQ just off the beach.

Rear Admiral Edward Gueritz CB OBE DSC

It had not been possible to clear many of the obstacles from the approaches to the beaches before the tide, accelerated by the wind, had swept over them. When the Naval officer in charge, Sword Area, Captain W. R. Leggatt came ashore, it was decided to hold incoming flights of landing craft to enable the beaches to be cleared. The reserve brigade, 9 Infantry Brigade, did not land until mid-afternoon.

As the day went on, there was sporadic shelling and mortar fire on the beaches; the first air raid, by a lone Focke Wolf, came about 5 p.m. Many ships flew barrage balloons, but later they lost their popularity among those on the beach when it was realised that German gunners were using them for ranging on beach targets. Some further enemy action occurred later, causing confusion as airborne reinforcements and resupply flights for 6 Airborne Division flew in towards the River Orne. These flights necessarily passed close to the ships lying of the beach and there was a good deal of trigger-happy firing.

Early afternoon 6 Beach Group, accompanied by RN Commando R, arrived ashore and we were able to reallocate responsibilities within the Sword Area. The commander of 6 Beach Group took command of both Beach Groups until he was wounded during the night; as was his second-in-command who relieved him.

Despite the confusion the landing had gone well. The last group of the assault brigade had landed only eighteen minutes behind schedule with the intermediate brigade following. Only the reserve brigade was held up due to the congestion on the beaches. Not far behind F Commando was R for Roger Commando. R Commando's Principal Beachmaster on D-Day itself was Lieutenant Commander A. C. MacDonald RN, but on D-Day plus 2 he was invalided out and replaced by Lieutenant Commander Jack D'Arcy RNVR.

Although R Commando landed after F Commando the dangers they faced were much the same.

Able Seaman Ken Barry, R Commando

The night was clear, with a moon and the phosphorence from the bow waves from the other craft in the formation showing we were not alone.

Our destination was Sword Sector, Queen Red Beach as Reserve, our touchdown was to be at 8.30 a.m. Dawn comes up early in June; so far no signs of any fighting. My feeling was that I was invincible; it was only other people who were killed or wounded. I checked my weapon again, put one up the spout in readiness. Orders came down that no weapons were to be loaded at this stage, so I unloaded. At about 6.30 a.m. the rumble of gunfire could be heard, but no sign of the ships concerned. As we drew nearer, we passed HMS *Roberts* firing salvoes: the noise from the big shells was like an express train. The columns we were in began to slow. We were now amongst smaller ships firing rapidly, and smoke was all around. Very confusing, but still no sight of land and what we had to face. We were not to know at this stage that the assault had gone in successfully, but that the beach was very congested with vehicles as few exits were open, and we were held off from beaching. In fact we were held off for four hours, then our turn came. As we neared the beach, the shore looked very indistinct with so much smoke, but most of the noise was from our own ships which were shelling positions inland. Even so, I remember many shell splashes amongst our flotilla coming from our left, then we were amid the beach obstacles. We could see the shoreline with some craft on fire and smoking. Then we began to make out some houses up behind the sand dunes. I remember they looked a long way from the water line; a lot of distance to cover without any protection.

The order was given to down ramps. My mate and me were down first. A wet landing just over our knees. We waded in to see a few figures at the water's side. We instantly recognised one of the lads from R1 Commando who was bringing in this wave of craft. We asked him, 'What was it like?'

He replied, 'You will soon find out,' and directed us to our beach assembly area at the back of the beach on top of the sand dunes. There were about five tanks knocked out. Further down the beach an LCI(S) and two LCTs on fire. As we progressed up the beach, many bodies from the initial assault were still lying where they had fallen. Firing from over to our right where a pillbox was still being engaged.

We were as nervous as kittens, dropping to the sand with almost every explosion. We made the assembly area and reported. We dug a slit trench as quick as we could. It appeared we were amongst two strong points. One was out of action, but the other was giving a lot of trouble. A destroyer was engaged in so close a range it seemed she would be grounded. She was firing into this strong point at point blank range, and it was late afternoon before it ended.

Lieutenant Commander Jack D'Arcy RNVR, Principal Beachmaster R Commando

When the ship's stern grounded on the sea bottom still about a hundred yards out from the Ouistreham beach somewhere around noon, the wind had got up unpleasantly, and although we embarked from the gangway platform into only chest-high water the onshore breeze had whipped up sizeable waves over the shallow reaches, and these were high enough to buffet the back of our heads as we struggled towards the land. The smaller chaps amongst us had the crests of the waves rolling over their heads, but at least we were being propelled in the right direction; unless of course one was knocked flat on one's face, as indeed some were. One thing was for certain – if one didn't fancy a stay-over in France that day, there was no way one could fight one's way back to the ship.

One of my smaller chaps had left the LSI (Landing Ship Infantry) with me and he was carrying my least favourite of all weapons, the strip Lewis machine gun. He was sent flying as the first wave hit him, and although he held on gamely to the wretched thing I motioned to him to hand the thing to me. It was no good shouting an order – the words would have been blown away by the wind and waves.

Two Pioneer Corps soldiers wading towards the shore ahead of me had reached slightly shallower water and were now only about waist deep, when they suddenly disappeared from view. Thinking that they must have tripped over some obstacle on the seabed, I quickened my pace as best I could to give them a hand if required. Then I too disappeared as I stepped down into the bottom of a deep bomb crater. As the sea closed over my head I jettisoned that damned gun and struck out for the surface, supported by my

Mae West lifebelt, firmly tied under my armpits. As my head popped up I saw the two soldiers floating face down in the water, with their lifebelts secured around their midriffs, forcing their bottoms up and their heads down, leaving them powerless to help themselves. Still swimming, I managed to grab one of them and push him shorewards into safety, but I regret I was too late to help the other fellow.

As I staggered up the beach, stepping over the prone but alive Pioneer soldier, a German Junkers 88 bomber swept in low along the beach dropping a cloud of anti-personnel bombs. I shouted out, 'Down for your lives!' at the top of my voice but this was more of an encouragement to myself than as a warning to others, because not a soul could have heard me in all the noise of the aeroplane engines, the explosions and the rough weather. I've always liked the sound of my own voice anyway.

We all rushed to our appointed places, apparently unscathed by the bombing raid, and I found Mac (Lieutenant Commander MacDonald) in a deep dugout at the top of the beach.

Able Seaman Ken Barry, R Commando

We decided to go in search of the rest of R2 Commando, but up in the dunes there was barbed wire with *Achtung Minen!* on them, so we went along the beach and shortly found the rest of our lads along with the Beachmaster dug in at the base of the dunes. We were detailed to go further along the beach and set up our beach sign for the left extremity beside an exit that had been made through the dunes to the road at the rear. Beyond the dunes was a row of bungalows without any roofs on them. Back to our dugout which was just below the strong point called La Breche that was to be our HQ. We were then sent down to the water edge to guide in some LCTs that were coming in with an assortment of vehicles on board. The craft were still experiencing trouble negotiating the obstacles on their run in. The Landing Craft Obstacle Clearance Unit teams had not managed to clear them all yet, and we waved to the best gaps for them to get unloaded. Some of us were set at points across the beach to guide the vehicles around the best route to the beach exits.

The Royal Engineers who worked very close with us used their AVRE (Amoured Vehicle Royal Engineers) and an armoured bulldozer. They carried steel matting in case any vehicles got stuck in the soft sand. Any hold-up caused chaos and attracted attention, so we kept urging the drivers to keep moving and we soon began to work as a team. We brought in three waves of various craft on the rising tide.

The day was very confusing with so much going on, the noise and smoke, all the activity on the water, self-preservation uppermost. I had not seen a live German as yet. The only thing I can really recall vividly during the rest of the day was a low strafing attack by three aircraft that looked like Lightnings with our markings on. They came in line abreast from the direction of Ouistreham. All hell broke loose from our retaliation; we heard they were all shot down before reaching Juno Sector. There is no protection on an open beach. I felt vulnerable; a very frightening experience.

Lieutenant Commander Jack D'Arcy RNVR, Principal Beach-master R Commando

We had been so busy that it seemed no time at all before the Principal Beachmaster grabbed my arm and took me along to the Beachhead Command Post situated in a large bomb crater. I was surprised by the number of us gathered there and, just as the Colonel was about to address us, another low-flying Junkers approached, heading straight for the bunker. This time, however, the enemy plane was being shadowed by two diving Spitfires, and, as the German reached us, the leading Spitfire opened up with his twelve wing cannons. The fuselage of the Junkers plane was sliced cleanly in two and the two halves fell twisting and hurtling down to their destruction. This was too close to us for comfort, and, as each senior officer formed his own judgement as to where the pieces would end up, a lot of undignified and un-gentlemanly pushing and shoving went on. The forward momentum of the bomber, I'm pleased to say, took the shattered remains a safe distance away from us, and we all tried to look as if we hadn't had that dreadful moment of panic a few seconds before.

The Colonel's opening remarks were not that reassuring: he explained that he was the deputy now in charge, as the Colonel originally appointed had been killed by a sniper's bullet, and the situation was still very confused. He felt unable to give us any clear orders that night but we would meet again at 08.00 hours the following morning. In the mean time he told us to place our men around the beach area in defensive positions, and he finished with, 'Please all of you keep alive until the morning.'

Later than evening, feeling a little forlorn, we stood on the edge of the sand dunes with tears in our eyes as a great black cloud of Allied planes slowly approached from the sea, all towing gliders, which they released over the land and, turning, made their way back to our islands. We could see the gliders clearly swooping down to earth as another enormous flight of transport planes arrived to drop hundreds and hundreds of paratroops. I have never felt so emotionally grateful and proud in all my life. So we set out our defensive positions, as instructed, and in good heart waited for the morning.

Able Seaman Ken Barry, R Commando

Towards evening 6 Airborne appeared. The planes and gliders stretching as far as the eye could see, a really impressive sight. A big cheer went up along the beachhead. It was a great morale booster; these reinforcements were landing right in amongst the Germans. They cast off just short of the coast and circled to find the best landing zone amidst heavy fire from the Germans.

D-Day night we were informed that a German panzer-tank column had counter-attacked, broken through, and was heading for the beaches to our right. We were stood to and given beach defensive positions and code words to challenge everybody. My position was right up in the dunes in front of the German trenches and barbed wire. Right alongside of me was a bay in which was a little tankette full of explosives which should have been set off electrically during the landing to run around until it hit something. My thoughts were if a bullet hit it I would go sky high. I was in the most forward position, and my imagination was really working overtime – every post was a German.

Sub Lieutenant Derek Dowsett RNVR, Assistant Beachmaster R Commando

Every so often, whenever I was awake, I would do the rounds and poke my head into the slit trenches to make sure everyone was alright.

Able Seaman Ken Barry, R Commando

I was certainly very tired from lack of sleep, and into the bargain my Assistant Beachmaster, Sub Lieutenant Derek Dowsett, made his rounds every half-hour and whispered, 'Barry are you still awake?' Who, I ask you, could sleep with the anchorage being bombed and all the pyrotechnic display from the flak like Guy Fawkes Night going on all around?

It was a long night.

It was the end of D-Day. Across all the Assault Areas, Sword, Juno, Gold, Omaha and Utah, the assault formations were securely established on shore and the beachhead was holding firm, although the extent of the advance inland was variable. There were more ships and landing craft on their way, but given the success of D-Day the main worry about their welfare was concentrated on the weather holding up.

With the Commandos dug in overnight the principal dangers came from the air. At 01.10 the next morning an enemy aircraft was shot down over Gold. Out at sea there was a constant threat from German U-boats and Allied aircraft spotted nineteen which they prevented from getting near to the convoy routes. At 03.36 the Royal Navy fought off an attack by eight German E-boats.

It was the start of the second day on the beaches.

CHAPTER 9

Normandy: The Beaches

Extract from the D-Day diary of Able Seaman Edward Blench, Q Commando

WEDNESDAY 7TH JUNE, SECOND DAY

News from the front line still good – armoured division passed
over beaches.
More prisoners.
Night air raids.
Heavy barrage.
Urgent demands for ammo.

Ordinary Seaman Mick Richmond, S Commando

On the second day, a Canadian cameraman took a film of me
kissing the first French girl to visit the beachhead. On the
same day I missed death by the width of this page. A
Messerschmitt fighter was machine-gunning all along the
beachhead. He had to swoop over a villa, and I dived into the
ground like a frightened rabbit. The bullets whipped an inch
over my head. Had I been to the right of this page instead of
to the left, I wouldn't be writing this.

By dawn on 7th June 1944, most of the men on the
beaches had not slept for two days and two nights. Out at
sea Admiral Ramsay and General Eisenhower sailed the
length of the beaches in HMS *Apollo* to gain a first-hand
impression of what was happening. What they saw was
both encouraging and discouraging. The weather was

improving, but the beaches were littered with stranded and damaged craft.

On the beaches themselves, some of the men had tried to sleep during the previous night, but the work of some others was so urgent and so necessary that they had carried on right through the previous night and were destined to continue through the day as well.

Able Seaman Colin Harding, Landing Craft Obstacle Clearance Unit No. 3

We worked for three and a half days without food or sleep, living on pills that our officer, Lieutenant Hargreaves, gave us if he saw we were getting tired.

The obstacles which had not been cleared on D-Day still represented a danger the next day. Therefore it was vital that the Landing Craft Obstacle Clearance Units worked as fast as possible to clear the beaches ready for the next wave of landings.

Able Seaman Colin Harding, Landing Craft Obstacle Clearance Unit No. 3

Our unit, and the Beach Party with their bulldozers, gathered up all the tetrahedrals and explosives into one area with fourteen ounces of TNT on *each* obstacle. There were about two hundred obstacles laid out over the beach, close together with cortex. We all had whistles that we blew when we were ready to blow up an area of obstacles and explosives for all those people nearest to them as a warning that we were about to blow.

What a lovely big bang, they must have heard it in England.

As well as running the beaches, the Navy was still inland with the frontline troops. The Telegraphists of the Combined Operations Bombardment Units not only had to face the hostile Germans but on occasion the hostile British as well.

Telegraphist Neil Gregory, No. 3 Bombardment Unit

We went over Pegasus Bridge and an Army officer saw us. Because we were the only two Royal Naval ratings in the area, he wanted to arrest us. Our Commanding Officer had to explain our presence in the area.

Being arrested by their own side was an occupational hazard for the Royal Naval personnel behind the lines with the Bombardment Units. Because of the secrecy surrounding their role, they were under strict orders to give only name and rank if arrested by soldiers suspicious of anyone wearing an RN badge so far inland.

Only the explanation of the unit's Commanding Officer could secure their release, and in cases where a Naval Telegraphist might have been dispatched alone to carry a message or escort a prisoner there might be a lengthy period of confinement before things could be sorted out. Fortunately for No. 3 Bombardment Unit, the Commanding Officer was on hand to explain so they could carry on with their mission.

Telegraphist Neil Gregory, No. 3 Bombardment Unit

Our officer at the time of this incident was Captain Bob Blower. He called for us to accompany him to 'Shell Fire Corner' where three roads joined to make a three-sided verge, and where three Telegraphists were having a bad time with mortar fire. We came to a piece of the road which had high sides for a short distance and then opened to a clearing. A German corpse lay on the side of the road. We slowed down to read the situation when mortar fire enveloped us. I was sat at the back of the Jeep with a 22 radio on my right and a C ration box on my left. The mortar splinters crashed through the Jeep's sides and windows. The Captain went out to the right as it was a left-hand drive, the Bombardier to the left with me following. I was smoking and chewing gum at the same time. After discussion we crawled back in the tank tracks which had left ruts in the soil road, me still chewing gum and cigarette together. Captain Bob was sitting on the far side of the road asking if we were OK. He said we were to go back. I didn't think anyone could drive in reverse at such great speed.

For the Combined Operations Bombardment Units, moving around a hostile countryside was not the only challenge they had to face. Calling in shells in extremely difficult circumstances was something else they had to take in their stride. The penalty for failure was Royal Naval shells landing on Allied soldiers instead of on German ones.

Captain F. Vere Hodge MC RA, No. 1 Combined Operations Bombardment Unit

About D-Day plus 2 I was asked to take my team into the grounds of Bénouville chateau where the fighting was a bit sticky. As we made our way there another COBU party met us coming back. The officer in charge, whom I knew slightly, told me that he had been up to the front but it was not possible to do a shoot.

When we reached the chateau, the company commander told me that the Germans were pressing him from the other side of a large field, immediately outside the wooded chateau grounds. This target was technically too close to our own troops to engage because a ship's shell could fall on us. However, things didn't look too good anyway, so I decided to take the risk.

The Tels got me a ship. I sent the fire orders and she fired but I couldn't see where the shots were falling. So I called for a battleship, thinking that as their shells weighed a ton or so (roughly the weight of a Mini car) if anything would show up on landing, they would. HQ attached me to a battleship codenamed PEG. The Tels told me afterwards that this was HMS *Ramillies*.

I had a couple of ranging shots; they were just audible as they passed over our heads before landing, which caused some men near me to look askance, but I reassured them – the shells' landing was very visible. The next shots were right on target and the Germans came out of their bunker with a white flag. I sent the conventional code for 'shoot successfully completed' and added in plain language, 'Enemy considerably discouraged.'

Back on the beaches, the days after D-Day itself were still full of activity and still full of danger. The first phase after D-Day lasted for eight days, during which time the landing organisation settled in and the bridgehead was consolidated. Across in the American Assault Areas of Utah and Omaha, there was a slightly different beach organisation. Whereas the Royal Naval Commandos were first in and ran the beaches under the NOIC from day one, the Americans only sent in their beach organisation after the beaches had been secured. The two weeks after the first phase lasted to the end of June and marked a period of relatively smooth organisation, although a violent storm caused much damage and meant that the wreckage had to be cleared and a fresh start made.

The Commandos on the beaches did not yet have the benefit of hindsight, so their world was confined to observing that the landing craft were still bringing in men, vehicles and supplies, and that no one was, as yet, going the other way. Therefore they could assume, reasonably, that things were going well on the frontline. Not that the frontline itself was still very far away, and neither was the ever-present reality of death.

Able Seaman Ken Barry, R Commando

D-Day plus 2. During the day, a large petrol dump behind the beach was hit and set on fire. Petrol cans bursting and hurled all over, leaving a big pall of black smoke high in the sky. Until now I had not slept properly for three days. My fingers had burns from cigarettes from falling asleep smoking them. While waiting for some more craft to come in we came under sniper fire from the direction of the houses at the back of the beach. We all went to ground to decide how to attack this menace, but we did not have to worry. A mad Irishman from R1 Commando called Stitt just walked up to the front door blazing away with an automatic gun. We never did find the sniper though.

Lieutenant Commander Jack D'Arcy RNVR, Principal Beach-master R Commando

A great pall of black smoke rose into the air about two miles away when the Lufwaffe hit one of our fuel dumps. Depressing in itself, when we had witnessed the effort required to build up our stocks, but probably of minor significance in the overall picture. And that was what we lacked in those first few days – information. Were we about to be pushed back into the sea? How far had our armies advanced? Well, the traffic across the beaches had not diminished, so it all must have been going somewhere.

We were fortunate that we did not get much attention from the Luftwaffe; there were no concerted or prolonged attacks on our beach, and any raids were made by single aircraft, either Junkers or Focke Wolfs raking the shore with their machine guns or dropping anti-personnel bombs. If we were caught in the open as the enemy flew over, there were a number of immobilised amoured vehicles under which we could dive for cover. On one of these occasions I had thrown myself under a knocked-out armoured car and, as I did so, a shattered torso thudded down onto the sand just a foot or so away. We were truly thankful that the Army Pioneer Corps were there to deal with the gruesome task of collecting up and dealing with these distressing casualties.

Able Seaman Ken Barry, R Commando

The next morning, the armoured bulldozer ran over a mine. The explosion hit Slinger Wood of R2 Commando. We rushed him up to the Dressing Station, but could see his injuries were too severe; he died on the stretcher. This upset us more than you could know as he was only eighteen years old.

Able Seaman Ken Oakley, F Commando

A great deal of my time was spent at the Beachmaster's HQ, and on the third day he asked me if I would attend the burial service of all those men who were killed in the Beach Area. I said, 'Yes,' I would go as a representative of Fox Royal Naval Beach Commando. We travelled a short distance from the beach to a large apple orchard. Here, the bulldozers had dug out wide trenches in which the wrapped bodies were laid side by side. The smell of rotting flesh was appalling, and I will never forget it. The burial service was attended by three padres, one of each of the main denominations.

Whilst we stood silent, among the laden apple trees, I reflected how lucky I was to have survived this one, especially after the experience of Sicily.

Able Seaman Ken Barry, R Commando

During the night we had an attack by two Junkers 88 bombers: one was caught in the searchlights from the ships. All hell broke loose, with the anti-aircraft fire well mixed with tracer. We reckoned he jettisoned his bombs before being hit and crashed in pieces. One blazing wing fell in our bivouac area, severely injuring and burning one of our Commandos, better known to us as 'Drip' as he was always moaning about everything. He was sent home the next day to hospital. Two weeks later we read of him in the *Daily Mirror* saying all he wanted to do was to get back to his mates in Normandy, which gave us a laugh as his 'drip' was that all he wanted to do was to get out of all this. In the night we could see tracer from the ships at sea being attacked by E-boats; never a dull moment.

Bodies from the main assault were still lying about amongst the obstacles and in the wire. The smell and flies filled the air. We were forbidden to bury them as they had to be identified as best as possible. The Pioneers had the unenviable task of collecting them to do this, and then transporting them to a mass grave at Hermanville just beyond the beach.

There was a chaplain covering Sword Sector named Reverend Maurice Wood. One day he came along to our beach to give a service. He set up his altar in a hollow in the sand dunes. A good crowd attended. We were saying our prayers and singing hymns when the Germans lobbed over a couple of shells. This did not deter him, or us. Mind you they were not directed at us personally; just to keep us on our toes.

The shelling from the German guns was a constant torment to the Commandos in Sword Sector, and although the German guns were close to the big guns of the Royal Navy they defied the best efforts of the Allies to destroy them.

Lieutenant Commander Jack D'Arcy RNVR, Principal Beach-master R Commando

The thing that gave us the greatest concern on Sword Beach was a gun battery hidden in a fissure of the rocky cliffs towards Le Havre. I'm not sure when we first became aware of this alarming threat, but as soon as the smaller vessels coming into the beach gave way to the larger landing ship tanks the large-calibre German guns opened up. Because of their draughts the LSTs had to ride into the shore at high tide and then wait for the ebb before they could discharge their non-amphibious cargoes of armour and heavy-goods vehicles onto dry land. The ships were then stranded until the tide rose again sufficiently for them to float off. This was the signal for the enemy battery to open up.

Able Seaman Ken Barry, R Commando

Because the gun batteries were causing so much havoc on Sword Beach they sent in five LCT(R) rockets and two LCGs to try and knock them out. They sailed in line ahead and fired two banks of rockets each at the gun positions. From where I stood it seemed like a volcanic eruption on the shore opposite, and from the noise of each bank of rockets taking off anyone would have thought nothing could live through such a barrage. But later in the day they fired on a Rhino Ferry that was coming in and set on fire the vehicles it was carrying. It was abandoned drifting off course towards Ouistreham. Later it was discovered Jerry was using mobile guns.

The ships at sea carried out a bombardment firing inland; the noise from their shells going overhead was terrific. During all this we unloaded a couple of thousand troops, along with about two hundred vehicles and some stores.

Across in Juno they were having similar problems. Air raids were always a problem although sometimes the British responded by firing before checking exactly what it was that they were firing at.

Petty Officer Telegraphist John Savory, Royal Naval Beach Signals Section No. B7

We spotted an anti-aircraft multiple .5 machine gun mounted on a Bren-gun carrier chassis, so we walked over and chatted to the crew. After a while an air raid warning came through, so we stood out of the way while they swung round to face south. We soon saw and recognised the distinctive shape of a Spitfire, which had black and white stripes painted under its wings – the extra identification marks for our aircraft for this landing – approaching from the south at about a thousand feet. As he got near, the gun crew received the all clear and stood down. Then, when he was just about overhead, six clouds mushroomed around him. Our local senior Naval officer aboard the cruiser *Scylla* had laid on a full salvo of her six-inch guns!

The plane flipped over and crashed down vertically. I saw a parachute open up and the pilot landed unharmed beside us. He was Fleet Air Arm and dressed in flying gear over pyjamas. We took him back by explaining that we were in touch with the *Scylla*. So, without further ado, he sent off a signal, 'Congratulations! Good shooting!' As he left us he said he thought he had been very lucky as the blast from the salvo had blown off his canopy, so that when the plane flipped over he just fell out!

Able Seaman George McAuliffe, L Commando

At this time I recall that we were regularly dive-bombed and strafed by German aircraft. They used to chase us up and down the beach, machine-gunning as we dived in and out of cover. We were also shelled by German artillery from inland. With so many dead bodies on the beach it started to smell pretty badly. On about the third day they placed as many dead bodies as they could into a mass grave.

Although the Normandy beaches were dangerous places, it did not take long after the initial landings for the Commandos to organise themselves and the beaches. As with everything else, there was a daily routine which carried on, and, because the Commandos were Royal Navy, it was right and proper that they should be organised in watches rather than in shifts.

Lieutenant Fred Killick RNVR, Beachmaster L Commando

We would rise in time to go on watch at 04.00 (we worked four hours on and four off whilst in Normandy). Assuming the tide was rising, flotillas of landing craft would be anchored off the beach waiting to be called in at dawn. The Beach Signals Unit would advise them the time. We would be advised what the craft were carrying so we could be prepared. Tanks and heavy vehicles would unload quickly, and we would direct them to the nearest tank exit from the beach. If there was a breakdown, an army REME vehicle would be called to tow them away. Heavy vehicles would leave the beach quickly.

The next flotilla to land would have a light-artillery group with a greater number of personnel. This would mean slower unloading and require more directing to correct exits. Lighter vehicles had more problems driving off the sand so that assistance from bulldozers was often needed. Some light artillery had breakages to their gun carriages requiring assistance from army engineers for repairs (in our training we learnt which army units to call on for assistance in any particular difficulty). The many motor personnel were well trained to deal with all types of terrain and therefore had no difficulty with sand.

If some of the craft were unloaded too slowly, the tide could change and the craft would be stranded. We would then call on heavy bulldozers to push them off. The bulldozers were water-proofed to five feet. We were relieved at the end of our watch and went to eat meals that were provided by the army kitchens for all beach personnel. We would then rest until we returned to the beach after four hours. We lived in primitive conditions in dugouts that we made from anything available on the beach.

The next watch may have started without much activity, as the tide could be falling. We would then check if there were any obstructions on the beach and have them removed. Later in the watch on the rising tide an LST (landing ship tank) would beach and it would take some hours to discharge its multi-deck cargo of vehicles. If we were lucky it would be an American ship and we would be invited on board for a meal. After another four-hour rest we would return for another variety of vehicles and supplies. A small Dutch cargo vessel called a *schoot* with a flat hull could beach and sit on the beach for several tides whilst it was unloaded by amphibious trucks.

Hours of daylight are very long at that time of the year, so that supplying the Army and Air Force could continue almost round the clock. This however was dependent on the weather, and at times this halted all landings. In the case of the major storm seven days after D-Day many craft were stranded, including an LST. This took a lot of effort by bulldozers and various vehicles as well as a tug to remove them. This general selection of events could occur during any day during our six weeks on the beach. At the end of six weeks the Mulberry Harbour and cleared ports were able to handle everything for the advancing forces.

Two weeks after D-Day a great storm blew up which effectively stopped work on the beaches and which caused much disruption to the supply operation. It also made life very miserable for the Commandos and everyone else who was living in the sand.

Able Seaman Ken Barry, R Commando

During the night a wind started to come up. By morning it turned into a gale. Small landing craft broke away from their moorings where they were sheltered inside the Gooseberry. The abandoned ones were swept further down towards Roger Beach where the shoreline curved inwards. This beach was unusable due to the deep runnels on it.

No craft could beach to unload. We just stood around huddled in our groundsheets, thoroughly miserable. It was then decided to send us in batches to Bayeux some fifteen miles away where the Army had erected a Bath Unit. We had a clean-up, fresh underwear and denims, and were issued with a hot meal into the bargain; very welcome.

Also during this period of inactivity we discovered a German BMW motorbike. Two of us went down to Arromanches to see the Mulberry Harbour we had heard had been built. It was a terrific sight to see. On the way back through Juno Sector, we saw some of P Commando and met Ron McKinlay. He was a townie of mine from Portsmouth and his father owned a pub just outside the station. He said that if we called into see him we could get a free pint. He was to get a Conspicuous Gallantry Medal for his part in the landing.

Sub Lieutenant Jack Gaster RNVR, Assistant Beachmaster J Commando

Forty barges were swamped and sunk on the beaches during those four days that the gale raged. We must be thankful that the DUKWs kept going the whole time with the loss of only one that tore its side out against an obstruction. They were worth their weight in gold for keeping the ammunition supply coming ashore from the ships offshore. It was from one of these DUKWs that Bobby Campbell made what I think was a very brave attempt to divert a mine from being swept onto one of these ammunition ships outside the harbour. On one of these ships, someone reported what they thought was a mine being swept by the tide onto their vessel. It was certainly a metal object lying deep in the water. Bob got one of the DUKW drivers to put him as close as possible, then dived over the side to push it clear of the ship. It turned out to be a smoke float, but Bob did not know that before he got to it.

Petty Officer Hugh Jones BEM, J Commando

The London barges were finding it too rough to land, so we laid a trot of buoys so that the barges did not have to come right up to the beach. We blew holes in the sand for a mushroom anchor and the buoys went out about a hundred yards from the beach.

Able Seaman Ken Barry, R Commando

A few of us went down the beach to see the shambles of the wrecked landing craft from the storm. On the first LCT an officer and a rating lay dead on the ramp. Up in the wheelhouse were two more, the Coxswain lying over the wheel. On the LCI(S) about twenty Army Commandos lay dead in the passenger space, a massive hole in the side where the tide had come in and out for over a week. It all seemed very eerie and we beat it back to our bivvy area and reported our findings.

The wind dropped and landings commenced again, stores were urgently needed after four days with no supplies. The German gunners pinpointed the main bivouac area with a creeping barrage. A panic started, with a few men running towards the fields at the back of the beaches. As the shells landed ever more forward it turned into a mass run to escape, a few sheepish faces on the return.

Across in Juno there was another potential hazard which could impact upon the daily routines of the Commandos. Patrolling the beaches in this Assault Area was the Naval Officer in Charge (NOIC), Captain Colin Maud DSO DSC RN. He was in all senses larger than life, and with his black beard, the shillelagh which he carried, and dog at his side, he prowled the beaches issuing orders. On occasion he would even swim out to landing craft to berate their commanding officers on the error of their ways. Being in charge on Juno beaches meant that junior officers had to look lively when Captain Maud wanted urgent action, whether it be an immediate report on German V weapons exploding close to the shore or special tasks which he wanted carrying out straightaway.

Sub Lieutenant Alan Dalton RNVR, Assistant Beachmaster P Commando

I arrived at Beach Headquarters and unwisely picked up a telephone which was unmanned and ringing impatiently. There then ensued the following dialogue.

'What was that?'

'What was what?'

'That thundering great explosion you idiot!' (This in a crisp and very nearly recognisable senior Naval officer's voice.)

'A thundering great explosion, Sir?'

'Where?'

'On the horizon, or thereabouts, Sir.'

'Who is that?'

'Sub Lieutenant Dalton, Sir'

'Well, don't just stand there doing nothing!'

'What do you suggest, Sir?'

'A deep-water recce, you fathead!' (I was now aware that I was talking to Captain Colin Maud RN.)

'But Sir, it's got to be ten to fourteen miles offshore!'

'Don't argue – get on with it!'

I tried to point out that deep water recces undertaken by even the tallest of men were impracticable in more than about five feet of water, and that soundings in the area of the explosion were probably fifty fathoms. All to no avail, 'Right Sir, at once,' was the only possible conclusion to that extraordinary conversation. I commandeered two DUKWs, joined them amidships with about a hundred feet of wire and took off. We cruised up and down quite pointlessly for several hours some hundred yards or so from the beach. It was a warm and pleasant day, and eventually, having carried out my orders to do a deep-water recce, we drove ashore. Our clothing consisted of tin hats and very little else.

Unhappily, a very considerable reception party awaited us. It was headed by a very angry Captain Maud, backed by an impressive staff of Navy, Army and Air Force officers, some of whom proved to be from Intelligence. The hilarious and undignified scene and interrogation which followed can be imagined. The upshot was a requirement for my 'reasons in writing', a time honoured preliminary to what was usually a rapidly deteriorating situation. In this case I heard no more beyond being warned by Maud's secretary to write more serious prose in the future.

Sub Lieutenant Ron Lawrence RNVR, Royal Naval Beach Signals Section No. B6

Once in the early stages of the invasion I was on duty as the Signal Officer to Lieutenant Commander Freemantle of S Commando, the Principal Beachmaster of Bernières-sur-Mer, when

Captain Maud appeared. He habitually carried a stout walking stick, which he pointed at me with the words, 'I have a special job for you – detail off four ratings to accompany you and report to me at the Alligator on the beach.' An Alligator was a large armoured vehicle with balloon tyres, as distinct from tracks, and completely open on top. I was told that the adjacent beach between Bernières-sur-Mer and St Aubin had been closed due to heavy defensive mining and beach obstacles. A large number of landing craft had been wrecked and were unable to withdraw. My instructions were to take the Alligator with a driver provided by the Army and visit every wrecked craft, remove all confidential books, portable radio and radar equipment, and if not portable destroy them.

Many of the vessels were badly holed and the job entailed frequently wading through sea water with diesel floating on the top, and in several instances dead crew. To this day I cannot bear the smell of diesel! On several vessels we found officers who refused to leave and I later reported their positions. It took sixteen hours to complete the mission, all the time very conscious that the beach had not been cleared of mines. However, we eventually returned unscathed but smelling strongly and soaking wet, having successfully completed our task.

But Captain Maud did support his officers when they found themselves in conflict with Naval officers out at sea. On 7th July 1944, Royal Naval Commando P for Peter was relieved by Royal Canadian Naval Commando W for William, who immediately settled into the routine of bringing in the landing craft in the Juno Area. But when this took place at night there could be particular problems.

Lieutenant Donald Sutherland RCNVR, Beachmaster W Commando

Signalling in a landing ship transport to a landing beach in the dark is a responsibility not to be taken lightly. An empty LST weighed 2,300 tons, but when it arrived at the invasion beaches with its mixed load of tanks, tracked artillery guns, Bren carriers, trucks, ambulances, jeeps and motorcycles, its gross weight rose to over 4,000 tons. An LST was 328 feet long, its beam 50 feet and its draught 14 feet. These statistics were a matter of deep concern to me one dark night in July when the Captain of LST 360 threatened me with court martial. I fully expected to have his LST on my slop chit.

On the night in question, as Beachmaster of Juno Mike Green Beach at Courseulles-sur-Mer, I was scheduled to expect three LSTs on my beach, which was separated from Juno Mike Red by a galvanised steel pontoon causeway. The purpose of the causeway was to permit the landing of LCTs or LCUs at any state of the tide. It did however constitute a navigational hazard for the LSTs, which could only be beached at high tide.

Watching the incoming LSTs approach my beach in the dark, I could see that four ships were approaching rather than the three I had been told to expect. Because I had adequate room for four ships I decided to allow the fourth LST to proceed. Regrettably, at the last minute, when it was already too late to change his mind, the LST's Captain realised he was approaching the wrong beach and started to turn his ship hard to port. Clearly LST 360's Captain was completely unaware that his course parallel to the beach would run his ship aground on the pontoon causeway. My beach Signalman with his Aldis lamp immediately began flashing V signifying 'You are heading into danger!' It was my hope that the LST's Captain might be persuaded to order 'Full speed astern!' Almost at once I could hear the LST hit the causeway. Even then full speed astern might have helped, but instead the Captain ordered 'Full ahead!' Hoping to push LST 360 over whatever obstacle his ship had encountered. He was still blissfully unaware that he was aground on a steel pontoon causeway.

Of course the ship stuck fast. As the tide ebbed one could hear in the darkness the sinister grating sound of buckling steel. With my vivid imagination I took this to be the breaking of the LST's back. With the ebbing tide, I was able to walk out on the causeway until I stood under the LST's bridge, the ship's vast bulk towering over me in the dark. I looked up into the apoplectic face of the Captain who shook his fist at me and screamed, 'I'll have you court-martialled for this, you bloody idiot!'

Quite intimidated, I retreated back to Beach HQ, where I reported the incident to my Principal Beachmaster, Lieutenant Commander D. J. P. O'Hagan GM RCNVR. O'Hagan suggested that I should report the matter at once to Captain Colin Maud DSO DSC RN. I told him I was afraid I had broken the back of LST 360 and that her Captain had threatened me with a court martial.

'Nonsense,' said Captain Maud. 'Stop worrying Sutherland! These ships are expendable you know!'

Although Captain Maud had been sympathetic, there was still an LST stuck on the beach with its cargo still aboard. Clearly the best course of action would be to unload the LST and see if there was any damage.

Lieutenant Donald Sutherland RCNVR, Beachmaster W Commando

I returned to my beach somewhat comforted and waited for daylight and the next low tide, having concluded that my next move would be to see if I could unload the LST. Unfortunately, LST 360 was lying parallel to the beach and beyond the point where firm sand gave way to pebbles and mud. However, I decided that the best course of action was to try to unload.

The bow doors were opened, the ramp lowered. Imagine my chagrin when, hoping for a lighter vehicle such as a Jeep, or a staff car, or even an ambulance, the first vehicle that had to be offloaded turned out to be a Sherman tank, all thirty-eight tons of it. I waved it forward. The tank came down the ramp at a good clip but slowed appreciatively as it hit the mud. It quickly ground to a halt and began subsiding into the ooze and then disappeared with remarkable speed, its driver scrambling from the hatch as his tank bubbled out of sight for ever.

My next move was to put down in front of LST 360 the so-called beach roadway. This consisted of chestnut palings – a sturdier version of a Canadian drift fence – covered with chicken wire held down with steel bands.

Alas, the second vehicle in the LST proved to be yet another Sherman tank. I waved it down. At first it seemed to be managing successfully, but in taking the first curve of the beach roadway it ran off the edge. Like the first tank it too disappeared into the mud, its driver making a hasty, last minute emergency exit. Concluding, quite reasonably I think, that I could not afford to lose any more Sherman tanks that morning, I instructed the LST's Captain to raise his bow doors and await the next tide.

When the tide flooded again the broached-to LST floated off the pontoon causeway. At once it became apparent that the horrible sound of buckling steel that had haunted me in the darkness had only been the noise of the causeway's steel pontoons yielding to the gross tonnage of LST 360.

The Commanding Officer of LST 360 put his ship on Juno Mike Green correctly the second time and we unloaded her successfully. At low tide he and I inspected the LST's bottom and could find no evidence of damage. On the next tide she pulled astern and departed, and was never heard of again by me. Happily, I can report that I did not get charged for an LST or even two Sherman tanks, nor was I court-martialled.

In an invasion sailors are expected to undertake a variety of unnatural manoeuvres such as running a ship aground on an alien unfamiliar shore in the pitch dark with only the dimmest of navigational lights to guide them. England still expects every man to do his duty.

Apart from the hazards of bringing in the landing craft, the beaches were still very dangerous places. The Germans had mined them thoroughly, as well as placing underwater obstacles to obstruct the landing craft on their way in.

Sub Lieutenant Jack Gaster RNVR, Assistant Beachmaster J Commando

I noticed a Royal Engineers mine-clearance team working in a section to the right of the beach exit road just clear of the beach. It had been marked off with the normal white tapes denoting it as uncleared and with the usual *Achtung Minen!* sign on the wire around the area. Apparently, these were known as shoe mines, and were undetectable using the ordinary detectors because they were constructed of wood and the detonator was brass, with just a small nail that activated the detonator when it was pressed down. It was shaped like a small shoebox.

The only way that the REs had to locate them was by using long steel rods pushed through the soil at an angle until they found something solid. They then very carefully scraped away the soil around them. Within a few minutes the mines claimed their first victim, a young Sapper who was badly injured around the face and eyes. Then the Sergeant who was trying to rally his now shaken unit. A Field Ambulance Unit removed the injured men and the young Subaltern who remained with the unit decided that he would have a go, again with disastrous results. By this time the IWT Captain responsible for the beach area called a halt, telling them to pack up, saying 'I don't know whose idea it was to clear that part. We are not using it, and I shall use a flail tank to clear it later.'

Able Seaman Ken Barry, R Commando

On D-Day plus 17, a small ammunition coaster, the *Dunvegan Castle,* was beached to unload her cargo and set on fire. There was a shortage of ammunition at the front line, so it was all hands to the pumps to remove as much of the ammo as possible; the situation was dangerous in case of explosion. This work went on even as the tide came in, and I drove our little amphibious Jeep with Midshipman J. H. Speed along with DUKWs to help clear it with no thought of the danger. The fire was eventually put out but the ship was a total loss. From this day onwards no more ammunition stores were unloaded on our beach.

For their parts in this episode, Ken Barry received a Mention in Dispatches and Midshipman Speed a Distinguished Service Cross. There was also the danger from the air. Across all the sectors were barrage balloons. These came in all shapes and all sizes, some were small enough to be carried by a single person. Because barrage balloons were there to prevent enemy air attack, their deployment was a matter for the RAF who used individual aircraftmen to carry them around the beachhead.

Telegraphist Eric Dove, Royal Naval Beach Signals Section No. 9

I noticed one of these young men disembark from a landing craft with his balloon flying about one and a half metres above his head secured by a hand-held reel of wire. Fascinated by this spectacle, I watched him stride up the beach in our direction, being careful to walk between the white tapes (indicating a clear passage up the beach from anti-tank mines). He reached me with a big smile on his face, only a boy; I think he was proud to be taking part in this operation. He asked if he could anchor his balloon near our dugout. He probably felt safer amongst company. We told him we didn't mind. Taking off his equipment, he assembled his entrenching tool to dig a hole to anchor his balloon. I saw him swing the pick above his head and strike it down onto the sandy ground. He hit an anti-tank mine that had been buried just below the surface of the sand. I felt the searing blast of the explosion as his body lifted ten feet into the air. We ran to his aid. He was still alive, but only just; his body held together by the rags of his uniform. Our CO gave him a sip of water, then the boy died.

Sub Lieutenant Jack Gaster RNVR, Assistant Beachmaster J Commando

One very sad occurrence happened whilst I was on duty one afternoon. An RAF Corporal approached me to ask where he and two airmen could bivouac in safety. They had been taking charge of balloons brought over by the landing craft to set up a defence against enemy aircraft in the Mulberry Harbour area. I advised them to see the Royal Engineer Captain in charge of the Beach Area as he would know of the cleared areas. Shortly afterwards I spotted them along the other side of the beach exit. They seemed to be coping well and I turned to look at a DUKW that was coming towards me from the roadway. I sensed rather than heard an explosion. Turning my head in their direction I saw almost in slow motion their bodies being lifted and thrown in a ghastly pirouette. Two were killed outright, the other survived for an hour. I was shaken by this incident, and the question always remained with me, could I have done more for these lads?

J Commando were in the Gold Assault Area which was just as riddled with mines as the other two areas. Most people treated them with the respect that they deserved, but some Commandos let their curiosity get the better of their caution.

Sub Lieutenant Jack Gaster RNVR, Assistant Beachmaster J Commando

A flail tank started to clear the field that lay on the other side of the drystone wall behind our tented bivouac area. Immediately several S-mines were detonated. These were a rather nasty anti-personnel device that was triggered by someone kicking against one of the three small prongs situated on the top of the mine. It would be fired from a metal cup buried in the soil, causing it to be lifted about four feet from the ground before exploding with a killing range of about fifty feet.

Our immediate concern was the damage done to our tents. Those alongside the wall were damaged by the flying shrapnel. Petty Officer Fedder brought several mines into the bivouac area and proceeded to take them apart. Needless to say, there was a general exodus from the vicinity where he was working. I suppose I should have had my head examined. I was so fascinated that I stayed to watch as he unscrewed the detonator with the three little prongs that would take a very sharp eye to spot in a grassy area. He then lifted the mine from its metal case which remained in the ground and acted as mortar. He dismantled the mine casing and poured out the contents. There were over two hundred pieces of rod iron cut at 45°, measuring about half an inch long from one sharp end to the other. There was no wonder they were so deadly.

On 26th June F Commando lost their Principal Beach-master, Acting Lieutenant Commander Edward Gueritz RN, who was badly wounded by shell fragments. This resulted in a general order to beach units to wear steel helmets while on the beach.

For all the dangers and deprivations on the beaches, the Commandos still found occasion, when they could, to take advantage of the fact that they were camped at the seaside, although, as always, senior officers sometimes took a dim view of their men enjoying themselves too much.

Sub Lieutenant Jack Gaster RNVR, Assistant Beachmaster J Commando

We managed to get hold of some salt-water soap for general usage. Bob Campbell and I were sharing a watch on the beach. It was high water and craft movements had been completed, so I suggested to Bob that he take his lads into the water for general bathing for half an hour. I would then follow with the remainder when they had completed their bathing session. It was my luck to be in the water when the Principal Beachmaster happened along, and to receive a rollicking for treating this as a seaside holiday.

I bit my tongue until my period of duty finished, and then went along to see him. 'I suppose you have come along to apologise,' he said.

'No Sir,' I replied, 'I have come to complain *re* your conduct towards me in front of the ratings. You did not ask why we were in the water.' I explained that we had been on the beach for two months without the facilities for bathing, and that I had managed to get hold of some salt-water soap so that we could freshen up. Also that we had not left the beach unattended at any time as Midshipman Campbell had bathed with his section first whilst I covered, and that I had only just entered the water with my lads when he arrived on the scene. I got my apology, also his approval for further bathing when circumstances allowed.

The Combined Operations Bombardment Units also had a few chances for some relaxation in between operations. But not before the Germans played a few tricks of their own on them.

Captain F. Vere Hodge MC RA, No. 1 Combined Operations Bombardment Unit

One day the German artillery played an old gunner's trick on me. Getting our range, they fired on us a few seconds after my ship fired on them, each time causing our troops to think I was hitting them by mistake. I just had to stop firing because I couldn't convince them that I wasn't.

Wilf discovered that I enjoyed table tennis, as he did, and he determined that we must have a match. During another lull he found a table in a canteen but it was 'Other Ranks Only' so I was not allowed in. Then we realised that our Airborne smocks did not have any badges of rank on them so we decided to play in them. Wilf also suggested that he should do the scoring so that I did not have to speak.

It was a hot day, and we proved evenly matched, so the games were long and we got appallingly hot. The audience could not understand the smocks, but they were not Airborne troops so they didn't like to say much and just assumed that we were mad.

At the end of June the Allied advance was moving out of range of the Naval guns, and the job of the Combined

Operations Bombardment Units was finished by early July. By 30th June 1944, Rear Admirals Rivett-Carnac and Wilks had established their shore headquarters, and Operation Neptune officially came to end. On 5th July the one millionth man landed in France.

Six weeks after D-Day, the Arromanches Mulberry Harbour was operational, as well as the ports along the coast which had been taken by the Allied forces. The Arromanches Mulberry handled on average 6,750 tons every day from 20th July onwards.

The Royal Naval Commandos were still in Normandy and it was not until early autumn that they were returned to England. S Commando were the last to leave.

Normandy had been the biggest amphibious landing of the war, and the Royal Naval Commandos had played a vital role in it. In addition, all this time the Royal Naval Commandos had been in action in Italy while the world's eyes had been focused on Normandy.

CHAPTER 10

Elba

Extract from a letter dated 14th July 1946 from Reverend Hyde Gosselin RN (retd) to the mother of a Royal Naval Commando

We assembled in Corsica some days before the landing was due to take place and were briefed by Admiral Troubridge, who revealed the plan to us and how each of us fitted into it. About 5 p.m. on 16th June [1944] we set out. It was a fleet of small vessels – as Elba was so heavily mined that only MLs and LCAs could hope to get across the minefields onto the beaches. Alas, some of them were blown up before reaching their destination.

Fortunately, it was a beautifully calm night – not like the landing on Sicily – and in complete silence the long line of attacking ships, loaded with the French Army, made their way under the stars to the venture lying just ahead. The Commando party had a very important and a very dangerous part to play. There was at Elba moored alongside the sea wall at Marina di Campo – the main town of Elba – a German flak lighter. Her guns covered the beach we purposed landing on and it was essential that they should be silenced and the German ship captured: this was the work of the gallant Commando party. They embarked in two parties just before 5 a.m. (then if one party was wiped out the other could carry on). They got alongside the flak lighter and in spite of heavy resistance boarded and captured her. But the Germans had an electric charge, fired from shore, ready for such an emergency and they blew up the ship as she lay there. The damage was worse to the men than to the ship. As soon as we could land I went round. German and British dead were lying huddled together. A Petty

Officer and one or two helpers were carrying our lads out and laying them along the quayside. I buried them the following day in a cemetery we made for the purpose.

The operation to capture Elba was given the codename Operation Brassard and was set for 17th June 1944. After the stalemate of Anzio the Allies had broken through and captured Rome on 4th June. The problem now was that the supply routes along the Italian coast ran under the German guns on the island of Elba, which is only eight miles from the Italian mainland. Allied planners therefore decided that the island needed to be captured.

Fortunately for the Allies, the French had already captured the nearby island of Corsica, and this, together with the island of Bastia, provided a convenient base from where to mount the attack. Because the French were already on Corsica their troops were given the job of invading Elba.

The 9th French Colonial Infantry, mainly Senegalese, French Commandos and Moroccan troops called Goums, were lined up for the attack. The Americans provided landing craft and air cover. The French, British and Americans each commanded one part of the attacking force. Rear Admiral Troubridge of the Royal Navy commanded the Naval forces. The French Brigadier General Magnan commanded the ground forces, and US Air Force Colonel Darcy was in command of air forces.

With many of the Royal Naval Commandos still on the Normandy beaches, A and O Commandos were dispatched to Corsica to lead the landings on Elba. Allied agents had already been to the island and reported the presence of a heavily armed German flak lighter in the harbour at Marina di Campo, the village in the deep-water inlet called Golfo di Campo which had been chosen for the main landings.

Flak lighters were used for carrying cargo like the Allied landing craft, but in addition they were bristling with artillery. They had 20-mm, 40-mm, 75-mm and 88-mm guns. The flak lighter therefore presented a real danger to the Allied troops as its guns covered the landing beaches. Capturing it would not only prevent the guns being used against the Allies, but they could be turned against the Germans in support of the landings. O3 Commando and A1 Commando were given the job and their operation had its own codename, Operation Cutout. The plan was for A1 Commando to capture the flak lighter and for O3 Commando to prevent any German advance onto the jetty in order to assist the crew of the flak lighter.

As the very first Royal Naval Commando, A Commando had already been in action in Madagascar and Anzio, but for O Commando this was to be their first operation. O Commando had been in India for a short while before returning to be in reserve for Anzio, and it was then sent to Corsica for the Elba operation.

The Allied agents on Elba reported that the German troops defending the island were ordinary garrison troops. They were wrong. It was later discovered that soldiers from the Hermann Goering Panzergrenadier Division were in residence and that these were battle-hardened frontline troops.

As was normal practice, the main landing areas were given code names. To the west of the Golfo di Campo was Louise Green Beach. Inside the Golfo di Campo the beaches were Kodak Red (at the village of Marina di Campo itself), Kodak Amber and Kodak Green beaches. To the east in the Golfo dell Acona was Glaxo Red Beach. Kodak Red Beach was right under the guns of the German flak lighter, and this was clearly why the cutting-out operation to capture it was essential to the success of the landing.

The landing craft set sail for Elba at about 5 p.m. on the evening of 16th June and made its way slowly overnight towards the dropping-off points. As dawn broke, the attacking forces were able to make out the inlet of the Golfo di Campo. One of the landing-craft crew later wrote, 'When I saw the harbour where we were to land I had a fit. A narrow opening as you went in. A death trap if I ever saw one.'

The first landings were made at 01.00 on 17th June, three hours before H-Hour, which was set for 04.00. Just before 01.00 the invading forces had their first encounter with the German flak lighter which was returning to Marina di Campo.

Able Seaman (Radar) Denis Blow serving aboard HDML 1301

We had led our landing craft in and were waiting for them to come away after their troops had disembarked, when a German flak lighter rounded the point. As it came abreast of us it opened fire, which we returned. During the ensuing action our Captain, Lieutenant Carter, was killed, along with a Telegraphist. The After Gunner and his assistant both received wounds, putting them out of action, and the First Lieutenant had a number of shell splinters in his back. All these later recovered, but Lieutenant Carter left a son he had never seen.

The forward Oerlikon Gunner went aft and took over the rear gun and I took over the forward Oerlikon. As we turned our bows towards the flak lighter she started to make off towards the bay and harbour, possibly under the impression we were a torpedo boat. As she did so, only one of her guns was firing, and it virtually became a duel between this gun and myself on the forward gun as our own rear gun could no longer bear.

The flak lighter then made its way back to Marina di Campo where it unloaded its cargo. The invasion forces were puzzled that there seemed to be no reaction to the invasion at this stage, and concluded that the Germans had no idea that an invasion was imminent. A different story was to emerge later. Also among these advance landing parties was one of the Bombardment Units, which was sent on ahead to take over the German gun emplacements

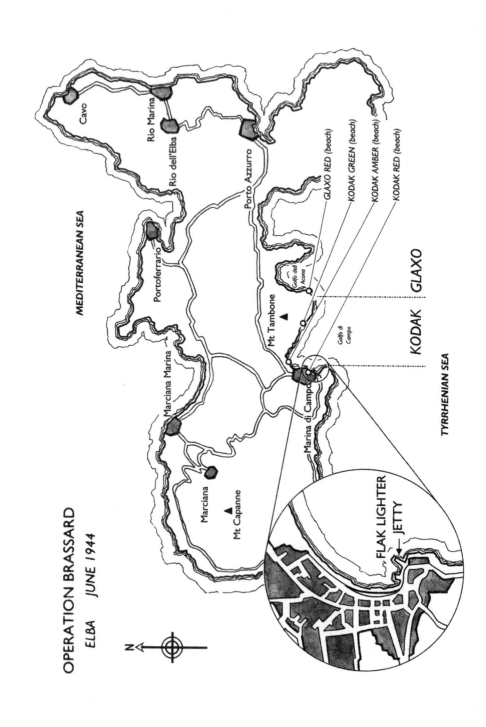

OPERATION BRASSARD

ELBA   JUNE 1944

N

MEDITERRANEAN SEA

Cavo

Rio Marina

Rio dell'Elba

Porto Azzurro

Portoferrario

Marciana Marina

Marciana

Mt Capanne

Mt Tambone

Golfo dell'Acona

Marina di Campo

Golfo di Campo

GLAXO RED (beach)

KODAK GREEN (beach)

KODAK AMBER (beach)

KODAK RED (beach)

KODAK   GLAXO

KODAK

TYRRHENIAN SEA

FLAK LIGHTER

JETTY

above Marina di Campo. However, in the event the greatest danger they faced came not from the Germans but from the French.

Leading Telegraphist George Gingell, B Troop No. 2 Combined Operations Bombardment Unit

We joined up with the 1st Batailon du Choc (Free French) and were made up as members with badges by the French Colonel Gambier, mine was number 422. The French were anxious to attack Elba following their horrendous losses in retaking Corsica. Our objective was to land three hours before H-Hour in silence (especially radio) and to take over German positions at Marina di Campo. The No. 18 radio set was on 'Net' to send one message to confirm capture of the said gun emplacement.

We were not aware that owing to a lack of secrecy heavy reinforcements were in place from surrounding islands, and more guns awaited our later landing parties. Previously our invasion convoy had paraded around the island of Elba for some hours in bright sunlight. Some secret!

We went into a little cove to the left of the beach at Marina di Campo in pitch darkness. We were not fired on and our single message was duly sent and the group advanced to higher ground over the beaches.

The landings proper were preceded by direct gunfire and a rocket attack ship. We viewed the following landings with horror as machine-gun fire, artillery and mortars attacked our invasion craft.

Moving in to take over a fortified post, we began setting up an Observation Post when we were attacked by a Moroccan Goum who was in high excitement (to say the least!). Our Royal Artillery Captain did look Italian, with a dark moustache and blue cap comforter. With rifle fire the Goum got us spreadeagled on the ground and screamed for support from his friends. It came – luckily with a French officer we could understand. Our rescue was a great relief to us all.

Down in the harbour, A1 Commando were set to attack the flak lighter which was at the mole, or jetty. It was up to A2 Commando to land on the beaches around Marina di Campo (Kodak Green, Amber and Red beaches). Their survival depended on the flak lighter being taken out.

The Germans first reacted to the fact that an invasion was taking place a quarter of an hour before H-Hour. This was perhaps surprising, given that the first landings had taken place nearly three hours previously. The Germans opened up on the landing craft heading into the Golfo di Campo with both machine guns as well as with the guns of the flak lighter.

Just after 04.00 the two landing craft carrying the cutting out party arrived at the jetty where the flak lighter was tied up. In overall command of the cutting-out party was Lieutenant J. Lukin RNVR, a Beachmaster from A Commando. On their way in the Commandos could hear the Germans shouting at them. Ominously the Germans were shouting that they were waiting for the Commandos.

On the way in to the jetty both landing craft were hit by enemy fire, with the loss of one killed from O3 Commando and several wounded from both landing craft.

Lieutenant Hodgson RNVR, another A Commando Beachmaster, was in charge of one of the assault craft and his men swarmed up the side of the jetty to capture the flak lighter, as planned. O3 Commando under Sub Lieutenant Alan Davis, Assistant Beachmaster, took their positions on the jetty itself.

Official report of Commander Duncan RN, Principal Beachmaster A Commando

The party from LCA 576-6, led by Lieutenant A. B. Hodgson RNVR and Sub Lieutenant E A MacDonald RINVR, threw their hand grenades as planned, scaled the wall on the seaward side of the mole and stormed the F-lighter alongside the mole, followed by the other party, led by Sub Lieutenant A. Davis RNVR, a few moments later.

Able Seaman Ken Hatton, O Commando

We went in aboard two assault landing craft. These brought us right in under the mole and this was where Sub Lieutenant Griffiths was killed by a grenade. We got out by first getting onto the other landing craft and then we scaled the wall of the mole throwing our hand grenades.

Official report of Commander Duncan RN, Principal Beachmaster A Commando

Opposition on the F-lighter was not serious and in a few minutes the capture was complete. It appears from interrogation of prisoners taken later . . . that about half the crew of the German ship went ashore to air-raid shelters when the 'rocketing' commenced, the remainder, about fourteen, were taken prisoner by the assault party, with the exception of two or three who were killed at their gun positions.

About 04.15, enemy small-arms fire, assisted by mortars and possibly field guns, was directed against the mole. Lieutenant Hodgson organised the party to defend the mole as it had been agreed with the French military commander not to proceed into the village, as French troops were engaged in clearing the enemy out of the village at this time. In this defence plan, use was made of the F-lighter's 75-mm gun manned by British Naval ratings. Enemy prisoners were concentrated on the seaward end of the mole under guard and the remainder of the party were spread out on the mole, Bren gunners covering the approaches. Concentrated fire was directed against enemy snipers and the situation was considered to be in hand.

During the assault insulated wires on the mole were cut with wire-cutters although it is not certain that all such wires were severed. At about 04.45 shells from a heavy enemy battery were directed against the mole from the eastward. This was considered to be from the battery near Mount Tambone.

The battery at Mount Tambone had been identified as a particularly important target and a Bombardment Unit had landed with the main assault and was on its way up to an Observation Post to direct the Naval shelling to put a permanent end to its activity. But the ship allocated to fire the shells to destroy the battery had only arrived on 15th June and consequently had had little practice with the attacking force. While the ship was trying to get into position to destroy the battery the same 155-mm shells which had done so much damage in the harbour below also found the Bombardment Unit and their wireless set.

Telegraphist Ken Simmons, No. 2 Combined Operations Bombardment Unit

Once we got into the assault craft the noise started up. It was terrific with machine-gun fire and flaming onions (tracer). When the ramp went down, I said to myself, 'I'm not getting out of the boat,' but of course our training took over and we ran for it. The assault craft had beached on a sandbar on the beach to the right of Marina di Campo. This meant we were getting out straight into deep water and we went in right up to our waists. We kept moving under continuous fire in the half-light of dawn. Still under fire we climbed the hill to our Observation Point where we were able to take cover in a small slit trench. About two or three hours after we had come ashore one of the 155-mm shells found our OP (the shells had been killing the Senegalese in the valley below us) and one caused us a bit of mayhem. I was holding onto my tin hit and the shrapnel from the shell went between my arm and my head. Apart from lumps of shrapnel in my arm and my body, I was speckled all over with smaller bits. Our Forward Observation Officer, Captain Marcus

Orpen, took a piece of shrapnel through the front of his tin helmet. This cut a nasty hole across the top of his head, exiting through the back of his helmet.

Meanwhile A1 Commando were on the flak lighter below in the harbour, so it was up to A2 Commando to land on the beaches in the Golfo di Campo where they faced intense German machine-gun and mortar fire. Added to this was the heavy shelling from the German battery at Mount Tambone, and it was not long before disaster overtook the Commandos.

Official report of Commander Duncan RN, Principal Beachmaster A Commando

The first salvo was over and landed in the village, the second and third landed on or about the extremity of the mole, exploding two heavy-demolition charges in this area, which blew the end off the mole and made a thirty-foot breach in the mole some twenty feet from the end.

Petty Officer Gordon Holwill, A Commando

On the way in we received a signal that resistance was being encountered from the Germans in the houses and to give assistance. As some of A2 Commando had been sent to open another beach there were about twelve of us left with the Goums on an LCT.

We landed, but the beach was covered by some German machine guns. An LCI had been hit and was burning, giving off clouds of smoke. Some of us ran along the beach to a house on the outskirts of the village, which luckily was empty. There were about five of us at this stage. Those who had run up the beach had not stood much chance of survival.

The time was 05.00 and the only light was from the burning LCI. Some of our friends had got onto the German ship and were firing one of the 88-mm guns at the houses and shells were falling all around the jetty.

Suddenly an explosion occurred on the jetty which was big enough to lift the ship and leave it at 90° to the jetty and with the bows resting on it.

Able Seaman Ken Hatton, O Commando

Ginger Bailey and I were at our positions at the A-guns at the front of the Flak Ship when it exploded. I was badly wounded – the pain across my chest and back was terrible.

Petty Officer Wallace Stanley DSM, A Commando

We landed on the headland opposite Marina di Campo on the right-hand side as you come through the harbour. There was a little cove there so the German battery firing on Marina di Campo couldn't reach us. We landed just after 4 a.m. in an LCA which was full of Goums. They were from North Africa and they took their women on the landings with them. The women carried the ammunition and loaded the guns for the men. But both women and men were terrified of the water, and I remember carrying several women ashore before someone had the bright idea of using a gangway, which was then set up. We were under fire the minute the ramp went down, but we dropped the Goums and went off back to the harbour again where there was chaos because of the explosion. We joined up with the main body of our party, and went from house to house as quickly as we could, winkling out any Germans with the Army's assistance.

Petty Officer Gordon Holwill, A Commando

Able Seaman Fraser joined us, although he had seen us disappearing in the direction of the houses – he had been unable to follow us and had spent the time until the Germans had left lying in the sea amid debris from the LCI. He was finding it difficult to move as his battledress had collected so much sand and it was like a board.

The explosion on the German flak lighter had killed two officers and eighteen ratings from A1 Commando and two officers, two Petty Officers, one Leading Seaman and thirteen ratings from O3 Commando. The total number killed was thirty-eight. More were wounded and the official report states that forty-eight out of the forty-nine Commandos who took part in the operation were casualties.

The force of the explosion had been so great that virtually all those in the immediate area of the flak lighter had been killed. However, there were some survivors, including a small group of O3 Commandos who had been stationed at the landward side of the jetty to fight off the Germans, although many of them were wounded in the blast.

With the flak lighter on fire and ammunition exploding there was an urgent need to take the survivors off the jetty.

Official report of Commander Duncan RN, Principal Beachmaster A Commando

This explosion killed a large number of the cut-out party and blew the stern of the F-lighter away from the mole causing a fire onboard and setting off ammunition. Two British ratings were found dead at the 75-mm gun. Able Seamen J. Johnson and W. McDonald, who had been lying on the foredeck of the German ship in a defensive position, were assisted ashore down the head ropes by Able Seaman C. Woodhall, and together with the remainder of the party still alive climbed over to the seaward side of the wall where they were taken off by Lieutenant Lukin in LCA 576-6.

In the mean time, Lieutenant Lukin had seen that the party under Lieutenant Hodgson had achieved their objective, so took off the wounded to LCF 19, from where he made a signal reporting progress. On his way back in he picked up ratings and troops from LCI 132 stranded and burning on Red Beach. As he was closing the mole the demolition charges exploded so that the remaining members of the party were evacuated shortly afterwards.

It is a high tribute to the courage and determination of the surviving members of this party that despite the fact that the mole was illuminated by the burning F-lighter, all the wounded were got over the wall and rescued from amongst the dead, with the exception of Able Seaman Ball who was unconscious and left for dead. Lieutenant Harland was in a large measure responsible for the conduct of the evacuation.

On the way out LCA 576-6 picked up further survivors from LCI 132. At this time, Sub Lieutenant Fynn displayed great coolness and persistence in rescuing survivors by diving overboard to bring them to the LCA despite considerable enemy fire. Surgeon Lieutenant Coffey RNVR, one of those rescued from the sea, did sterling work amongst the wounded in the LCA and later in LCI 176. LCA 576-6 transferred these survivors to LCL 176 and was taken in tow to Bastia where they arrived about 13.30.

Although Able Seaman Ball had been left for dead, he was brought out later by Able Seaman Slyfield of A Commando. Later Able Seaman Thomas from the O3 Commando cutting-out operation was found wounded on the jetty as well. The surviving Commandos were puzzled that what had seemed to be a straightforward operation had ended with such heavy loss of life.

Petty Officer Gordon Holwill, A Commando

The Germans told us that they had known for some time that we were going to invade Elba from Corsica and had kept watch. They had seen us leaving Corsica and had made preparations to receive us. They had evacuated the local population from Marina di Campo and placed landmines at the end of the jetty, wired to be detonated from one of the houses.

On the hill above the village a *Nebelwerfer* (six-barrelled rocket launcher) had been placed, which was aimed directly at the jetty. This I believe (contrary to the official report) exploded the landmines as some of the tubes had been fired.

Meanwhile, the main landings had not been going as well as had been hoped. Only Green Beach in the Golfo di Campo could be used at first, because of the heavy shelling on Amber and Red Beaches, and it was not until after midday that the village of Marina di Campo was captured and the invading troops could be put ashore on all the landing beaches.

It had been a day of bloodshed and bravery. From A Commando Lieutenant Commander Scott-Wilson RN was awarded the Distinguished Service Cross. Petty Officers Francis Smith and Wallace Stanley along with Able Seaman Henry Goddard and Able Seaman Malcolm Slyfield received the Distinguished Service Medal. Also from A Commando, Sub Lieutenants Thomas Howell and David Phibbs were Mentioned in Dispatches. From O Commando Able Seaman Cyril Woodall and Able Seaman Victor Parsons received the Distinguished Service Medal. Telegraphist Ken Simmons from Bombardment Unit No. 2 was awarded the Croix de Guerre with Silver Star.

For O Commando Elba was both their first and their last operation. For A Commando it was to be their last operation. Both Commandos were sent back to the UK and both were eventually disbanded without being called upon again.

Elba's German garrison finally surrendered after two days of fighting. Knowing that they had no hope of relief, the German garrison had put up very fierce resistance, and the Goums and the French Commandos had had to clear the German strongpoints one by one. A few members of the German garrison did manage to escape after the surrender, among them the garrison Commander.

But before the Commandos left Elba they marked the sacrifice made by their dead comrades. The service was held the day after the invasion.

Petty Officer Wallace Stanley DSM, A Commando

The next day we buried the lads in a cemetery which was made for them. It was a beautiful strip of ground, like a bowling green, only half the length. As many that could come attended the burial service and the Army supplied a firing party. We laid them to rest there, at the back of the bay.

CHAPTER 11

Final Operations

After the D-Day landings on the Normandy beaches, most of Royal Naval Commando J for Jig had several reasons to celebrate. First, they had survived. Second, they were on their way back to Scotland. And last, but by no means least, they had seen off the taxman.

Sub Lieutenant Jack Gaster RNVR, Assistant Beachmaster J Commando

We arrived at Waverley Station, Edinburgh, in time for breakfast. The lads had theirs laid on for them at a nearby canteen, whilst the officers were invited to take theirs in the Great Northern Hotel.

We had a quick wash and brush up in the cloakroom before making our way into the dining room where we were met by the maître d' who earnestly requested us to leave our weapons outside the door in case they offended the other guests. We had been so used to wearing them that they had become part of our everyday life. Having humoured him by placing them in a corner where we could keep a watchful eye on them, we enjoyed a breakfast of sausage, powdered egg, beans and toast with a nice pot of tea. It was all served with clean linen tablecloths and napkins. The bathtubs at Hopetoun were beckoning, where we would enjoy a good long soak, then change into our blue uniforms. We were given a great welcome when we arrived back. Arrangements were made for payment to the lads, and leave was granted for fourteen days on the next morning.

I did have one upset when a Customs and Excise man turned up demanding that the lads could only take a hundred cigarettes home with them as we had been missed when we landed in

Portsmouth. I could not get over this, and went to see him to ask how he would have liked to have spent nearly four months on the beaches with just six cigarettes a day rationed, then to have someone like him come along and say you are only entitled to a paltry fifty cigarettes from the NAAFI Canteen that were not even duty-free. I think he took my point and left.

But not all of J Commando were on their way home. Some of the Commandos were going east with the advancing Allied armies, where their skills were needed for a series of landings and river crossings, albeit on a much smaller scale than the landings they had just taken part as part of Operation Neptune.

After the success of D-Day, the Allied forces moved through France and into the Low Countries. On 4th September, to the surprise of the German Army stationed there, General Montgomery's 21st Army Group reached Antwerp. In fact, so surprised were the Germans to see the Allied tanks that they did not manage to destroy Antwerp's port facilities. Any attempts they did make were frustrated by the local resistance.

Crucial to the onward progress of the Allied armies into Germany itself was a port to supply the land forces. The British and Canadians alone needed 12,000 tons of supplies a day, and they desperately needed a port closer than in Normandy.

Antwerp was therefore ideal, the more so since the failure of Operation Market Garden at Arnhem meant that neither the ports of Rotterdam nor Amsterdam could be used for the time being. But the problem with Antwerp was that the docks were forty miles up river along the Scheldt. Clearly, the Germans needed to be cleared from their strongpoints on the river banks, so that their guns no longer threatened the Allied supply route up the river.

In early October the Canadians started the process of clearing the banks of the River Scheldt. By the end of the month the South Beveland Island was cleared in an operation codenamed Operation Vitality, and Operation Switchback had taken the defensive positions around Breskens, known as the Breskens pocket.

The last remaining obstacle was Walcheren Island. Like South Beveland this was an artificial island recovered from the sea by the Dutch. Walcheren was therefore below sea level with a protective rim of dykes to keep the sea out. These dykes were thirty-feet high and over two-hundred-feet wide.

Between South Beveland and Walcheren there was a 1,200-yard-long narrow causeway which repulsed all the efforts of the Canadians to cross it, although the 52nd Lowland Division eventually found a way over. Meanwhile, the Allies launched two amphibious landings against Walcheren. One, at Flushing in the south of the island, involved No. 4 (Army) Commando and the 52nd Lowland Division, and was codenamed Infatuate I. The other, at Westkapelle on the western tip of the island, was codenamed Infatuate II and involved a British Commando brigade.

Leading the way in at both Westkapelle and Flushing was Royal Naval Commando L for Love, accompanied by part of J Commando for the Flushing landing. For the two landings they were split. L1 and L2 Commandos were sent to Westkapelle and L3 Commando was sent into Flushing.

Apart from a number of German batteries which were an obvious danger, the Royal Air Force had made a series of bombing raids and opened a gap in the dykes at Westkapelle and Flushing, leading to extensive flooding.

The Flushing landings went in first and were launched from Breskens at 04.00 on 1st November 1944. J Commando and L3 Commando then crossed the Scheldt and made for a jetty whose marker was a windmill silhouetted

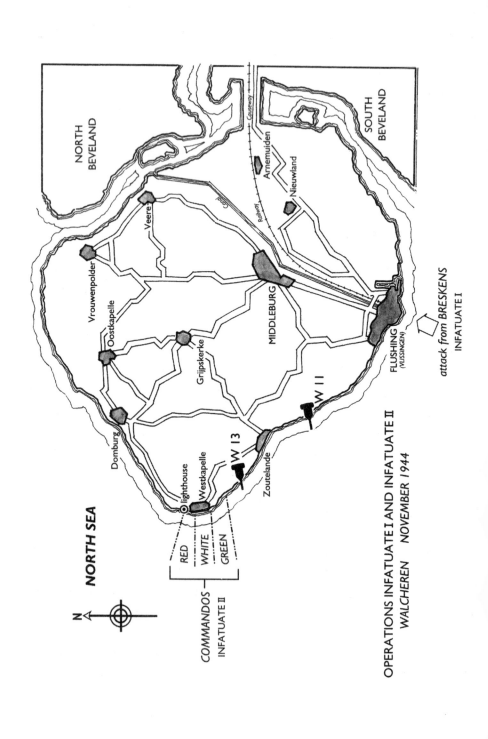

NORTH SEA

NORTH BEVELAND

SOUTH BEVELAND

Veere

Vrouwenpolder

Oostkapelle

Domburg

lighthouse

Westkapelle

Grijpskerke

MIDDLEBURG

Arnemuiden

Nieuwland

Zoutelande

W 13

W 11

FLUSHING
(VLISSINGEN)

attack from BRESKENS
INFATUATE I

Causeway

Railway

Canal

RED
WHITE
GREEN

COMMANDOS
INFATUATE II

N

OPERATIONS INFATUATE I AND INFATUATE II
WALCHEREN   NOVEMBER 1944

against the fires started by RAF Mosquitos, which had managed to drop several bombs before the Flushing landing.

Also with the Commandos, spearheading the assault, was a Landing Craft Obstacle Clearance Unit to clear any obstructions. Except there were none there.

Able Seaman Colin Harding, Landing Craft Obstacle Clearance Unit No. 3

The LCA in front of our boat took a direct hit from a German 88-mm gun firing from the island. We found a mole and the officer went ashore to recce the area. We waited about five minutes until the officer returned.

Why were we here? There were no obstacles to destroy, so we ended up searching the prisoners in six inches of mud between the two piers.

Able Seaman Alexander Hutton, J Commando

We made our landing on the beach at Flushing and then realised we probably could have walked most of the way across the river because the water was so shallow. There was a lot of shelling and machine-gun fire but we landed the troops.

Able Seaman Michael McFadden, L Commando

We were surrounded by pillboxes and on one occasion a few of us and some International Brigade soldiers from 10 Commando went up to one of these pillboxes. One of the soldiers with us who could speak German called out to the Germans to come out with their hands up. A small group came out with their hands up. Suddenly a shot rang out and the last prisoner in the line fell. We remonstrated with the soldier but he just said, go and look. Sure enough when we looked we saw that the prisoner he had shot had a stick grenade in each hand. The landing craft were coming in when my mate Petty Officer Hough was killed next to me.

Further north at Westkapelle, the landings had not yet commenced when the Flushing operation was underway. There were just three beaches. Red to the north measuring just 800 yards. White in the centre measuring just 380 yards. Green to the south measuring just 450 yards. None of them were very wide and all were next to one another. White Beach covered in the gap in the dyke which had already been blown.

Due to bad weather, the air support was limited to an advance raid on Flushing, which meant that the early bombardment at Westkapelle had to be provided from the sea in the hours leading up to H-Hour, which was set at 09.45 on 1st November 1944. Given the cluster of German gun positions around Westkapelle, this was clearly a dangerous job in itself.

Able Seaman (Gunner) Aubrey Puttick, Landing Craft Gun No. 1

A landing craft gun (LCG) is basically a landing craft tank with a gundeck and the front ramp sealed shut to keep out the water. We had two 4.7 guns on the deck, two Oerlikon guns on the bridge and two at the rear. I was manning one of the bridge Oerlikons.

We arrived at Walcheren at about 06.00. Because of the lack of air cover we came in two hundred yards off the beach and cruised up and down firing at targets. The skipper had his binoculars and directed our fire as we only had a general view of the beach and the German 77-mm gun positions.

Later in the morning, my magazine loader was killed, and at about 10.00 we were hit by a 77-mm shell. The craft rocked but we carried on. Everyone on the bridge was injured, so we carried them down to the gundeck and hailed a passing LCI which came alongside and took us all off. Our LCG went over onto its side and later sank.

The Principal Beachmaster, Commander Redvers Prior DSO DSC RN, who had been with the original Beach Parties at Dieppe, also had two Landing Craft Obstacle Clearance Units, a Beach Signals Section as well as L Commando. Although there were three beaches, the gap in the dyke was on White Beach and this was where most of the forces would land.

Extract from the official report of Commander Redvers Prior DSO DSC RN, Principal Beachmaster L Commando

White Beach was divided into two parts by a water gap. At low tide the centre of the gap was a very swiftly flowing stream; at high tide the gap was covered with water. The northern portion of White Beach where nearly all the craft touched down was very irregular, varying from sand and soft clay on the right, to boulders on the left. These boulders had been part of the dyke and had been formed into mounds by the bombing. At the extreme left of White Beach was a cliff twelve feet high. At the right of the northern portion was an anti-tank obstruction. The southern portion was sand and anti-tank obstructions with an upturned pillbox on the right limit.

Able Seaman George McAuliffe, L Commando

In October 1944 we left England for Ostend. There we were informed by Admiral Ramsey, who was in charge of all operations, that our next operation was to be the landing on the Walcheren Islands. He told us that 'the landing would be straightforward and we would just have to pick our way through the minefields'. He couldn't have been more wrong. On 31st October 1944 we boarded LCTs in Ostend for Westkapelle.

In my view, this landing was more difficult than D-Day because we had to operate on a much smaller beach and bad weather prevented our aircraft from providing cover. We received intensive bombardment from enemy coastal defences and mortars, and many landing craft were either sunk or damaged. Our LCT was hit and damaged and we had to wade onto the beach from about a hundred yards out. I got ashore OK. I had received orders from the Beachmaster and moved away when a mortar bomb exploded next to me and John Lindsay. I received injuries to my knee from fragments of my rifle which had been blown to bits. John was badly wounded in the chest and couldn't move, and I was having trouble trying to carry him because of my knee wounds.

Cover was quickly found by the Royal Naval Commandos in one of the bombed-out German gun emplacements. No. W13 was close to White Beach where L Commando had a base.

Able Seaman George McAuliffe, L Commando

I decided to return to our base at gun emplacement W13 for help. On the way to W13 I came under machine-gun fire but got through. Our people were hard pressed and in no position to help, so I was told to bring John back by myself. I didn't like the prospect of going back alone but there was nothing else to do. On the way back I again came under machine-gun fire but reached cover, and returned fire using a Sten gun I had taken from a dead Royal Marine. I got to John and was attending his wounds when five Germans approached with their hands up. I now thought my luck had changed and I ordered the Germans to carry John back to base. Luckily, they seemed to have had enough and were very co-operative. On the way back we were not machine-gunned, so I can only assume that these five Germans must have been firing at me earlier. As we returned, one of the Germans who was leading the way stopped and pointed to where a land mine was placed. At that moment a Royal Marine stepped out and hit him across the face with his rifle butt. I lost my temper because the German was clearly unarmed and trying to help, so I fired a warning shot into the sand at the Royal Marine's feet and told him to piss off. The German recovered and we made our way back to W13. John was later taken away for treatment and survived his wounds. Unfortunately, another of the captured Germans was killed by mortar fire during our return to base.

I resumed duties and was ordered to recce W13 for booby traps and mines. Inside the gun emplacement we found all the Germans were dead. Under W13 there were tunnels, storerooms and sleeping quarters. In one room we found a safe and blew open the door with a grenade. Inside there were no papers but there were thousands of Deutschmarks and a few hundred Dutch guilders. The Deutschmarks were worthless but the guilders were not so we shared them out. We also found a suspect booby trap in a doorway – a packet of cigarettes placed conveniently on the top of a big tin – and attempted to detonate it by firing a shot at the cigarette packet. It did not explode so we opened the tin to find several packets of cigarettes. These were also shared out and that's when I became a smoker.

Meanwhile the main landing force was coming ashore. Also on White Beach was an anti-tank obstruction which was doing its job well and stopping the vehicles from proceeding. The LCOCU were ordered to blow them up and in doing so lost three men from mortar fire. On Green Beach the Commandos came under sustained fire and the Germans succeeded in shooting down their beach sign. The fire from the German guns was persistent and accurate. They were using the Westkapelle lighthouse as an Observation Post for their artillery spotters, and it was only when this was burnt out by the Allied troops that the German fire became less accurate and less intense. After the first day, the Commandos normally settled into the routine of running the beaches. But at Westkapelle this was not possible and they were reduced to less interesting activities.

Lieutenant Fred Killick RNVR, Beachmaster L Commando

During the following days the weather deteriorated so that follow-up supply craft were unable to reach the beach, resulting in severe shortage of food and ammunition for forty-eight hours. The casualties and POWs could not be evacuated. As we were not required for unloading stores we were given the task of guarding the POWs. They were held in an enormous bomb crater on top of the dunes near an area occupied by the field hospital.

Extract from the official report of Commander Redvers Prior DSO DSC RN, Principal Beachmaster L Commando

On D plus 1 on Green Beach at 13.30 the craft and beach area were subjected to heavy and accurate shell fire from W11. Several LVTs were hit and ammunition exploded. The German prisoners then sang 'Deutschland über Alles'.

Five days after the landings the weather moderated and normal service could resume once more. Three days later, the beaches were finally closed as the island had been captured. The Royal Naval Commandos went back to their normal routines.

Able Seaman George McAuliffe, L Commando

We went back to beach-landing duties and many craft continued to be hit, sunk or damaged. One LCT was having trouble getting ashore and was moved alongside the jetty. I was ordered to go down and grab a line to secure the bow mooring. As I did so, I came under machine-gun fire from inland which scared the living daylights out of me. Luckily there were thick wooden supporting planks which ran the length of the jetty and I was able to find cover behind them. I crawled to the end of the jetty and secured the bow-mooring line and then sprinted back – MacDonald Bailey never ran faster. My oppo John Long secured the stern mooring and was out of view/range of machine guns so he never came under fire – if I'd known I would have changed places.

Later I was ordered by the Principal Beachmaster (Commander Prior) to search an LCT that had washed up broadside onto the beach. The craft was full of water up to the gunwhales and awash with dead bodies, but there was a chance someone was alive inside the hold. There was a dead frogman alongside the LCT and I could have used his gear, but I didn't fancy the idea of undoing the wetsuit and finding body parts or whatever inside. I chose to strip down to my underpants and swim underwater to try and open the hatch to see if there was anyone alive. Because of the water pressure and cold I could not open the hatch and after several attempts returned to shore – wringing wet and blue with the freezing cold. There was no way I could dry myself so I resumed duties in a cold and wet uniform. A large tot of rum helped get me back on track.

A few days later I had found refuge under cover in a dugout with John Mahoney when I was woken up by a loud explosion and the cover of our dugout caving in around us. The roof of the dugout collapsed and John was hit on the head by a piece of timber. As we clambered out, we saw that an armoured personnel carrier had hit a landmine nearby and a length of its tracking had landed on the roof of our dugout. We helped medics with the injured and wounded and reported back to base where it was found that John had a fractured skull. Tragically, I think he later died of his injuries in England.

The island was taken a few days later and we returned to Belgium, where I had my first shower and decent meal in two weeks. It's funny but I don't remember eating during the operation – I guess I was preoccupied with other things. I had my wounds attended to when I returned to Ardentinny.

It took two days of street fighting before the Germans in Flushing surrendered. On 5th November the island's principal town, Middleburg, surrendered. During this time Army Commandos who had landed at Westkapelle had swept north-east and south-east to link up with the landings at Flushing and to capture the German batteries which crowded the shoreline. Finally by 8th November the beaches were closed and the last German resistance had folded. The island was in Allied hands. By the end of November the approaches to Antwerp had been cleared of mines.

The Allied armies were still moving east into Germany itself and Royal Naval Commando J for Jig was still with the advancing forces.

Able Seaman Alexander Hutton, J Commando

Again we were loaded onto lorries and taken to Nijmegen. Whilst there, the paratroopers were having a terrible time at Arnhem with the Germans knocking hell out of them. We went across the river and brought back as many as we could, all the time under fire from the Germans.

From there we crossed the Rhine to a place called Emmerich, and once we landed the Germans were surrendering in droves. When Germany surrendered it was chaotic as there were a lot of refugees, many of whom were Germans. There was a fraternisation ban on us at the time so we weren't allowed to talk to them.

With the Allies in northern Europe moving further east, the Allies in Italy were still moving north. After the fall of Rome, the Allies moved slowly northwards through the autumn and the winter of 1944. Field Marshal Kesselring's Army Group C had put up stubborn resistance as it withdrew slowly towards the Alps.

By the spring of 1945 the Germans had fallen back to the Po valley. At the point where this reaches the coast is a shallow lagoon called Lake Comacchio on the Adriatic coast south of Venice. To assist with their defensive positions, the Germans blew a hole in the Argine dyke and flooded a large area of the Po Valley.

Along the dyke, which included the towns of Argenta,
Longastrino and Comacchio itself, the Germans had
strongpoints ready to repulse the Allied attack which was
codenamed Operation Roast. At the forefront of the attack
it was planned that three squadrons (A, B and C Squadrons)
of Fantails, or Buffaloes, should assist the main assault.
These were armoured amphibious carriers with tracks that
carried British and American tank companies and troops.

By the time of the assault 2 Commando Brigade had
already attacked German positions on the narrow stretch
of land separating Lake Comacchio from the Adriatic.
Their attack had persuaded the Germans to move in more
troops so that Operation Roast to the west now stood
more chance of success.

By this time Royal Naval Commando H for How had
returned from Burma and India and were in northern
Italy where they were employed on different duties, the
main ones being to look after stores in Naples. But one of
their Beachmasters was sent off to assist with the crossing
of Lake Comacchio in early April 1945.

Lieutenant John Hill RNVR, Beachmaster H Commando

A problem foreseen by the planning staffs was the difficulty
the soldiers might encounter in navigating their vehicles
over the flooded valley to arrive at the exact place to put the
troops ashore. Two Navy officers were seconded to cover this
difficulty. B Squadron were to be piloted by a red-bearded
Lieutenant Commander, and C Squadron by Lieutenant John
Hill, Beachmaster of RN Commando H3. Major John
Abrahams commanded the RASC unit of C Squadron.

The attack on Argenta was timed for dawn on April 8th,
the starting gate was the recently shattered village of San
Alberto. As only A and B Squadrons were to be used in this
first incursion on the western dyke, owing to congestion at
the village, caused by debris from the recent battle and the

narrow roads, I thumbed a lift on my red-bearded friend's Pilot tank. There was plenty of room, it having been decided not to encumber the leading vehicle with soldiers. We mustered near the dark waters just after midnight where the road dipped into the flooded valley, making an ideal launching pad for the Buffaloes. At 03.00 A Squadron moved off. It was by no means a silent departure as the tanks were fitted with aero engines and made the most appalling row. The theory was that the Germans would think there was a flight of bombers heading in their direction and, very sensibly, keep their heads down. A comforting thought.

At 03.30, Lieutenant Commander Red Beard received the order, over the RT, to start the procession, and the vehicles waddled in line ahead down into the water. After the first few miles navigation was no problem. The sound and flame of the battle beginning around Argenta were a tocsin and a brilliant beacon to mark our destination. The Pilot pushed on, taking the shortest line commensurate with safety. That is, avoiding drowned houses, barns etc. showing just above the water, darker shapes in the greyness of pre-dawn.

We came under fire from 88-mm guns and mortar shells as A Squadron passed us, returning for more troops. The fighting ranged along the dyke behind which lay Argenta, and we landed at a point where about forty yards of sloping turf made a convenient approach in the lee of the high ground.

The first wave, carried by A Squadron, were Marine Commandos, and the open ground held many of their dead, sadly recognisable by their green berets. B Squadron carried the Queen's Regiment, and they boiled out of the Buffaloes and up the twenty-foot-high dyke like singleminded berserks and we turned away, back to San Alberto, for reinforcements, ducking below the gunwhales of the amphibian to avoid bullets and shell splinters from the air bursts. By the time we returned, the Germans had been blasted out of Argenta and the main force (Indian 4th Division and New Zealand Division) were driving along the captured highway, northward.

The enemy regrouped and held a strong position near Longastrino, while the main British force drove towards Ferrara along the better roads. It therefore became the task of our small force to dislodge the Germans from Longastrino, attacking from the water gate as at Argenta. As the American pilot had been killed and Red Beard called away for other duties, and, as the Buffaloes were many less in number because of breakdown or destruction, the remaining vehicles and their crews came under the command of Colonel Forbes and were entirely manned by the RASC with myself as the pilot. The job was a sinecure really, as the crews became familiar with the flooded valley and they were not so dependant on the pilot. Only sometimes.

In three days we were ready for a bash at Longastrino, and at the usual unearthly hour we took to the water. Taking a longer route and curving away towards the eastern spit to stay out of range as long as possible, and with the intention of keeping the enemy guessing as to our landing point, we arrived about two miles offshore from the small town and lay silent, engines stopped, waiting for the 25-pounder barrage which would be the overture to the battle for Longastrino. We waited as dawn crept slyly over the muddy liquid that was once an onion field, its soggy, rotten fruit bobbing around the Buffaloes. There we were as the sky lightened and the red roofs of Longastrino became visible over the wall of the high dyke.

'Like a bloody Cowes regatta,' John Abrahams growled over the RT. Looking back along the line of amphibians, details were becoming clearer. Close up in the van the green berets of the Commandos were plainly evident, and further back the anonymous helmets of the line regiment made a dull carapace for those water-borne monsters in the rear.

We were spotted, of course, and shells from the shore batteries began falling around us. Several mortars joined the orchestra and matters soon became serious as the close misses threw up dollops of muddy water. The first pale gleam of sunlight lightened the roof tops and, as if this woke up the artillerymen, 25-pounders began their bombardment. A few ranging shots cracked a sharp warning and within minutes the full schtonk was thundering down on luckless Longastrino. The barrage was short, accurate, and totally destructive. The red roofs disintegrated into swirling clouds of pink dust. The walls of the tiny houses collapsed and crumbled. In twenty minutes nothing much remained of that small Italian town.

'Bloody Hell,' boomed an involuntary (and unlawful) voice over the RT. Two red flares curved upwards from the command vehicle and my radio man repeated the order to commence landing. The aero engines lifted their register from a menacing growl to a high-pitched scream as we churned towards the shore in an uneven line abreast, making for the point where the flames still licked and smoked in the shattered dwellings. Our Brens hammered viciously, while the enemy mortars hurled their bombs over the protecting Argine dyke, causing many casualties. The Bren guns kept raking the top of the bank until the soldiers landed and surged up and over the embankment and battled away among the ruins. Such was the momentum of the assault that the noise of street fighting soon receded northwards to the far side of Longastrino. A flight of rocket-firing Spitfires zoomed in low and vented their destructive spite on the town of Comacchio and on the remnants of enemy still holding the eastern spit. It was time to go back for the reinforcements.

When we returned, leading the second wave, the sheltered side of the flood bank was crowded with prisoners and a few guards. The majority of the captives were very young and very, very glad to be done with the war. The flower of a mighty army had withered and fallen on the frozen wastelands of Russia, on the burning sands of North Africa and in the mud of France and Holland. The dross remaining could sight a gun and pull a trigger but soldiers they were not. The Spitfires came again with their rockets to clear the high road of the fleeing enemy. They destroyed the retreating transports and artillery, littering the road north with the debris of a broken army. The Buffaloes regrouped on the southern side of the river Po, at a point almost midway between Polasella and Crespino on the opposite side, and three days later we were ready to ferry the 2nd Guards Brigade across. It might be supposed the Germans would take the opportunity to make a stand here – they held all the tactical advantages, but we met with very little resistance. A few *Schmeissers* and some mortar fire were all they could offer, and the Welsh Guards cleared them off in very quick time. We spent a few hours more ferrying troops over the river and in that time the Engineers shoved a Bailey Bridge over the Po at Occhiobello, making the Buffaloes redundant. Still it was a glorious memory, John Hill leading the 8th Army over the Po River.

The amphibious vehicles lumbered on. Crossed the Adige in the wake of the New Zealanders, but we never really caught up with the war again, and VE Day found us encamped in another olive orchard, near Terranova. After a few hectic days of celebration, I said goodbye to Major John Abrahams and my tank crew and rejoined part of H Commando at Leghorn.

On 8th May 1945 VE day was celebrated and the war in Europe was over. H Commando made its way back to Scotland where it was disbanded in November 1945.

But the war was not yet over in the Far East. Royal Naval Commandos C, E, U and V were sent out to assist with the potentially costly task of taking the Japanese on in the final stages of the war. And if Japan itself had had to be invaded the Royal Naval Commandos would, as usual, have been the first into what would have been a very bloody campaign. Other Royal Naval Commandos at home were on standby to go out to the Far East. But to their relief in August 1945 the Americans dropped the two atom bombs and the Japanese surrendered.

The campaign in the Far East did have its lighter moments. In May 1945 the Beach Signals had accompanied the seaborne landings at Rangoon as part of Operation Dracula. Although signals work was vital to the war effort, sometimes everything had to be dropped for even more important missions.

Lieutenant Cyril Jackson RNVR, Commanding Officer Royal Naval Beach Signals Section No. B1

One morning while we were working away in the Signal Distributing Office we received a visit from Admiral Cunningham. We had a Jeep with each unit and ours was parked outside. Admiral Cunningham enquired as to who was in charge of this Jeep. On finding it was myself he said to me, 'Right, Jackson, you are now my chauffeur. The first thing you can do is to take me back to the Commissioner's building.' And so I became his chauffeur.

One morning he said to me, 'I want you to take me to the HQ ship.' This I duly did and he disappeared into the wardroom. After half an hour had gone by I could hear a heated argument taking place. Suddenly the door burst open and out stormed Admiral Cunningham. He came up to me, slapped me on the shoulder and said to me, 'Come on old chap, they're all bloody mad on this ship!'

The Japanese signed the surrender document on 2nd September 1945 and the Second World War was finally over. One week later, the British landed in Malaya, landings which were codenamed Operation Zipper and which, unsurprisingly, were unopposed.

Able Seaman Alf Humberstone, U Commando

As we approached the beach a launch with the Union Jack and the Japanese flag flying came out with the surrender party on board. The only fire came from an Indian soldier who stumbled and tripped down the ramp of his landing craft and his Sten gun went off by mistake.

The war was finally over.

CHAPTER 12

Endings

For the Royal Naval Commandos the end of World War II meant the end of the road. As early as 1944 in a report on Operation Neptune after the D-Day landings the Admiralty commented, 'It is Admiralty policy for the Royal Marines to provide the personnel for the Naval Beach Organisation in future.' From late 1944 through 1945 each of the Royal Naval Commandos was disbanded.

After World War II the role of the Royal Naval Commandos passed to the Assault Squadrons of the Royal Marine Commandos. The landing craft they operate today are very similar to the ones used in World War II, although today's Royal Marine Commandos expect to have a very accurate and very intensive aerial bombardment of any beaches before they land. The name Royal Naval Commandos was transferred to the medics who belonged to the Royal Navy but who worked with the Royal Marines and who underwent Commando training.

On 25th September 1944 HMS *Armadillo* sent out the latest memoranda. Sandwiched between the usual amendments to regulations, changes to pay rates and administrative bumf was a piece of paper with the number 91 on it.

Beach Commando Memoranda, HMS 'Armadillo', Ardentinny 25.9.44

NO. 91 – DUTIES OF A BEACH PARTY

1. The Beach Party, in conjunction with the control ship, should do its utmost to delay the landing of the assault party and to interfere with the subsequent ferry services.

2. It is the duty of the Beachmaster and his assistants to confuse as much as possible the landing craft approaching the beach. Considerable ingenuity may be exercised in the alternate use of coloured lights, triangles and the indiscriminate waving of flags.

3. The ratings of a Beach Party, especially trained in boat destruction and confusion of signals, should be given every opportunity to become qualified menaces (this latter achievement being marked on page 3 of the service certificate).

4. The Beachmaster must act quickly if he is to prevent the arrival of the first series on time. On landing he is at once to look out for any natural obstruction, making full use of deep water recces to find shoals, rocks and patches of seaweed. Landing lights will then be placed over the obstructions. The Beachmaster is to ensure that one of two red or green lights is obscured so that it is impossible for incoming craft to get any two lights of the same colour in transit. If there are no natural obstructions then the Beachmaster is to direct the placing of artificial ones. As a final precaution all coloured lights are to be put up at least half an hour after zero hour, this should give ample time for the first flight to go astray.

5. The best opportunities for the Beach Party to carry out its duties occur in daylight hours. The Beachmaster should conceal himself behind a tree and shout loudly and unintelligibly through the Ardente. All craft should be called in at once and should be stopped as soon as they move, preferably of course after they have dropped their kedges. Flags of all nations should be waved from the beach and every endeavour should be made to keep the craft on the beach until they are high and dry.

6. When a variety of craft appear to be converging on the same beach, are fouling one another's kedges, and are finally running on the rocks, the Commanding Officer of the Beach Party should give the order to all and sundry, 'Get off the beach!' supplemented with, 'Get the hell out of here!' and is to withdraw the party a short distance inshore, light a fire, make cocoa, and carry on smoking.

Today it is hard to find any physical signs of the Royal Naval Commandos' activities during World War II. The beaches where they landed are still there and some, especially in Normandy, have displays and museums to tell the story of the landings.

But the spiritual home of the Royal Naval Commandos was, and remains, the Highlands of Scotland. At their base, HMS *Armadillo* at Ardentinny, the Commandos were trained and it was from here that they started their journeys to the beaches.

It does not look today quite the same as it looked during the war, but parts of HMS *Armadillo* still remain, and the Royal Naval Commando Association has placed two plaques in the church which commemorate the Commandos.

If you visit the site of HMS *Armadillo,* do take a moment to pay your respects at the church. And when you wander round the site keep a lookout for the Commandos who return from time to time. Today the youngest of them is in his late seventies, most are in their eighties, and some are in their nineties.

The Royal Naval Commando Association formally disbanded in May 2003. It organised a return trip to HMS *Armadillo* in May 1993 when the Commandos marked the occasion with a suitable farewell to the their wartime home.

'Jungle' George Fagence, Founder and Honorary Vice President, the Royal Naval Commando Association, formerly H Commando

We merrily boarded the charabanc, in full song as we set out for the nostalgic happy hunting grounds. On arrival the awe and foreboding, recalled to mind of the old place, gave way to regret and past sorrow of the place which had become run down and overgrown. Familiar landmarks were of comfort. Each made his way hither and thither along the single track alongside the loch leading to the end of the campsite in ones and twos. All having reached the end of the track, for some reason, which to this day I do not comprehend, each individual fell into columns of three, one behind the other, and automatically began to march in step, back along the track, singing at the top of their voices, 'Onward Christian Soldiers!'

This was completely spontaneous and uncoordinated, each one in step, the only sound was the 'Battle Hymn' from the brotherhood.

Archie Carey, former Landing Craft Signalman

I served all over the Mediterranean in the same operations as the Royal Naval Commandos. Not many people knew about what they did or where they were but they were a handy lot.

Bernard Stone, formerly Royal Naval Beach Signals Section No. B5

My travels took me halfway around the world. Mixed with fear, hardship and excitement, it was an adventure in my life not to be missed, but never to be repeated.

Eric Gear, formerly Q Commando

I can only say that I am on reflection very glad to have served with such a lovely gang of blokes – and my friendship with Paddy Bell lasted until he died in 1997.

Ken Simmons, formerly No. 2 Combined Operations Bombardment Unit

We had a hell of a time, one way or another. I wouldn't have missed it for the world.

Appendix 1

RN Commando Formation and Operations Timeline

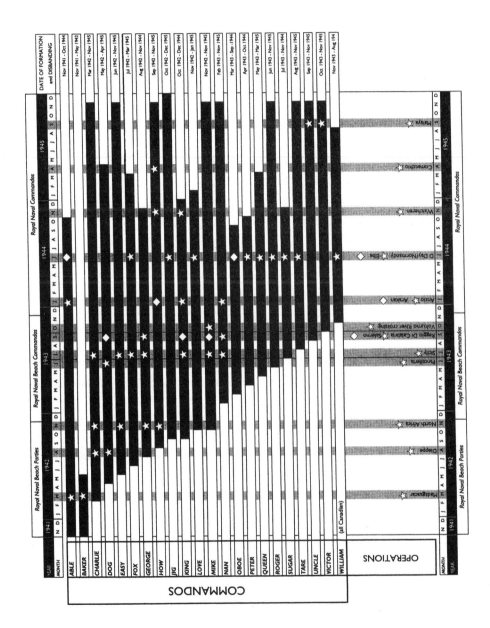

Appendix 2

Known Medals Awarded to Royal Naval Commandos
Based on information collected by Ken Barry, ex-R Commando

George Cross

Commander Anthony Cobham MBE RN   H Commando (1929 *HMS Devonshire*)

Order of Bath

Vice Admiral Sir Patrick Bayly KBE CB DSC and two bars	M Commando
Rear Admiral Edward Gueritz CBE OBE DSC	F Commando

Distinguished Service Order

Acting Commander H. R. M. Nicholl RN	G Commando
Commander Redvers Prior RN	L Commando *London Gazette* 23/3/43
Captain W. F. N. Gregory-Smith, DSO and bar, DSC and bar RN	T Commando (Normandy) *London Gazette* 14/11/44
Lieutenant Frank Brinkley RN	Commando (Sicily) *London Gazette* 21/12/43

Order of the British Empire

Commander Arthur Havers DSC RN   K Commando *London Gazette* 2/6/43

Distinguished Service Cross

Lieutenant Commander A. H. Ballard RN	A Commando
T/Sub Lieutenant David K. Phibbs RNVR	A Commando (Madagascar) *London Gazette* 25//8/42
T/Lieutenant James Scott-Wilson RNVR	F Commando (Sicily) *London Gazette* 21/12/43
T/Lieutenant Commander James Scott-Wilson RNVR BAR	A Commando (Elba) *London Gazette* 7/11/44
Lieutenant D. T. Bibby RNVR	C Commando
T/Sub Lieutenant Robin L. Coppock RNVR	C Commando (Sicily) *London Gazette* 21/12/43
T/Sub Lieutenant Douglas T. Kent RNVR	C Commando (Hardelot Raid) *London Gazette* 7/7/42
T/Lieutenant Lieutenant Douglas T. Kent RNVR BAR	COPPS (Sicily) *London Gazette* 7/12/43
Lieutenant Commmnder T. Pearson SANF	D Commando
T/Lieutenant Richard J. Franklin RNVR	D Commando (Anzio) *London Gazette* 23/5/44

Lieutenant Frank E. Brinkley RN — E Commando (Sicily) *London Gazette* 21/12/43

A/Sub Lieutenant David F. Goodale RN — E Commando *London Gazette* 5/7/40

Lieutenant Edward F. Gueritz RN — F Commando (Madagascar) *London Gazette* 25/8/42

A/Lieutenant Commander Edward F. Gueritz RN BAR — F Commando (Normandy) *London Gazette* 29/8/44

Lieutenant Michael H. Collar — F Commando (minesweeping) *London Gazette* 4/9/45

Sub Lieutenant William Pittendrigh RNVR — F Commando (Normandy)

Sub Lieutenant Sis E. Willis RNVR — F Commando (Normandy)

T/Midshipman Norman E. Draper RNVR — G Commando (Italy) *London Gazette* 9/5/44

Lieutenant Thomas L. Martin RN — G Commando (Messina) *London Gazette* 25/1/44

T/Sub Lieutenant Oswald Cook RNVR — G Commando (Messina) *London Gazette* 25/1/44

Sub Lieutenant J. C. McPherson RNVR — G Commando

Sub Lieutenant P D Alderton RNVR — F & H Commando (Normandy)

Commander Geoffrey Ransome RN Retd — F & J Commando (Sicily) *London Gazette* 21/12/43

Commander Geoffrey Ransome RN Retd BAR — F & J Commando *London Gazette* 24/4/45

Commander Arthur Havers DSC RN — K Commando (Salerno) *London Gazette* 23/5/44

Lieutenant Herbert V. Veal RNVR — K Commando (Salerno) *London Gazette* 23/5/44

Lieutenant Roger C. Norwood RN — K Commando *London Gazette* 17/3/42

T/Lieutenant Richard Blackwell RNVR — K Commando (Anzio) *London Gazette* 1/8/44

T/Lieutenant Thomas E. Hope RNVR — K Commando (Anzio) *London Gazette* 1/8/44

Commander Redvers M. Prior RN — L Commando (Dunkirk) *London Gazette* 7/6/40

Commander Redvers M. Prior RN BAR — L Commando (Walcheren) *London Gazette* 22/12/44

Lieutenant J. K. Matthias RNVR — L Commando

Lieutenant Aldrin RNVR — L Commando

A/Lieutenant Commander Patrick U. Bayly RN — M Commando (Sicily) *London Gazette* 21/12/43

A/Lieutenant Commander Patrick U. Bayly RN 1st BAR	M Commando (Salerno) *London Gazette* 23/5/44
Commander Patrick U. Bayly RN 2nd BAR	HMS Constance (Korea) *London Gazette* 19/5/53
T/Lieutenant Ernest A. Berry RNVR	M Commando
T/Lieutenant Harry Seely RNVR	M Commando (Salerno) *London Gazette* 23/5/44
Lieutenant H. A. Venn RNVR	M Commando
Lieutenant John B. Russell RN	HMS Exmoor *London Gazette* 23/4/42
Lieutenant John B. Russell RN BAR	N Commando (Anzio) *London Gazette* 5/8/44
Lieutenant John B. Russell RN 2nd BAR	N Commando (Anzio) *London Gazette* 15/8/44
Commander P. W. F. Stubbs RN	N Commando (Torch) *London Gazette* 16/3/43
T/Lieutenant Ian A. Harris RANVR	N Commando (Anzio) *London Gazette* 9/5/44
Lieutenant Commander G. Phillips RNVR	Q Commando
Lieutenant Commander Edmund S. D. Freemenatle RN	P Commando (Normandy) *London Gazette* 14/11/44
T/Sub Lieutenant James H. S. Speed RNVR	R Commando (Normandy) *London Gazette* 27/3/45
Lieutenant Commander F. Gregory-Smith RN	T Commando
Lieutenant Commander F. Gregory-Smith RN 1st BAR	T Commando (Normandy)
Rev Maurice A. P. Wood RNVR Commando's Padre	—
Lieutenant Robert Billington RNVR	No. 1 LCOCU (Normandy)
Lieutenant Robert Billintgton RNVR BAR	No. 1 LCOCU

Conspicuous Gallantry Medal

Petty Officer Ronald Harry George McKinlay P/JX 245579	P Commando (Normandy) *London Gazette* 29/8/44

George Medal

Lieutenant Commander D. J. O'Hagan RCNVR	W Commando (Mine Disposal) *London Gazette* 29/7/41

Distinguished Service Medal

Petty Officer Francis Sidney Smith
P/JX 95994

A Commando (Elba) *London Gazette* 7/11/44

Petty Officer Wallace Victor Stanley
C/JX 241463

A Commando (Elba) *London Gazette* 7/11/44

Able Seaman Henry John Goddard
C/JX 279669

A Commando (Elba) *London Gazette* 7/11/44

Able Seaman Malcolm David Slyfield
P/JX 325864

A Commando (Elba) *London Gazette* 7/11/44

Petty Officer Henry George Oag
P/SSX 20886

E Commando (Sicily) *London Gazette*
21/12/43

Able Seaman Kenneth Addison
D/SSX 29363

E Commando (Sicily) *London Gazette*
21/12/43

Able Seaman Sydney Compston
D/JX 169001

F Commando (Normandy) *London Gazette*
14/11/44

Leading Seaman Albert Charles Davey
D/SSZ 25236

F Commando (Normandy) *London Gazette*
21/12/43

Able Seaman Edward George Saunders
D/JX 237823

F Commando (Normandy) *London Gazette*
14/11/44

Able Seaman Donald Emery P/SSX 29684

F Commando (Normandy) *London Gazette*
14/11/44

Able Seaman Thomas Hunt D/JX304950

F Commando (Normandy) *London Gazette*
14/11/44

Leading Seaman Thomas William Gooding
D/JX 161420

F Commando (Normandy) *London Gazette*
14/11/44

Able Seaman Charles Frederick Maylon
C/JXD 167181

H Commando (Arakan) *London Gazette*
4/7/44

Petty Officer William Charles Fedder
C/JX 140885

J Commando (Normandy) *London Gazette*
10/4/45

Petty Officer Ronald Marshal Hall
P/JX 149429

K Commando (Anzio) *London Gazette*
1/8/44

Petty Officer Raymond Thomas Henry Sims
D/JX 133648

K Commando (Salerno) *London Gazette*
23/5/44

Petty Officer Stanley Fearn D/JX 142689

K Commando (Anzio) *London Gazette*
1/8/44

Able Seaman W. W. R. Walker P/JX 383736
!/8/44

K Commando (Anzio) *London Gazette*

Petty Officer James Reginald McClure
C/SSX 2424

L Commando (Walcheren) *London Gazette*
17/4/45

A/Petty Officer Harry Best C/JX 159393

L Commando (Walcheren) *London Gazette*
22/12/44

Petty Officer A. D. Chaplin P/JX 156000	M Commando
Able Seaman J. O'Rourke D/JX 392953	M Commando
Able Seaman Victor William Parsons C/JX 374660	O Commando (Elba) *London Gazette* 7 /11/44
Able Seaman Cyril Woodall P/JX 161762	O Commando (Elba) *London Gazette* 7/11/44
Petty Officer Frederick Raymond Perrin P/JX 157866	R Commando (Normandy) *London Gazette* 14/11/44
Petty Officer George Colin Richards D/JX 142919	R Commando (Normandy) *London Gazette* 14/11/44
Petty Officer John Grahame Tapley D/JX 139148	R Commando (Normandy) *London Gazette* 4/11/44
Able Seaman William Dennis Cook C/JX 377978	R Commando (Normandy) *London Gazette* 14/11/44
Able Seaman Charles William Day C/JX 379987	R Commando (Normandy) *London Gazette* 14/11/44
Petty Officer Henry Colin Lynas Foreman P/UDX 1241	S Commando (Normandy) *London Gazette* 14/11/44
Telegraphist Leonard D. Rowland P/JX 360009	Levant Schooner Flotilla *London Gazette* 11/12/44
Telegraphist William George Quinn C/JX 361334	RNBSS B18 (Normandy) *London Gazette* 14/11/44
Coder Geoffrey Harris	RNBSS B2
Telegraphist Abraham Acton Parr P/JX 232311	RNBSS B18 (Normandy) *London Gazette*
Telegraphist Kenneth Eifon Penny D/JX 342823	FOB (Normandy) *London Gazette* 14/11/44
Telegraphist Alexander John Boomer D/JX 358442	FOB (Sicily)
Telegraphist Geoffrey James Bennett P/JX 341030	FOB (Anzio) *London Gazette* 1/8/44
Leading Telegraphist Robert William Brown C/JX 357188	FOB
Ordinary Telegraphist Roland Arthur Batson C/JX 308577	FOB (Normandy)
Telegraphist Alan Gwillym Dixon P/SSX 33052	FOB (Sicily)
Telegraphist Harry Monks P/JX 321640	FOB (Normandy)
Telegraphist Donald Stewart Paterson C/JX 271970	FOB (Sicily)

A/Petty Officer Telegraphist Geoffrey
Harvey Scholey C/JX 15132

FOB (Sicily)

A/Leading Telegraphist Edwin William
Sutton P/JX 223185

FOB (Normandy)

British Empire Medal

Petty Officer Hugh L. Jones

J Commando

Petty Officer W. J. Feltham

D Commando

Mention in Dispatches

Signalman Raymond C. W. Priddle
D/JX 340303

RNBSS B6 (Normandy) *London Gazette*
14/11/44

T/Sub Lieutenant Thomas E. H. Howell
RNVR

RNBSS B7 (Torch) *London Gazette* 4/5/43

T/Sub Lieutenant David K. Phibbs RNVR

A Commando (Madagascar) *London Gazette*
25/8/42

T/Lieutenant David K. Phibbs RNVR

A Commando (Elba) *London Gazette* 7/11/44

Able Seaman Clarence Brind D/JX 213610

A Commando

T/Lieutenant Benjamin C. Farthing RINVR

A Commando (Arakan) *London Gazette*
10/7/45

Lieutenant John A. Jones RN

C Commando (Sicily) *London Gazette*
21/12/43

Leading Seaman Robert Baldwin
D/MDX 2177

C Commando (Sicily) *London Gazette*
21/12/43

Lieutenant David F. Goodale RN

E Commando (Sicily) *London Gazette*
21/12/43

T/Sub Lieutenant Edward H. Hannaford
RNVR

E Commando (Sicily) *London Gazette*
21/12/43

Sub Lieutenant Charles N. Reid RNVR

E Commando (Sicily) *London Gazette*
21/12/43

Able Seaman Stanley Beck D/SSX 2643

F Commando (Sicily) *London Gazette*
21/12/43

T/Lieutenant James A. Scott-Wilson RNVR

F Commando

Lieutenant Michael H. Collar RN

F Commando *London Gazette* 21/12/43

Petty Officer John Thomas Howard
C/JX 110175

F Commando (Sicily) *London Gazette*
21/12/43

Petty Officer Eric G. S. Milne C/JX 160081

F Commando (Normandy) *London Gazette*
14/11/44

Able Seaman John McCann C/JX 351309

F Commando (Normandy) *London Gazette*
14/11/44

Able Seaman Willaim D. Walsh C/SSX 27179 — F Commando (Normandy) *London Gazette* 14/11/44

Able Seaman Alan Waterworth D/JX 363891 — F Commando (Normandy) *London Gazette* 14/11/44

T/Sub Lieutenant Richard H. Donger RNVR — F Commando (Normandy) *London Gazette* 14/11/44

T/Lieutenant Herbert Vine-Jones RNVR — F Commando (Sicily) *London Gazette* 21/12/43

Able Seaman Kenneth G. Oakley D/SSX 32778 — F Commando (Sicily) *London Gazette* 21/12/43

T/Midshipman Norman E. Draper RNVR — G Commando (Sicily) *London Gazette* 21/12/43

Able Seaman Harry Kimberley C/JX 169896 — H Commando (Arakan) *London Gazette* 4/7/44

T/Lieutenant Henry G. Leeke RNVR — H Commando (Arakan) *London Gazette* 4/7/44

A/Leading Seaman Edward J Peasley P/JX 166792 — H Commando (Arakan) *London Gazette* 4/7/44

Petty Officer Edward H. Pirks C/JX 136995 — H Commando (Arakan) *London Gazette* 4/7/44

Lieutenant Roger C. Norwood RN — K Commando (Sicily) *London Gazette* 21/12/43

Lieutenant Roger C. Norwood RN — K Commando (Salerno) *London Gazette* 3/5/44

A/Commander Arthur A. Havers RN — K Commando (Anzio) *London Gazette* 1/8/44

T/Lieutenant John Palmer RNVR — K Commando (Salerno) *London Gazette* 23/5/44

Able Seaman Thomas W. Taylor P/JX 201278 — K Commando (Salerno) *London Gazette* 23/5/44

Able Seaman Arthur W. Pudney P/JX 323658 — K Commando (Salerno) *London Gazette* 23/5/44

Able Seaman Joseph Glover C/JX 375393 — K Commando (Anzio) *London Gazette* 1/8/44

Sub Lieutenant Samuel E. A. Ellman SANF(V) — M Commando (Volturno) *London Gazette* 9/5/44

T/Lieutenant Alex Varley RNVR — N Commando (Anzio) *London Gazette* 9/5/44

T/Lieutenant Thomas J. Turton RNVR — N Commando (Sicily) *London Gazette* 21/12/43

T/Leading Seaman Ernest F. Gilbey C/JX 354144 — M Commando

T/Sub Lieutenant Oscar A. W. Dodd RNVR   M Commando (Europe 45) *London Gazette* 11/12/45

Lieutenant Commander Edmund S. D. Freemantle RN   P Commando (Calabria) *London Gazette* 11/9/40

Able Seaman Kenneth M. Barry P/JX 388551   R Commando (Normandy) *London Gazette* 14/11/44

A/Lieutenant Commander Jack Orchard D'Arcy   R Commando (Normandy) *London Gazette* 14/11/44

T/Sub Lieutenant Kenneth Keys RNVR   S Commando (Normandy) *London Gazette* 29/8/44

A/Leading Seaman Hugh H. Laird D/JX 150456   S Commando (Normandy) *London Gazette* 14/11/44

Leading Seaman Patrick Moran P/JX 170231   S Commando (Normandy) *London Gazette* 29/9/44

Ordinary Seaman Frank Richmond P/JX 425580   S Commando (Normandy) *London Gazette* 4/11/44

Able Seaman William P. Watson C/JX 397187   S Commando (Normandy) *London Gazette* 14/11/44

Telegraphist Wilfred Fortune C/JX331059   FOB (Normandy) *London Gazette* 14/11/44

Telegraphist Kenneth Norman Simmons C/JX 342384   FOB (Sicily)

Telegraphist Leonard G. Townsend C/JX 425031   RNBSS B1 (Normandy) *London Gazette* 14/11/445

Coder William B. Leggat P/JX 227523   RNBSS B17 (Normandy) *London Gazette* 14/11/44

T/Sub Lieutenant David B. McArthur RNVR   RNBSS B2 (Normandy) *London Gazette* 11/12/45

Coder Geoffrey Harris P/JX 405338   RNBSS B2 (Walcheren) *London Gazette* 22/12/44

Telegraphist Stanley C. Paul C/JX 358108   RNBSS B2 (Normandy) *London Gazette* 1/12/45

Telegraphist Ronald Hobman P/JX 308549   RNBSS B6 (Normandy) *London Gazette* 1/411/44

Telegraphist Robert N. Mitchell NZ 4492   RNBSS B6 (Normandy) *London Gazette* 14/11/44

Signalman Robert Moffitt D/JX 248258   RNBSS B6 (Normandy) *London Gazette* 14/11/44

T/Lieutenant Theo C. Morgan   RNBSS B6 (Normandy) *London Gazette* 14/11/44

Croix de Guerre

T/Sub Lieutenant Richard H. Donger RNVR	F Commando (Normandy)
Petty Officer Eric G. S. Milne C/JX 160081	F Commando (Normandy)
Able Seaman Alan Waterworth D/JX 363891	F Commando (Normandy)
T/Sub Lieutenant John Barr RNVR	S Commando (Normandy)
A/Leading Seaman Hugh H. Laird D/JX 150456	S Commando (Normandy)
Ordinary Seaman Frederick Richmond P/JX 425580	S Commando (Normandy)
Coder William B. Leggatt P/JX 227523	RNBSS B17 (Normandy)
Telegraphist Kenneth Norman Simmons C/JX 342384	FOB (Elba)

Select Bibliography

Chambers, William Scott, *Full Cycle: The Biography of Admiral Sir Bertram Home Ramsey*, London: Hodder & Stoughton, 1959

Combined Operations 1940–1942: Prepared for the Combined Operations Command by the Ministry of Information, London: HMSO, 1943

D'arcy, Jack, *The Teller's Tale*, n.p.: privately published, 2000

Dunning, James, *It Had to Be Tough: The Fascinating Story of the Origins of the Commandos and Their Special Training in World War II*, Edinburgh: Pentland Press, 2000

Finley, E. G, *RCN Beach Commando 'W'*, n.p.: privately published, 1994

Ford, Roger and Tim Ripley, *The Whites of Their Eyes: Close-Quarter Combat*, London: Sidgwick & Jackson, 1997

Gilchrist, Donald, *Castle Commando*, Edinburgh and London: Oliver & Boyd, 1960

Hampshire, A. Cecil, *The Beachhead Commandos*, London: William Kimber & Co., 1978

Ladd, James, *Commandos and Special Rangers of World War II*, London: Macdonald and Jane's, 1978

The Normandy Landings: A Facsimile Reproduction of the Special Supplement to the London Gazette, Containing the Despatch from Field Marshal Viscount Montgomery of Alamein to the Secretary of State for War about the Normandy Landings and Subsequent Operations in NW Europe June 1944–May 1945, London: HMSO, 1994

Pugsley, Anthony Follett, *Destroyer Man*, London: Weidenfeld & Nicholson, 1957

Slim, Field Marshal William Joseph, Lord, *Defeat into Victory*, London: Cassell & Co., 1956

Warner, Philip, *The D-Day Landings*, London: William Kimber & Co., 1980

Index